Praise for *Feed the Baby Hummus*

An easy-to-read parenting book with a twist. Complementing the usual pediatrician guidelines for safe baby care, Lewis concludes each section with tips from global baby-care routines. Indian massage. Jamaican rosewater bath. Sumatran rocking. Jewish naming rituals. American parents will find a treasure trove of practical and time-tested suggestions here. This reader-friendly guide will make a charming baby shower gift.

—DR. ALMA GOTTLIEB, coauthor of *A World of Babies: Imagined Childcare Guides for Eight Societies*

Dr. Lewis's new book offers parents a truly unique guide to child-rearing. *Feed the Baby Hummus* not only provides traditional and time-tested parenting advice from the West, but is also interspersed with parenting stories, customs, traditions, and even baby food recipes from around the world. In reading this book, we realize how much there is to learn from the global parenting village. Dr. Lewis's pediatric expertise combined with examples from around the world makes this book an insightful and comforting companion to new parents everywhere.

—LEENA SAINI, author of *Around the World in 80 Purees: Easy Recipes for Global Baby Food*

A delightful and practical read for all expecting moms and dads. I wish I read it before becoming a parent!

—RINA MAE ACOSTA, coauthor of *The Happiest Kids in the World: How Dutch Parents Help Their Kids by Doing Less*

Celebrate their life, hold them when they cry, feed them food that is nourishing. The baby-parent-community oneness is age-old common sense. The careful reader should find inspiration from this book and reflect on how to respectfully honor this precious time in an infant's life while relying on practical guidance from a pediatrician who values human connectedness and culturally grounded wisdom regarding babyhood.

—PATRISIA GONZALES, PhD, associate professor and author of *Red Medicine: Traditional Indigenous Rites of Birthing and Healing*

I have often thought that if we pooled together the most positive elements of each culture across the world we would create one strong thriving society. And what better time to do this than at the start of new life. This book provides parents with the wisdom and traditions from across the globe and ultimately the knowledge to follow their own natural intuition. A great read for new parents.

—LOUISE WEBSTER, founder of Beyondtheschoolrun.com and author of *A New Way for Mothers*

FEED THE BABY HUMMUS

FAMILIUS

For my mother.

Published by Familius LLC, www.familius.com

Familius books are available at special discounts for bulk purchases, whether for sales promotions or for family or corporate use. For more information, contact Familius Sales at 559-876-2170 or email orders@familius.com.

Library of Congress Cataloging-in-Publication Data
2017958506

Print ISBN 9781945547799
Ebook ISBN 9781641700504

Printed in the United States of America

Edited by Lindsay Sandberg
Cover design by David Miles
Book design by Brooke Jorden

10 9 8 7 6 5 4 3 2 1

First Edition

FEED THE BABY HUMMUS

Pediatrician-Backed Secrets from Cultures Around the World

LISA LEWIS, MD

CONTENTS

A Note from Dr. Lewis

Every family has their own traditions, values, and child-rearing philosophies. This book isn't written to change your current parenting style. My hope for you, reader, is that you gain practical parenting advice with insight and guidance from cultures around the world.

Throughout the book, I note when parents institute changes that differ from society and their own upbringing, they may encounter skepticism from family members and friends. In these situations, I suggest you gently guide those who haven't encountered the delightful flexibility that world parenting styles can offer.

As a reader of *Feed the Baby Hummus*, what an attentive parent you must be! Your baby's needs are simple: food, clothing, shelter, access to healthcare, and, most important, lots of love. Keep your parenting style simple while recognizing that no perfect parent exists. You will be a more effective parent if you offer your child and yourself forgiveness and acceptance of any imperfections.

I wish you the best of success and enjoyment on your parenting journey.

PART 1

Behavior and Development

Give the ones you love wings to fly, roots to come back, and reasons to stay.

—Dalai Lama XIV

Chapter 1

BONDING WITH YOUR BABY

F resh out of the hospital's delivery room, Derrick and Samantha lie with their firstborn baby they've named Sophia. Samantha went into labor at 4 p.m. Sunday and didn't give birth until 6 a.m. Monday morning. Tired and quiet, each of them is thinking about the road ahead with their new baby. Derrick is afraid that if he holds Sophia, he might harm her little body or accidentally drop her. How will he know what to do to make her happy?

Samantha is so thrilled Sophia has arrived. And what a relief. But she's also afraid she doesn't know how to bond with her baby. Will Sophia love her back if she just holds her, feeds her, and changes her diaper? What does she need to know about nurturing her daughter?

Amid the exhilaration, they both have a consistent worry: "How do I get this right?"

While there's no strict formula for "getting this right," there are certainly methods that make it easier. The first three chapters of *Feed the Baby Hummus* address bonding, nurturing, and soothing as slightly different but intertwined aspects of building a relationship with your new little one. All three aspects add up to a loving, ongoing process of bonding—a feeling of unfailing devotion between parent and child like an ongoing affair. Although newly born or adopted babies might immediately love their parents, it takes time, patience, and attentiveness to experience true attachment and bonding.

Instinct kicks in after the baby's birth. If your baby is hungry, she expects you to feed her. If she's wet, she wants you to change her diaper. If she cries, you have to figure out why and soothe her. As a new parent, you will naturally tend to your baby's needs, which leads to bonding and attachment.

All this attention combines to create your baby's nurturing. You don't need to provide attentiveness constantly, though. Babies are able to relax and enjoy themselves while you do other things. But be conscious of providing the care your baby deserves. This will help her trust in her environment, strengthen her confidence in the world, and lead her to be more content overall.

Care and attentiveness help build the bond between you and your baby, and your instincts will guide the process. It comes especially easy for parents who have grown up in big families caring for siblings. They have plenty of experience with babies!

You might be among those who worry they aren't properly caring for their new baby or won't know what to do if their baby fusses. To improve your skills and increase your bonding, try the suggestions presented in these first three chapters. In effect, you're creating a nurture plan for bonding with your baby.

Throughout this book, you'll discover what mothers in other countries do to bond with, nurture, soothe, and care for their babies. Let's start with Indonesia.

Indonesia: 105th Day Ceremony—Holding Extensively

When babies are held, they feel calm. Their heart rates slow down, and they become more peaceful. People in Bali, Indonesia, have known for centuries how the act of relaxing babies boosts bonding and attachment. For the first three months of life (or the first 210 days, depending on the family's background), the feet of Balinese babies are not even allowed to touch the ground. Referencing this practice, in the first edition of *A World of Babies*, Marissa Diener wrote, "Having just arrived from Heaven, your infant should be treated as a celestial being. Provide the attention that a god deserves, and address your child with the high language suitable to a person of higher rank. You should hold your newborn high, for gods and members of higher rank should always be elevated relative to their inferiors." During this time period, "Never put your baby down on the ground or floor, which is too profane for a god. Until then, your baby should be carried at all times."[1]

Balinese babies are surrounded by lots of love at home, with multiple generations tending to their needs. After birth, babies are passed around to those who enjoy holding them—grandparents, uncles, aunts, and kind, tradition-loving Balinese neighbors. Anyone who visits the family compound after the baby's grand entrance into the world is welcome to join in on extra cuddles.

The Balinese tradition of keeping babies' feet off the ground centers on a spiritual meaning. On the 105th Day of Life, the high priest and close family members perform a ceremony. After sprinkling holy water and offering prayer, family members then allow the baby to place his or her feet on Mother Earth.

The concept may seem unreasonable to independent societies, but extensive holding can happen with planning and care. Many independent-minded parents try to do everything on their own, yet people in a wide range of cultures work as a group to care for babies in the community. You can learn from this practice by holding your baby in the first few months as much as possible. During this period, when you do put your baby down, place him on a flat surface, positioned on his back or stomach. If he is on his stomach, ensure you stay in the room with him to make sure he has good ventilation around his face.

I suggest you enlist the help of family and friends to provide extensive holding. Although the group approach may seem invasive to those who desire solitude, when a baby arrives, more hands available to hold him will decrease the new parents' stress.

Also soothe babies as much as possible when they cry. You risk nothing, and there's absolutely no way to spoil a baby in the first year of life. (Spoiling in toddler years are another topic and require a different approach than the one for infants.)

When you are not holding your baby, keep him close so you can soothe him if needed. You can put him in a bassinet, a swing, a special baby chair, or even a baby hammock. However, take care that the baby is not able to roll over in the hammock.

Switzerland: Soothing Frequently

In Switzerland, a baby in daycare (and sometimes at home) might sleep in a *hängematte*—a kind of sturdy hammock made of natural, breathable fiber. The *hängematte* safely positions babies on their backs.

Make sure your baby's sleep area has good airflow. To provide adequate ventilation for the baby, the *hängematte* should not be made of mesh or net. If you decide to use one, make sure it is a device that is safe for your baby. For more information about the safety of a *hängematte* or baby hammock you might purchase, check with the United States Consumer Product Safety Commission or a similar organization that examines product safety in your home country.

Keeping your little one close to you in their hammock will give you the freedom to be hands-free while your baby is comfortable and secure in knowing you are near.

MAKING EYE CONTACT

Besides soothing and meeting basic needs, your baby wants you to look in her eyes. In the newborn period, baby's eye muscles are exercising a lot. It may even appear that your baby is looking at everything except you. Do you notice that when you are nipple-feeding, whether via breast or bottle, your baby's eyes are on you?

Your infant will naturally look at you while feeding. Especially as your baby grows past the first year, it's important to maintain good eye contact during your interactions. It's easy to get busy and maintain a task without looking at her. Let her know you are present and focusing only on her.

LETTING YOUR BABY FEEL YOUR SKIN

Soft blankets and clothes feel good, but he will enjoy and be especially soothed by the touch of your skin. When your baby is relaxed, undress him (except for his diaper) in a warm room. Then lie down and gently place him on your bare chest or belly. Put your hands on his back and arms. Cradle him while your skin touches his. If you are breastfeeding, feel free to do so without wearing a shirt while in the privacy of your own home.

Skin-to-skin contact, also called "kangaroo care," has been found in studies to benefit the overall health and well-being of babies. For example, a 2002 study published by the American Academy of Pediatrics concluded that kangaroo care had a "significant positive impact on the infant's perceptual-cognitive and motor development and on the parenting process."[2] Simply stated, premature and full-term babies relax and have better development when they have had frequent skin-to-skin contact.

So do it often, and feel your baby's positive reaction. Note how content he is after a loving period of skin-to-skin contact.

TRY BABYWEARING

Babywearing means placing a baby in a cloth carrier of some type and literally wearing her—a common practice in Africa and other parts of the world for centuries. The practice likely developed out of necessity, but we now know the benefits of babywearing beyond a hands-free method of carrying a baby around.

The greatest benefit of babywearing is the security your baby feels being with you. Your baby may be worn on your body when you're busy during the day. She can be upright and looking at the world. And she'll learn a lot from being at her level of incline on your body. If your baby is upset when she's apart from you because she wants to be close to you, you will notice how quickly she calms down once you place her in the carrier attached to your body.

Africa: Babywearing Supports Contentment

Thema, a young mother from the Ivory Coast in Africa, is gazing at her baby and tickling his tummy. Her teenage sister, Akosua, is looking through a British magazine given to her at the market. Akosua is practicing her English; she'd like to travel the world, and knowing English makes that easier. In her magazine, she sees a picture of a red-headed lady pushing a baby stroller and says, "Thema, maybe you need one of these for Kojo." Thema looks at the stroller, perplexed, and then laughs. "Why stroll the baby around when I can care for him more easily by wearing him on my body?"

Many African women are appalled at the idea of using strollers and call them an unnecessary waste of resources. Mothers in Africa see babywearing as a practical maneuver that results in a more content baby.

Guidelines for Babywearing

Babywearing is not complex, but it's a skill that must be learned. Some carriers are more intricate than others. Unless you have already learned to use one, start with an easy-to-understand carrier specifically made for babywearing. Carriers that can be adjusted and fitted readily to your body are easiest and safest to use.

Wear your infant on the front of your body. Doing this increases the odds that your baby will get used to babywearing quickly. It feels simply like holding her except that your arms and hands are free. You can wear your baby in the house or even outside if she's properly clothed and protected from the weather with a hat and sunscreen.

Because safety for babywearing is important, be sure to follow these twelve guidelines from the Consumer Product Safety Commission and Babywearing International.

1. Babies who are premature, visibly sick, or less than four months of age should be worn in a carrier only after consulting your pediatrician.

2. Always make sure you are able to see your baby's face to ensure she is getting adequate ventilation. Her face should be at or above the rim of the sling and never covered by fabric.

3. The baby's head should be upright and never slumping forward. Don't let her get into a curled position with her chin touching her chest or her face burrowed into the carrier.

4. Never jog or exercise with your baby in a baby carrier on your body. The jolting motion of the sling may be harmful to your baby's brain and neck.

5. Use only carriers that are clearly marked for your baby's height and weight.

6. Always check your carrier before use to ensure it's not damaged. Look for tears or weaknesses in the fabric. Visually inspect and test the fasteners, seams, and buckles.

7. When bodywearing babies older than six months, be aware of what they can reach. Just like babies crawling on the floor, they might grab small objects or toxic items they could not ordinarily access.

8. Carry your baby and nothing else in the carrier. That means no items such as toys riding in the carrier with your baby.

9. Do not cook while your baby is in the carrier. It increases the risk of burns and severe injuries.

10. Never wear your baby in a carrier while on a boat. You both should be wearing life jackets, but especially your little one should have one.

11. Remove the carrier before placing your baby in a car seat. When a baby in a carrier is buckled into a car seat, the carrier takes up extra space and prevents the car seat straps from properly securing your baby.

12. Don't make your own baby carrier. You risk injury to the baby or even suffocation.

Babies also enjoy being carried on your back. However, don't do this until your little one is at least six months old and can safely sit on her own. Use only a carrier made for the back. Be sure to fasten her in with her head above the rim of the carrier. Always adhere to the twelve guidelines stated here.

Babywearing International (www.babywearinginternational.org) is an excellent resource to view the different types of carriers available for safe use. For further information on babywearing safety as well as a list of slings or carriers that have been recalled, consult the Consumer Product Safety Commission at www.cpsc.gov.

DIFFICULTIES WITH BONDING AND ATTACHMENT

What do you do when you don't feel attached to your baby? Sometimes a parent may not feel bonded at first and require time for bonding to develop. This can happen to any parent, and it's especially common if the baby is premature or has been ill. If this occurs, know that your baby is *ready* to bond with you. You can apply the guidelines in this chapter to enhance this process for both of you. If more than two weeks go by after birth and you don't feel as if you're bonding with your baby, talk to your doctor to figure out why.

WAYS TO ENHANCE BONDING AND ATTACHMENT

Chapter 1 suggested five ways to enhance bonding with your baby:

1. Holding extensively
2. Soothing frequently
3. Making eye contact
4. Letting your baby feel your skin
5. Babywearing

In Chapters 2 and 3, you'll discover further ways to bond with your little one through various forms of nurturing and soothing.

Chapter 2

NURTURING YOUR INFANT

N urturing can and should happen in many forms. You want to feed not only your infant's body but also his senses and his heart, mind, and spirit. Let's look at a few ways to support the development of a well-rounded, happy child.

PLAYING MUSIC, SINGING, AND DANCING

Music shared between a baby and parent promotes a relaxing bonding experience. You will note that your baby's senses are sharp in the first year of life, especially the sense of sound. Babies often feel afraid of loud, unfamiliar sounds and might cry or scream in response to them. On the positive front, babies like to listen to sounds that appeal to them, especially music.

A study in 2009 from the University of Tel Aviv in Israel concluded that energy expended was significantly lowered in healthy preterm babies who heard Mozart music compared to babies who did not. Further, babies who listened to Mozart gained more weight than those who did not.[1] Music can relax, soothe, stimulate, and improve a sad disposition. It can also calm a crying baby, which, for most new parents, is an excellent reason in and of itself to incorporate music into your baby's life on an ongoing basis.

Maori, New Zealand: Storytelling through Music

Maori people tell stories through music. The Maori are traditional Polynesian people who have lived in New Zealand since the eleventh century. Many Maori people have made their music more contemporary. But old or new, it's still an important part of their culture when used for gathering family members and rearing children.

Added to the music is storytelling, which serves to pass vital information from one generation to the next. Singing is often accompanied by dance moves integrated into the music. Instruments may be used, adding a variety of tones. However, singing with no instrument to tell a story is also common. So are lullabies. To provide continuous singing for long segments of time, singing in groups is common. A unifying and universal language, music brings families and friends together to build relationships today and for generations to come.

Enjoy your own relationship with music and pass it on to your baby. If you have favorite songs, play them. When your baby is feeling most relaxed and close to naptime or bedtime, it's a good time to play calm, soothing music. But when your baby is alert and playing, select music you like. It can be soothing, relaxed, or energetic. Babies like the simple, homogenous sounds of classical music, easy listening, and even modern pop culture. Do avoid introducing rap, heavy metal, or any music with harsh sounds. Typically, babies are overstimulated by loud, irregular beats.

Watch your little one for clues to what music is best. When your baby is tired, play soft music, but while your baby is active, any upbeat music that you appreciate will likely be enjoyed by your baby too. If not, adjust the song choice until both you and your baby are enjoying it together.

Using Instruments

If you play an instrument, your baby will likely love hearing you play it. But if your instrument is loud, watch out. Look for your baby's cues—crying, wincing, fidgeting, or looking fearful—to ensure you aren't making her uncomfortable. If your baby doesn't look relaxed, happy, or content as you play, stop for a time and try later. But don't give up. Sharing your instrument expresses your musical ability delightfully. And if you don't play an instrument, make music by gently tapping a spoon or hairbrush to a pleasing rhythm. To create a variety of tones, tap against different cups as you sing along.

Singing about Anything

Lullabies are universal songs sung with a tender, loving voice in any language. Sing any song you know that you enjoy sharing. Sing a conversation. Sing even if you can't carry a tune. Your baby will love the sound of your voice. You can find words to lullabies in the library, in children's books, or by searching the internet. If you don't like to sing, enlist family members or friends to sing, then sit back, listen, and watch with enjoyment.

Dancing Like No One (Except Your Baby) Is Watching

Dance around the room for great exercise and to put on a wonderful show for your baby. As with singing, if you don't have dancing talent, who cares? Clap your hands to the music. Stomp your feet. Sway your hips. Clap your baby's feet together. Your baby will squeal with pleasure watching you move, sing, or play a musical instrument.

How can you enjoy Maori and Pacific music with your baby from birth and throughout life? Check out the possibilities at https://www.library.auckland.ac.nz/ampm/.

FEEDING TO NURTURE YOUR BABY

Have you tried loving feeding? This term sounds unusual, right? And who doesn't feed their baby in a loving manner? But to make feeding time a bonding experience, take it to the next level. Commit to making it an event that focuses totally on your little one. What in your life can't wait? Very little. While you're feeding her, put all other duties aside and look your baby in the eyes. Touch your skin to her skin. Relax your movements during feeding and make them deliberate. Show her you are enjoying this special time. Do your best to make nipple-feeding by bottle or by breast a pleasant experience. Talk to her lovingly when the timing is right. You might say "Oh, it looks like you're hungry," or "There's a nice burp," or "Are you finished with your feeding?"

After feeding, hold her as long as she would like (or as long as you can manage). Life will continue to happen around you and draw your attention into other activities. Still, you can put aside nonessential issues until your baby is fed and content. These times pass by quickly, and you won't regret giving her extra attention at feeding time.

READING TO YOUR BABY

Do you like to read, or do you read only when you must? Reading to your child early in life sets the foundation for school success. According to the National Institute for Literacy, research has repeatedly shown that babies and children whose parents read to them are likely to read at an earlier age than those whose parents don't.[2] Children whose parents read to them are more likely to enjoy reading and model it throughout their lives than those whose parents don't.

Reading also improves early speech development. Before your baby can talk, he listens to your words carefully and processes them. Reading to him enhances his brain development in many ways. The more you talk to him, the wider his vocabulary becomes.

Most of all, reading to your baby facilitates bonding, stimulates memory, motivates him, and enhances his development. It's just an all-around good thing to do. As your child gets older, reading can even help him cope with stress.

You want to set up a relaxed environment for reading to your baby. If you pick up a book when your little one is sitting in your lap, you both get entertained. It's good to read when he's calm and relatively attentive. Most babies fare better with reading close to naptime or bedtime, but any time of the day can work just fine. Board books are best for babies because they can chew them, throw them, and play with them without causing damage.

Start your reading session by showing him the front of the book and discussing what it's about. As you begin to read, point to pictures and discuss them. He may not be forming words yet, but talking to your baby about them will help develop his mind, and he'll eventually point to pictures too. As you read, change your voice from high to low and make various sounds to hold his interest. Use a different voice for different characters in the story or make the sounds of the animals he sees on the page. Most of all, set the stage to make reading fun.

Read every day, even if it's for a short time. Put books where you and your baby will spot them. As he gets older, encourage him to turn the pages, which gives him a sense of accomplishment and develops his fine motor skills. As your child advances in months and years, sprinkle books all over the house. (You can find multitudes of used books at garage sales.)

Visit your library often. You can sit and read books aloud, and your early reader will grow into a child who loves books!

Books with Pictures of People—and Especially Babies

Seeing people—both in person and in books—is important for your baby's healthy brain development. Research published in the *Stanford News* in 2012 shows that infants are able to process and recognize faces more quickly than other objects.[3] Think back to how your baby gazed around in her first months and then the thrill you felt when her eyes followed you around the room. Being social, babies crave human interaction.

Have you noticed that babies love looking at babies? Watching themselves in a mirror can entertain them for half an hour. And books featuring babies' faces have been around for decades. In 2007, The Global Fund for Children published *Global Babies*, a board book with images chosen specifically to stimulate a baby's social senses.[4] Babies love contrast, and *Global Babies* shows infants in a distinctive array of colorful traditional clothing. Their complexions vary from page to page. The expressive baby faces feed an older baby's need to imitate. The book features colorful photos of babies from seventeen cultures around the globe presented in cultural context. It demonstrates that babies are universally nurtured by the love, caring, and joy that surround them.

An added benefit for parents and caregivers is the book's nurturing approach to parenting around the world. The outcome is the same in all cultures: people love and take care of a cherished baby. I suggest you read *Global Babies* again and again to stimulate your baby's brain development. Seeing babies from an array of backgrounds will spark a lifelong interest in learning about people from different cultures.

Chapter 3

SOOTHING YOUR BABY

L et's now look at soothing activities that bring your baby peace and joy while creating a long-lasting bond.

CALMING BABY BATH

A bath for your baby should be enjoyable and loving as well as just plain functional. Consider this bonding time, not just a chore! The following tips will make bath time fun and special for you and your baby.

Have a relaxed environment. Turn off your cell phone or place it in another room on silent. Play soft classical music during each bath. If you start the music each time before you bathe your baby, he will understand that it's a cue for his bath.

Run lukewarm water. Water temperature should be no higher than 100 degrees Fahrenheit. You can use a thermometer or dip your elbow in the water to make sure it's comfortable.

Do not give a bath immediately after your baby eats. Ideally, bathe your baby at least a half hour after a feeding, and never bathe your baby when he is hungry. It will be difficult for him to relax and enjoy the experience if his little tummy needs to be fed.

Get your supplies ready. Before the bath, ensure you have the necessary items available. It's inconvenient and perhaps unsafe to stop your bath so you can retrieve items. You will need the following:

- Unscented lotion
- Unscented soap
- Towels
- Washcloth
- Medium-size cup or ladle
- Diapers
- Diaper wipes
- Clothes for the baby to wear after
- Blanket
- Bath toy (optional)
- Baby shampoo
- Rubber bath mat or soft cushion
- Warm water
- Bathing chair (optional)

Initial setup: use a sink or a baby bathtub for infants younger than six months. Once your baby is sitting up, it may be easier to bathe him in a tub using a bath chair. A bath chair is a waterproof, portable seat used to keep a slippery baby in place in the tub.

To start the calming baby bath, talk to your baby and gently remove his clothes. Bath time for a baby should be relaxed and peaceful, supplemented with playful fun and laughter. If you feel a draft in the bathing room, wrap your baby in a towel before placing him in the water. Once his clothes are off, place one of his feet in the water first followed by the second foot. Next, move his buttocks and upper body into the water. This will get him used to the temperature and feel of the water. Make sure the bathwater doesn't go over his chest level, and keep his head visible. If you can't hold your baby at an angle to keep his head out of the water, then use a seat made specifically to hold your baby at an inclined angle.

Slowly pour water on the baby's body during the bath to keep him warm using a cup or a ladle. If he's in a sink or tub that has a faucet, let warm water trickle in via the faucet to keep the bathwater warm.

Use a warm washcloth on the baby's face and scalp. A warm washcloth provides the best way to clean your baby's face and scalp. A soft washcloth feels more comfortable than a sponge. Besides, a sponge can drip water onto the face or scalp, startling the baby.

Forget using soap for every bath. It's not necessary. And soap can be especially drying for a baby's skin. Unless you think your baby is particularly dirty (perhaps he's been crawling in the dirt), it doesn't harm him to skip the soap and avoid drying out his skin. However, if you use soap, be sure it's a *gentle* soap made specifically for babies. If you notice your baby's skin is red or dry after a bath, switch to an unscented soap, such as unscented Dove. You'll find liquid soap easier to use than bar soap, which can be quite slippery.

Wash the hair two to three times a week at the end of the bath. Your baby's hair doesn't need to be washed at every bath. To shampoo it, place him in a reclining position with his head facing upward and water no higher than chest level. If your baby bathes in the tub, have another adult hold him securely at a forty-five-degree angle or use a bathing chair to hold him in position.

You could also wash his hair after the bath by wrapping him in a towel and laying him flat on his back on the countertop with his head over the sink. Using your ladle or cup, gently pour water onto his head, then apply a dime-size amount of baby shampoo and gently massage it into the scalp. While rinsing, put a dry washcloth on his forehead to stop water from trickling onto his face. Then rinse the scalp until all of the shampoo is gone.

If he becomes upset during the hair washing, stop and console him. Try to figure out what's bothering him. Is the water warm enough?

Did it get on his face? Perhaps use a bath toy to entertain him or sing a song to distract him.

Wrap him up post-bath. After your baby's bath, lay him on a soft towel and wrap him in it. Pat dry the exposed areas of his body rather than rubbing them to avoid causing chafing. If he has dry skin, you may apply an unscented lotion recommended by your doctor. Most important, take time to hold your baby and let him enjoy the sensation of being swaddled after a relaxing bath.

Bathing together is a pleasurable option for skin-to-skin contact. As long as you're in a secure position and can't slip, you can safely bathe with your infant. Try breastfeeding in the bathtub, which can be enjoyable and relaxing for both mother and baby. Just be sure the water doesn't go above your baby's chest level and his face has good ventilation while breastfeeding. Once you are in the bathtub, have another adult hand you the baby and remain available to call if needed as well as help you take your baby out of the tub. Be sure you're alert enough that you won't fall asleep!

Important Bath Safety Recommendations

- To prevent burns, permanently set your hot water heater to 120 degrees Fahrenheit or less.
- Ensure your baby can't bump his head on the faucet. Special covers that fit over the faucet to prevent injury can be purchased if needed.
- Be aware that accidentally placing electrical devices in the water may cause electrocution.
- Don't keep electrical devices such as a hair dryer or flat iron close to the water. Babies might grab nearby electrical devices before you can stop them.
- Never leave your baby unsupervised during a bath. Babies can drown quickly in shallow water. Know that a baby lying on his stomach won't be able to breathe if his mouth is covered with just one inch of water.

- Line your tub with a rubber bath mat or soft cushion to reduce slipping.
- For newborns, do not submerge them in a bath until the umbilical cord has been detached for more than a week.

Malaysia: Calming Ladle Bath with Telon Oil

In Malaysia, it's common to use a large container and a *gayung* (ladle) to give a baby a bath. The baby is initially placed in a baby chair or secured in a washing bowl. Then warm water is put into a separate large container, and the ladle is used to scoop the water from the container to bathe the baby. Because it's not put back into its original container, the water remains clean. Refreshing the bath with warm water keeps the baby's body warm. In addition, the smooth movements created by the ladle simulate a waterfall, which can add to the fun and relaxation for your baby. This traditional method of ladling a bath with water is referred to as *mandi*.

After the baby's bath, telon oil is often applied. This oil is believed to keep the baby warm as well as provide certain health benefits. Telon oil is a mixture of cajuput, coconut, and caraway (or, sometimes, its cousin fennel) oils.

Telon oil should be used only on babies more than four months of age who don't have highly sensitive skin. If you try it, select a brand made specifically for babies. With no known absorption studies of telon oil, its safe dosage is unknown. For this reason, I suggest using it no more than three times a week after a bath and applying it to the skin only. Like any topical bath product, telon oil should never be ingested or put close to the eyes. With those simple precautions, there should be no trouble. It has been used safely for many centuries in Malaysia.

MASSAGING YOUR INFANT

Babies love contact with your hands, skin, and entire body. Your baby enjoys feeling the warmth of your touch and breath while hearing your soothing voice. To connect with her on a tactile, nurturing level, experiment with infant massage. Many countries use it not just as a treatment but also as a tradition for a baby's body and mind.

India: Massage as Normal Baby Care

One culture that uses infant massage as a tradition is India. The techniques may be different in each family, but the goal is the same: to promote good health and strengthen bones. Some mothers hire a *dai* or midwife to give a massage; others turn to their grandmothers and even learn from them.

After the birth of a baby in India, massage may be performed with a soft wheat dough ball and oil. The dough ball is used to apply gentle pressure on the baby. Because natural oil is considered best for newborns, their options include olive oil, coconut oil, mustard seed oil, and almond oil. Some parents also add a touch of turmeric.

Benefits of infant massage include enhanced bonding and nurturing as well as better sleep. The greatest benefit is the healthy skin-to-skin contact combined with a relaxing, rhythmic massaging motion.

Getting Ready for Massage

A good time to massage your infant is after a calming, loving bath. The following guidelines ensure the massage is healthy for your baby while stimulating her senses and brain and making her feel loved.

You may start massaging your baby right after birth, if desired, but take care with the products you use. The month after birth should be regarded as a period of adjustment from the shock of birth by using light massage and tactile stimulation. At this time, the baby's skin is a delicate barrier adjusting to the reality of a world outside the womb. In the first four months, use only unscented oil or lotion. Even babies with sensitive skin respond well to unscented lotion as a massage agent. After four months, you can transition to olive oil, almond oil, mustard seed oil, or coconut oil. But the day before you want to do the massage, test the unscented lotion or oil for a skin reaction on your baby's lower leg. Look for any type of skin reaction within twenty-four hours, such as a rash or redness. If the test goes well with no skin rash, it's time to begin your newborn massage.

Make sure your baby is relaxed. (It's not hard to find a calm baby in the first month of life, because newborns sleep a lot.) For a newborn, give a massage one-and-a-half to two hours after a feeding. However, an infant older than one month can be massaged any time.

Place all necessary items close by: oil or lotion, towels, a comfortable blanket, a fresh set of clothes, diaper wipes, and a diaper.

Wash your hands with warm water and soap prior to the massage. Remove any jewelry on your hands and arms. Make sure your nails aren't long; you don't want to scratch your baby.

Warm your oil or lotion. Place a small container of oil or lotion in a warm cup of water or a sink full of warm water thirty minutes ahead of time. You want to avoid having it so warm that it causes discomfort.

Place your baby on a comfortable, covered surface with your body close. It's best to use a place where you can sit comfortably and the baby can be relaxed. A changing table works well, or your baby could also be massaged on the bed. For a covering, place a soft towel on the surface where the baby will lie. This will also make the area comfortable.

Gently remove your baby's clothing, including the diaper, as you create a calm atmosphere. Cover your baby in a soft blanket that's easy to wash. Do not use one of your favorite blankets in case the oil or lotion stains it or your baby poops or spits up. Loosely wrap your baby in the blanket with his face exposed.

Steps of the Massage

1. *Place your baby on his stomach with his head to the side.* In this position, the head should be turned so you can see that the nose and mouth are open for good ventilation.

2. *Place the oil in your hands and then rub them together to warm it up.* Using lotion or oil that's cold defeats the purpose of giving him a warm, loving massage. Do not use a lotion or oil heater, since these devices may cause overheating and burn the skin. Use a very small amount of oil, and don't let it drip on your baby.

3. *Gently move the blanket off his legs and keep his back covered so he won't get cold. Rub your hands together again and start with the feet.* Clasp your hands around both feet and gently hold them to get him used to the feel of the oil. Then, with your fingers, make circular motions to rub the feet and legs. Gently apply pressure to each individual toe as you continue to massage his feet and legs. Experiment to ensure you're using the right amount of gentle pressure. Avoid tickling. It's unpleasant for the baby to be tickled during a massage because it increases tension in his body. If he seems uncomfortable, reposition him so you can add more pressure. If he seems fidgety, put one hand under the blanket and directly touch the skin on his back, applying light pressure to calm him.

4. *Move on to include a massage of the knee and hip joints.* It's okay if your baby moves or interacts during the massage. Just be sure he is secure and won't roll off the massage area.

5. When you feel the lotion or oil lessen on your hands, add some. Be sure to warm the lotion by rubbing your hands together. If you have a favorite song, sing it. Your baby will enjoy hearing the relaxing rhythm of your voice.

6. *After massaging the baby's legs, move on to the buttocks and back.* For these areas, you can use your fingers and the palms of your hands in a circular motion. As you move toward his back, cover the legs so he won't get cold.

7. Don't worry initially if you feel that your baby isn't responding to the massage. As you learn more about his rhythms and temperament, you will discover what works well for him. The main point is to not be afraid to use light pressure while massaging. Babies like feeling that amount of pressure.

8. *Gently turn your baby on his back.* If he seems to dislike the change of position, hold your hand on his belly and gently calm him. If he still seems uncomfortable, wrap him in his blanket or a towel to make him feel more secure and ensure he isn't cold.

9. *Start again at the feet, work your way up the legs to the abdomen (belly), and then massage the arms.* Include the elbow and shoulder joints. Massage the fingers gently by placing them between your thumb and forefinger. Massage the chest and work your way up to massage the earlobes and outer ear. You don't want oil or lotion to get inside the ear, so use a light coat in this area.

10. *Wind down the massage by picking up your baby, holding him, and repeating the massage on the back.* While holding your baby, lightly massage his scalp, ensuring that no oil or lotion drips onto his face. In time, if you find an area your baby seems to like best, repeat that area at the end of the massage.

Important Safety Concerns

Be sure you stay with your baby at all times to avoid accidents. When you walk away, expect your baby to roll around searching for you.

Support your baby's head during the entire massage. Allowing an excessively floppy head is uncomfortable for the baby. It increases tension in the body and is dangerous for the baby's neck.

Avoid the eyes, nose, mouth, inner ears, face, genitals, and anus. All of these parts have openings that may be adversely affected by applying lotion or oil.

Stop the massage slowly and delicately, not abruptly, while holding the baby and finishing with the back or noted favorite area.

Do stop the massage for discomfort. If you feel your baby is uncomfortable, gently stop the massage, wrap him in his blanket, and hold him. Babies want to be held when they are upset, and holding him will help him feel more secure.

Summary for Massaging Your Baby

1. Wrap your baby in a blanket.
2. Use warmed lotion or oil.
3. Place him on his belly, ensuring good ventilation around his mouth and nose.
4. Start with the feet, using a circular motion, and move up the legs toward the buttocks and back. Then move to the arms.
5. Turn the baby over while using the blanket to wrap him. Repeat the process, starting with the feet and moving up the legs toward the abdomen and arms.
6. At the end of the massage, hold him close to your body, repeat the back massage, and lightly massage the scalp. Feel free to massage other areas he seems to enjoy.

BABY ROCKING

Historically, many Western doctors viewed baby rocking as an indulgence. Parents who live at home with crying babies may beg to differ.

Rocking is a universal custom. Across the globe, families have created unique ways of rocking to soothe their babies and foster a sense of security. Baby rocking is not only practical; it also reduces the caretaker's stress. And less baby crying reduces life's worries.

Sumatra: Vertical Baby Rocking

Rocking in Western society is predominantly a horizontal activity. In some parts of Sumatra, Indonesia, though, people rock their babies in an up-and-down fashion. Babies can see the world better that way, and they enjoy the stimulation.

What is the right way to vertically rock a baby? You can do it either with a rocker or without. You can find vertical rockers for sale in the United States and Europe, although many are advertised as "bouncers." (Be sure to check its safety standards before purchasing a bouncer or vertical rocker.)

To rock your baby vertically, hold her in a secure position called a "football hold." This hold has the baby lying on her back along one of your forearms, with the baby's head supported by the other. Her body is now lying against your chest as you gently move your upper body up and down. Provide adequate ventilation around the face and ensure her body appears comfortable. Don't move too fast. Simply use a gentle, rhythmic up-and-down (vertical) rocking motion rather than swinging your baby side to side.

SPEAKING TO YOUR BABY

Peaceful speech relaxes your baby and helps her feel content and comforted. Speaking to your baby in soft, sweet tones ensures she will stop and listen. Loud, tense speech often offends a baby's ears and increases the risk of dealing with a high-strung, anxious baby.

Japan: Gentle Speech

In Japan, families regard their babies as gentle beings. The concept of a "difficult baby" is unheard of because babies are regarded as inherently decent souls. Mothers and other family members naturally speak to them in quiet, loving tones and closely observe their needs. They follow and respect the baby's rhythms and responses. Loud, boisterous speech with a baby is discouraged.

Using the Japanese's gentle speech concept can create a tranquil environment for your whole family. It's fine to have noise in the house and to talk in normal volume, but when you get close to the baby, let go of any tension you have so she can relax.

Making a deliberate decision to release your day's stress is also healthy for your own mind. Yes, life happens, and you can't always be relaxed, but if you make a deliberate effort to calm yourself and your speech, you'll be rewarded by having a more relaxed baby.

SOOTHING TECHNIQUES FOR CRYING

Still can't figure out why your baby is crying? The following techniques might help.

Pick him up and hold him. It takes time and experience with your child to learn what consoles him. Some babies like to be held upright; others, on your lap. Some want to be held like a football, and others prefer you to hold them while both of you lie down. To calm your baby, try gently bouncing him up and down while holding or rocking him.

Lay him down and pat his back, rub his tummy, or gently rub his arms. This helps if your baby is crying and doesn't want to be held. Lie down with him on the floor or the bed. Just having your body next to him with skin-to-skin contact might soothe him right away.

Change environments by finding a calm, quiet place for him to relax. Go to a different room or otherwise leave the place where he's crying. Moving to a different room can distract him. Sometimes babies cry when they are overstimulated or tired. If the crying continues, find as relaxing an environment as possible and relax with him.

Give him something to suck on. For prolonged crying in a baby who won't be consoled, offer your breast and see if he will attach or give him a bottle. Sometimes it's hard to tell when a baby is hungry, especially if he has fed recently. If he does not take your breast or the bottle, then offer a pacifier.

Sing a soothing song or play calming music. Your baby might like the soothing sound of your voice or music. Hold him or lie next to him while you sing songs or play relaxing music.

Nigeria: Crying It Out Not Allowed

In Nigeria, the cultural expectation is for babies to cry minimally. Women frequently wear their babies so they can be held a large part of the day. If a mother goes anywhere in a community where she's known, friends and family often take the baby, passing her from person to person with glee.

Dr. Ijeoma Nnamani, a Nigerian-born pediatrician who practices at the Ivy Children's Clinic in Euless, Texas, says, "Nigerian people refuse to let their babies cry because it's a sign that something is wrong. There is no concept of 'crying it out' in our culture. If you are in your home and your baby is crying, your neighbor may knock on your door and ask you what is wrong. The neighbor may reach out to hold your baby and help console her."

Nigerian babies are not spoiled. They simply are not left to cry it out.[1]

SPOILING BABIES WHEN THEY CRY IS IMPOSSIBLE

Children usually believe they are the center of the universe. And, as you have seen, babies in many cultures are the family's center of the universe. A spoiled child believes that the whole world and everyone in it revolves around him. This typically results when well-meaning parents don't set limits with a toddler or older child. *Spoiling a baby during the first year of life simply cannot be done.*

Jamaica: Rose Water Soothing

Mothers in Jamaica and other parts of the Caribbean have been known to use rose water to soothe babies who have a fever. Try it for your baby. Use rose water for babies four months and older. You can buy wonderful-smelling rose water or make it yourself using this recipe.

Rose Water Recipe

2 quarts fresh rose petals
Water
3 trays of ice (or 1 bag)

1. Place a small, clean brick in the center of a large pot that has a rounded lid. Put the rose petals in the pot; add enough flowers to reach the top of the brick. Pour in enough water to cover the roses. The water should reach just above the top of the brick.
2. Place the lid upside down on the pot. Turn on the stove and bring the water to a rolling boil, then lower the heat to a slow, steady simmer. As soon as the water begins to boil, toss three trays of ice cubes (or a bag of ice) on top of the inverted lid.
3. Strain and collect the rose water in a dark glass container. Depending on the size of your pot, it should yield 2–4 cups. This rose water should last six months.

Make sure your baby doesn't drink the rose water. Rather, to calm him, put one tablespoon of rose water into two cups of warm water. Dip a soft washcloth in the water and squeeze it. Then cradle your baby in your arms and lay the washcloth on his tummy. The scent and warmth are relaxing to both of you.

You can also give him a warm rose water bath. Some crying babies will relax in a calming baby bath, though others may become more agitated. Do it if all other measures have failed or you already know it relaxes him. Add two tablespoons of rose water to the warm bathwater, but don't use soap, because the combination of soap and rose water may irritate his skin.

If your baby cries excessively for several hours, has a fever, or shows any symptoms of illness, promptly call or visit your pediatrician.

BABIES CRY FOR A REASON

A baby's cry is his sole form of communicating distress, so never ignore cries from a young baby. Many sources of advice suggest letting the baby "cry it out" (CIO) in order to sleep or for other reasons a baby may be distressed. I do not recommend letting your baby cry it out in the early months. *A crying baby needs your attention.*

Babies in the first twelve months of life may cry three to four hours a day on a regular basis. That is a lot of crying! For parents, this may provoke anxiety and even feelings of inadequacy. Your strong instinct to protect your child may cause you concern, tension, and even anger whenever your baby cries.

Crying usually occurs for a reason, so when your baby cries, go through this checklist of what could be wrong:

1. Does she have a dirty or wet diaper?
2. Is she hungry?
3. Is she sleepy?
4. Is she sick?
5. Is she angry?
6. Is she cutting teeth?
7. Is she uncomfortable, cold, or hot?
8. Does she want attention?
9. Does she want to be held?

When your baby cries, pick her up and tend to her. *Do not let her CIO.* You may be able to let toddlers do so in certain situations, but when babies are learning to trust, this is not the time to let them CIO.

If your baby is crying but safe and you can't tend to her immediately, go to her as soon as you can. Perhaps you're in the shower, on the toilet, cooking, or caring for another child. Quickly finish what you're doing and pick her up. Rock her, hold her, and talk sweetly to her. Let your warm hands touch her body. Rub her back. Massage her. Show her you are there for her and will always take care of her.

EVERY BABY'S TEMPERAMENT IS DIFFERENT

If your baby cries more excessively than you think is normal, discuss it with your doctor. Perhaps your baby has a temperament such that almost anything makes him cry and only picking him up and cuddling him makes him stop. This can be quite difficult for you. After all, holding and consoling your baby around the clock is impractical during your daily life. I suggest you try babywearing, as discussed earlier. It's a safe technique to physically wear your baby with a sling or body carrier.

Some babies are little cuddle bugs who want to touch you, listen to you, and know you are present. They feel most secure knowing you are there. If this is your baby's personality, reinforce your presence. Then, when he is content, put him down. Place him in a position where he can see you and you can talk to him while going about your activities.

BABIES JUST CAN'T BE SPOILED. REALLY.

Having a baby comes with the responsibility of making her feel secure. If she is crying, she doesn't feel secure, so figure out why as best you can.

Of course sometimes the reasons are unclear. If she is consoled when picked up and held, you know she needed you. Despite what many people say, you are not overindulging (spoiling) her by doing this. Rather, you're helping her learn that the world is safe and her parents will take care of her.

This will change as your baby moves into the toddler years. But you can't spoil a baby during her first year of life by giving her too much holding and attention.

BABIES LOVE TO STAY OCCUPIED

Holding your baby is not the only way to soothe him and keep him content. Many parents work during the day and are busy in the evening. As you learn what your baby enjoys while you are busy, you can keep him active.

One of the best methods, as mentioned, is to keep him close by while you're doing things. If you're cooking, discuss what you are making, how your day went, or anything else that comes to mind. He may smile and respond. If he cries because he wants to get out of his seat, distract him with a toy or a song before you pick him up.

In time—especially when she is more than six months old—your baby will learn more about you and your response to situations. If you react quickly every time she needs something, she will learn to rely on you to take care of her needs rather than think independently. So balance your reactions to her needs. For example, if she cries when she wants a toy that's out of her reach, call out that you will tend to her in a moment. As a result, she might be distracted or redirected into another activity. Allow her to explore and not pick her up for every discontented episode or whimper. She may fuss because she is frustrated, and she has to work that out.

Don't fix or set up everything for her. Let her move to other areas of the room and allow her to explore without your interference (in safety-proofed areas only, of course).

As the months march on, it becomes easier to distract your baby with activities and engaging moments while you are busy. If your baby has an older sibling, often that child can engage him in play and conversation. Also, while you're busy, let him explore items in your home that don't pose choking hazards. For example, if you are cooking, hand him a wooden spoon. Then, after he has explored the wooden spoon, hand him a silver spoon. You're showing him two different textures and items to play with. If he gets bored with them, hand him a nonbreakable plate, and so on. You can use the same technique while working at your computer when he hangs out with you in your office. Hand him a board book or a small washcloth. Keep a favorite toy close by.

India: Distraction Creates a Helpful Reaction

Charu Chhitwal, a mother from India and cofounder of www.ketch-upmoms.com, says, "In India, we have this lovely tradition where the maternal side gives the baby a silver glass, spoon, plate, and bowl. They cannot really be used for eating; they are toys for kids to play with, to hold and pick up and explore so they can improve their fine motor skills."[2]

Babies like to explore. Once he's bored with one toy, hand him something else. If he has been in one position too long, change it. Once he's mobile (crawling, pulling up to stand), put him in a room or play yard where he can't get injured. Make sure he has plenty of fun items to stimulate him. And stay nearby, because he will like seeing you walk by as you talk to him, smile at him, or wink playfully.

Chapter 4

STAGES OF DEVELOPMENT

Your baby's development is exciting to watch. From one month to the next, the changes may seem subtle, yet they happen quite quickly. If you compare videos or photos of what your baby was doing two months earlier, the progression can be surprising. One minute, she's a newborn, and within six to eight weeks, she's following you around the room with her eyes and smiling.

The key to helping a baby's development progress is providing a loving and interesting environment. For many parents, stimulating a baby through tender, loving care and play comes naturally. Others prefer to read and hear advice on how they can enhance their child's development. This chapter identifies what's normal in your baby's developmental progression and characteristics to look for at each stage.

DEVELOPMENT: THE FIRST MONTH

A new baby is born—pink, crying, wrinkled, with squinting eyes—all perfect. It seems like a miracle, and it's no wonder you feel in awe of this experience.

What to Look For

Eye contact. You may notice your baby seems to look at you, then look away. At times, it appears he's looking at everything *except* you. Do you see he's quite intrigued with lights and bright colors?

I suggest the best time to work on gaining full eye contact with your baby is during feeding. At birth, your baby can see up to twelve inches away, so when his face is close to yours, he is more likely to fix his eyes on your eyes and gaze lovingly at you. At other times, you see your baby exercising his eye muscles trying to fix on an object and follow it routinely. Sometimes his eyes appear crossed, but they will likely look normal by three to four months of age. If his eyes appear crossed on a regular basis, though, consult your pediatrician.

Head bobbing. In the first month, your young baby can pick up his little head, but the head remains wobbly. Use your hand to gently hold his head while carrying the baby or reposition him altogether. You may touch his head and delicately cradle all parts of it in your hands. It's okay to gently touch the soft spot (the fontanel) on his head. Babies are typically born with two fontanels, anterior and posterior—located at the top and back of the head, respectively. The gaps in the cranial bones form the two fontanels to allow flexibility for bone growth. Blood vessels just underneath the head's surface are carrying blood to nourish the skull and brain. Because of this, you can even see a little pulse over the soft spot.

Hearing and loud sounds. Notice that babies with normal hearing are often startled by loud sounds, with some being more sensitive to sound than others. If your baby heard a lot of noise while in the womb, he may be used to loud noises and not seem affected by them.

Your baby may startle for reasons unclear to you, particularly when you are tending to him. In fact, he has a normal reflex called the Moro reflex that causes him to startle. This reflex shows his brain is working properly. If your baby startles, mostly likely he'll calm to your voice when you speak gently. Cuddling, holding, and rocking may soothe a baby who gets startled.

In addition, after experiencing extreme comfort in the womb, he's especially sensitive to his environment. His hands will flail as if he's grabbing the air, and his legs will flex.

In the first month, babies sneeze, hiccup, and make sounds like they're snorting. You may hear little grunts or squeaky noises. These sounds are, in most instances, normal early vocalizations. If other symptoms are also present, though, the sounds may indicate a problem. For example, babies who are having respiratory or feeding problems may grunt or make squeaky noises. If you hear the vocalizations persistently or recurrently, point them out to your pediatrician during your baby's next examination.

Closed fists. Initially, your baby's hands will often stay closed in fists while he moves. Over the months to come, though, his hands will relax. When you put your finger in his hand, he will grasp it. Look for this sweet handshake to continue at varying times throughout the first year of life.

Deep sleep breathing. While in a deep sleep, babies might pause for a few seconds while breathing. After the pause, they will breathe faster for several seconds. This is called periodic breathing—a normal breathing pattern that ensures a baby gets plenty of airflow. In fact, a baby's brain is wired to remind him to take breaths.

Danger Signs of Distress

Call your doctor if your baby:
- persistently makes grunting or squeaking noises
- breathes fast continually
- snorts all day, not just off and on
- has a fever exceeding 100.4 degrees Fahrenheit (38 degrees Celsius)
- exhibits difficulties while feeding or doesn't feed well
- fails to pass urine for more than six hours

DEVELOPMENT: MONTHS ONE TO THREE

During her first three months of life, your baby changes rapidly. By six weeks, your sweetie is typically smiling and showing off her personality. Some babies are more serious than others, and you practically have to beg for a smile, while others smile readily. How exciting to watch her evolving personality!

Compared to her first month of life, you'll notice she seems to communicate with you more with her eyes, her expressions, and her body movements.

What to Look For

Picks up the head. Your baby's head control gets better over time, but it still remains somewhat floppy and needs support. By the end of the third month, most babies will pick up their heads easily when placed on their bellies. Watch them demonstrate a delicate act of balancing their large-in-proportion-to-the-body head.

Watching your moves. During months one and two, expect her eyes to want to track and follow you. She will gaze at you and follow the face she loves as you move. Keep talking, cooing, and enjoying this time. It means so much to her—bonding at its finest. Following with her eyes is one of many important milestones that show brain development stimulation. When talking, put your face in front of her so she can see you well. She clearly wants you to converse with her! Relish in the delight on her face as she watches you.

Tummy-time exercises. Ensure your baby has tummy time by placing her on her belly on a flat surface at least four times each day. If she enjoys lying on her tummy, you may place her on it as much as she'd like while awake. And when you can't watch her when she's asleep, roll her on her back, ensuring good ventilation around her face.

If she doesn't like lying on her tummy or cries when placed in the belly-down position, feel free to pick her up and console her. If she seems unhappy with her position each time you place her on her tummy, try again later. She's likely to get used to tummy time if she's positioned on her belly regularly.

An alternative tummy-time position is with you lying on your back and her tummy in contact with yours. In this position, she's facing you and can make good eye contact. It also allows her to easily move her arms and legs, and you can lift her if she requires a change. You'll benefit from this soothing body contact and easy communication between parent and baby.

If you lay your little one on the floor on her tummy, put her on a mat or blanket. Some babies get rashes from floor-cleaning agents or carpet fuzz, so it's best not to expose her to chemicals. When she's lying on her belly, supervise her at all times so you can see her nose and mouth. The floor should be clear of objects so she can breathe with ease.

Still sleeping like a newborn. After the first month, your baby will continue to enjoy lying with her legs bent and often curl up into her original womblike position for sleep or snuggling. This is normal. As the months progress, she will relax her arms and legs more, flexing them less as they stretch out over time.

Because she still enjoys her newborn sleep position, encourage her to stretch and move her legs. While stretching her legs, sit her up in her car seat or infant seat so she can see the world. An upright position continues to foster and stimulate her curiosity. Ensure that her body and head are not slumped over in the seat. A good angle for a seated position is forty-five degrees; any higher angle could cause her head to slump forward. Practice having her sit up with her head back so she can breathe easily.

Dangle playful items. For playtime, find a bright object to dangle in front of your child. She will bat at the object but not yet deliberately grab for it on a recurring basis. At this point, she's working out the differences in colors.

You don't need to go to a lot of trouble stocking up on commercial stimulation toys. They are fun, but I can't say this enough: *Show her any object in your environment.* If you are cooking, show her the pan, then talk to her about the pan. Let her feel the coolness of the side of a clean spoon. When you get to the potty, show her the toilet paper, and even rub a piece of toilet paper on her leg. She wants to see everything, feel everything, and hear your voice. Don't offer several objects at once, as this might be too stimulating for her brain. Among the best objects to show are pictures in books and bright toys.

Chatty baby. You will notice your baby cooing more and more. As these months march on, she may coo for periods of time while smiling. Yes, that means she's talking to you! She will soon have lots to say.

Listening and soft sounds. Your baby wants to hear different noises and will get calm when hearing familiar voices (especially yours!). Sometimes it may seem that friends or family can't calm her. It's not that they aren't connecting with her; she simply prefers *you*. More and more, she'll turn her head toward sound. You'll note during this time that she pauses and listens. You may notice this particularly with music that you play. It's because music is engaging for her brain, and classical music is a soothing choice. If you don't like classical music, feel free to play any music that's not harsh or loud. Babies tend to like soft sounds. Hearing soothing music allows them to focus on other areas of their sensory input.

Expose your sweetie to different sounds in her environment. For example, if you're using an eggbeater while cooking, show it to her and let her listen to the sound. If she's afraid of a particular sound, console her and remove it from her environment.

Processing speech. This stage is a good time to introduce a second language. Your baby is learning to process speech. If anyone in the home speaks a second language, then speak it around the baby frequently. If you are hiring a caregiver, look for someone who speaks a language you'd like your baby to learn. For example, four of our southern states border Mexico. There, the most practical second language for children and adults to speak is Spanish. Or perhaps you have roots in Syria or other parts of the Middle East. Then you may want your child to speak Arabic. You get the idea.

If your family isn't bilingual, you might think having a person speak a second language around your child is daunting. Ask your friends, family, and trusted professionals for their experiences. If you get negative responses ("It's too early!") yet you really want your child to be bilingual, don't let their opinions dissuade you. Select the language and seek immigrant groups in your area. For example, in our hometown, a group of people who have immigrated from China and Taiwan have created a Chinese school for children. Perhaps a parent can call the school to find a Chinese person who might become a caregiver and speak Chinese to their child. Ensure your caregiver knows your priorities upfront: (1) caring for your baby and then (2) nurturing and speaking a second language.

DEVELOPMENT: MONTHS FOUR TO SIX

By four months of age, most babies are talking more and more in the form of cooing. They smile quite a bit. Many babies will start babbling and laughing when they feel happy or amused.

However, how much they laugh depends on their personalities. Some babies are serious little guys, making you work for a giggle or smile. By six months, though, they're likely to squeal with delight. When you talk to your baby, he will likely turn and look at you with a contemplative look or a sweet smile.

What to Look For

Baby's fist. You'll notice your baby's hand won't stay in a fist as it did in the first few months. He's batting at objects and, with both hands, reaching to grab them. By six months, he's grabbing whatever you give him and putting most objects in his mouth.

Ready to roll. Some babies roll over as early as four months. By six months, most babies will roll one way or both ways. Because it's easy for them to roll off of a soft surface, such as the couch, never leave your baby unattended. Most babies roll *from* their stomach *to* their back first. However, because we tend to place babies on their backs to sleep, many have stronger back muscles and may roll back to front first.

Tummy-time exercises. Continue doing your tummy-time exercises at least four times a day. Tummy time will get easier during this stage because your baby is better able to pick up his head to see things in front of him. Give him one object at a time to explore, or simply get on the floor and make faces at him.

Startle reflex. By the age of six months, the Moro (startle) reflex should be mostly gone. If you notice a persistent Moro reflex, discuss this with your pediatrician. Your baby may be overly sensitive, but a persistent Moro reflex can signal other medical issues that need addressing.

Teething. The ability of babies to place objects in their mouths comes just in time for the teething phase. Many babies grow their first teeth between four and six months. On average, babies cut their first tooth at six months, although some little guys wait as long as one year to sport it. Handing him objects to chew helps soothe a painful teething sensation. You are welcome to use teething toys, but realize that you have many objects in your home your baby would love to chew on. An example would be the end of a large spatula. You'll want to make sure the objects you offer are safe and not a choking hazard. For example, keys can be dangerous and cause mouth injury.

Sharper vision. As colors and details have more clarity for your baby, you may find him looking at his hand for some time as if studying the miracle of its beauty. Sensing the awe of his hands and other items teaches him about the permanence of objects in his environment.

Seeing and smelling. Your baby will become excited when he smells and sees food. He's ready to start pureed foods whenever you feel ready to offer them. With his heightened sense of smell, he might turn toward a certain odor if it's strong enough for him to notice.

Engagement and distraction. At this stage, your baby can easily find you when he hears your voice. If you keep talking, he will keep looking for you, though he might become distracted by something else.

Babies are easily engaged by any change in the environment. If an object is dropped, he follows its motion. If he sees something interesting, he reaches for it. Once the object is out of sight, he stops looking for it and thinks about something else. At times, it may appear he can't focus, but he can. He just wants to see it all!

Babies love to look at faces. Family, friends, strangers, and even their own images engage them, so bring out the mirrors for play and recognition.

Sitting up. Your baby will sit up better than before at the beginning of this period, although his back isn't quite straight enough to sit on his own yet. By six months, most babies can sit if they're lightly propped; some even can sit on their own. Keep your baby in an upright position while awake to allow him to view the world around him.

Southern Africa: !Kung's Side Sling Efficiency

If you don't already have a sling-style body carrier, six months of age is a great time to purchase one. Consider the !Kung San people, who come from northwestern Botswana.

Between 1969 and 1971, !Kung parental practices were studied extensively, and parents were praised for their nurturing skills. !Kung babies are carried in a sling on the mother's side instead of front or back. (!Kung mothers typically carry their babies, but some !Kung infants may be carried by their fathers.) In this position, the baby is able to move his head forward or backward and align with the mother's or father's view of the world. Skin-to-skin contact continues, and the parent wearing the sling can make eye contact and talk to the baby. !Kung moms don't wear bras so that their breasts can be freely available for their babies' midafternoon snack. The babies are able to breastfeed on demand from this sling position. Many !Kung mothers wear brightly colored necklaces. The colorful adornments around a !Kung mother's neck can serve to keep their babies entertained.[1]

The best time to use a side sling is when your baby has good head and upper body strength. You can tell this if she can easily hold her head up in the vertical position without flopping and can pull up on her arms when on her tummy.

If you purchase a sling-style carrier, try on different types with your baby in the carrier to get a good fit for both of you. Check safety standards of the side sling. (For more information, see the baby-wearing section in Chapter 1.)

United Kingdom: Affectionate Nursery Rhymes

Your baby will love listening to your voice. Rhymes and songs will make her smile and giggle. Here's a rhyme from England that also describes how to include touch as you say the rhyme.

> Round and round the garden . . .
> (*Run your index finger around baby's palm.*)
> Like a teddy bear.
> One step, two step . . .
> (*Walk your fingers up the baby's arm.*)

Tickle you under there!
(Tickle under the baby's armpit.)

And here's an Irish version of the same rhyme. Use the same tactile stimulation with your hands.

Round and round the racecourse . . .
Catch a little hare . . .
One step, two steps . . .
Tickle under there!

The English version traces back to the United Kingdom in the 1940s when teddy bears became popular. The Irish version dates back further with exact origins unknown. Both rhymes are still popular today.

To stimulate your baby's auditory (hearing) and visual response, change your voice each time you repeat the rhyme. And repeating it on a regular basis can teach your child to anticipate the fun last "tickle." For more international music and culture, visit http://www.mamalisa.com.[2]

DEVELOPMENT: MONTHS SEVEN TO NINE

Your baby is starting to sit up on his own and is likely beginning to crawl. Super fun!

What to Look For

Crawling. Some babies start with a standard crawl on both hands and knees. Others use one side then the other while crawling, and the movement appears asymmetrical. Many babies start by sliding on their stomachs then pulling up on both knees and hands. While in the position and ready to crawl, your baby will often rock forward as if he wants to lunge at an object. Once his hands and knees get together to move equally and symmetrically, look out! He's on the go, and you'd better keep his path clear.

Standing. Around the time your baby begins to crawl, you can prop him up next to a table or couch so he can stand while holding on. Keep a careful arm behind him, though, as he will topple over easily. Many babies are pulling up to stand by nine months, but some wait until later. After your baby pulls up, he will independently stand while holding on without propping. What a wonderful upright view of the world!

Fine-tuning the grasp. At seven months, your baby picks up objects by raking them with the palm of his hand. By nine months, he is likely using a "pincer grasp" in which small objects such as finger foods are grasped with his thumb and index finger. Also by nine months, he is feeding himself with his fingers. "One piece at a time" is the best rule of thumb for two reasons: he can practice his pincer grasp more easily, and it will help prevent choking. He will also learn to pass objects from hand to hand. He's not quite juggling yet, but he's practicing early!

If your baby isn't using a pincer grasp at nine months, check to make sure he's doing it between nine and twelve months. The change may be quite subtle, so you may not realize he's using his thumb and index finger to collect objects. If you notice your baby isn't using his pincer grasp by age twelve months, check with your doctor to ensure his fine motor skills are developing properly.

Playing. He loves to play interactively with you and look at books. When reading to him, point to objects he will enjoy, using simple words to describe them. He'll find it fun to listen to you talk as he looks at the object. When you drop a toy or an object he's interested in, he'll look for it, but not for long. He can be easily distracted by other engaging activities.

Copycat. Expect your baby to imitate even more of your sounds and gestures. He's chatting a lot, using single syllables, and may be saying "Mama" and "Dada." It's difficult to tell if he's addressing you or saying words randomly, but he definitely wants to engage your attention with conversation. You will notice him echoing many of your word sounds. Even though he's not saying distinct words yet, you'll hear noises that seem like a common word used in the family.

Sometimes your baby chooses to imitate a movement such as clapping or bobbing his head. Notice that his gestures are more animated than ever, and if you persistently wave at him, he might just wave back.

Ways of Greeting in Other Countries

Consider this a good time to have fun teaching your baby to greet others in ways used in other countries. For example, in Belgium, giving three kisses back and forth from one cheek to the other is a common greeting. Try walking in the room, smiling at your baby, saying "Hello!" and then greeting her with a Belgian kiss.

In New Zealand, people in the Maori tribe greet each other by rubbing their noses and foreheads together. According to the Maori people, the breath of life is exchanged during this simple greeting. Try this enjoyable stimulation by greeting her with a gentle nose and forehead rub. Your baby will love getting close to your face and rubbing noses. But watch out! She's getting strong and may pull your hair.

In northern Mozambique, hand clapping is a common greeting your little one might enjoy. People there greet each other by clapping their hands three times then saying hello. Your baby will enjoy all kinds of clapping games. Imagine her delight if you walk in, smile, and clap your hands three times before saying hello.[3]

DEVELOPMENT: MONTHS TEN TO TWELVE

Your baby's development in the last two months of the first year is a whirlwind of excitement. Sometimes it may feel like you can't keep up as you make your house safe for all this new mobility and increased laughter. The race begins.

What to Look For

Mobility. Most babies become highly mobile at this point, crawling frantically and pulling up to stand. The average baby starts walking at twelve months, though some walk earlier and others later.

Many fast crawlers have no incentive to rise off the floor, because standing up and toddling around doesn't appeal as much as reaching their destination with a fast crawl. Keep the floor clear of small objects that your little one could accidentally pick up and choke on.

Pincer grasp. During this time, your baby is perfecting his fine pincer grasp. He rakes objects with the palm of his hand less frequently and uses his thumb and index finger more often to pick up objects. This activity is fine-tuned by giving him finger foods—fruits, vegetables, grated cheese, and soft whole-grain breads. These foods allow him to perfect the pincer grasp, build confidence with self-feeding, and experience various food textures.

You may find that eating is fun yet challenging. Many babies are predominantly interested in finger foods once they're eating them regularly. If you still want to spoon him purees, he may refuse them. Until around eighteen months, your baby may seem uninterested in a spoon coming at his mouth when he can put it into his mouth himself. Place only one piece at a time on the eating space to avoid setting up a choking incident due to too much in his mouth.

Babbling. Your baby's ability to babble improves, and, by twelve months, many babies are saying one or two words deliberately. Often, the first words are the obvious "Mama" and "Dada" or even a favorite object. Keep reading to him and repeating words he enjoys. He will absorb them and belt them out more between ages one to two years.

As your baby gets more mobile, it may seem he doesn't want to stop to look at books, so keep a stash of books nearby for him. While he's playing with toys, make sure books are within his reach. If he picks up the books and plays with them, take this opportunity to jump in and read to him.

Another opportune time to read is when he's tired and sitting in your lap. Read until you are out of time or he falls asleep. Remember to read slowly enough that he can understand your words and look at the pictures. Consider changing your voice frequently so he can hear different inflections. During the exciting parts, add physical movements such as hand clapping, tapping on the table, or bumping your child up and down on your leg.

Exploring. With your baby's increased mobility, you will notice he wants to explore, learn, and stimulate his senses. I suggest giving him several different objects to touch and explore. If you have something in your hand or within reach that's safe (such as a plastic cup), hand it to him to explore. The more he explores colors, textures, shapes, and different temperatures, the more he learns. Plus, exploring keeps him alert and happy.

Separating. Separation anxiety is closely related to stranger anxiety. *You* are his world, and he wants to spend most of his time with you right now. Yes, he can enjoy being with others, but he's attached to his parents. Often, he will reach for one parent over the other recurrently. This doesn't mean he's not bonded with the other parent. He simply needs the parent he reaches for at the time so he can feel safe, nurtured, and loved. If that parent leaves the room, the other parent won't feel left out after all.

Stranger danger. Stranger anxiety is often present at this age. When your baby is playing with others, he will often look back at you and feel comforted by your presence. If you aren't in the room, he will come searching for you or even cry out for you to find him. Stranger anxiety happens most commonly with people he doesn't know well. Understand that he's still deciding if he is safe with others.

Making friends. Introducing your baby to new people will help decrease his fear of strangers and of leaving you. He will be intrigued with children his age and older, even though he may not play interactively at this point. Most babies, though, like to sit beside other babies and play. They explore each other's features and enjoy looking at each other. They also like touching each other's clothes, skin, and hair. Mostly, they imitate the sounds and facial expressions their baby friends make.

Being rough. Some babies begin to express themselves with an excited hit, pinch, or bite. This is a common, normal behavior when they feel happy, excited, or anxious. Typically, if this occurs, redirect or distract them. Punishments such as verbal reprimands or time-outs (placing him in a separate area to teach him a consequence) do not work at this age. Babies won't respond to such tactics, so save these forms of discipline for when they are toddlers. Instead, distract your baby away from any negative behavior so it doesn't become a habit.

For example, if your baby gets upset and smacks you across the face (Ouch!), a good response would be to put him gently in his playpen or on the floor and hand him a toy. Removing him from the scene takes the emphasis off the negative behavior and gives you a moment to compose yourself if you are hurting. It's okay to say "No," but yelling at your baby will scare him. A loud or stern voice directed at him may stop a negative behavior due to fear, but a baby who feels afraid is more likely to cry and be more anxious and emotional overall. He could grow into an insecure child who doesn't express himself well. If you're a yeller and can't control it, talk to your healthcare provider or a counselor to get tips on how to express yourself without instilling fear in your baby. Further, if others in the environment yell at him, tell them not to do so and/or get help to understand and correct the behavior.

No spanking or hitting. Understandably, some of your baby's behaviors such as hitting may be frustrating. If you're feeling stressed, take a step back to cool down. Don't spank or hit him. It's okay to put your baby in a playpen if you need time to collect your emotions after a negative behavior. Chances are your baby has plenty to play with and will keep himself entertained.

Allowing self-consolation in a loving way. If your little one is upset or frustrated, let him work it out. If he fusses and whines, let him deal with that too. You can talk to him so he knows you're there to support him, but give him space to figure out what he needs to do. If his discomfort is obvious and he can't tend to it himself (such as being hungry), meet that need. But if no reason is apparent, give him time to learn to console himself.

If your baby is upset and crying, hold him and try to calm him. If he clearly doesn't want to be held, put him down and allow him to console himself. At the same time, let him know you are present so he feels your support. When you're unable to calm him, sit beside him and hand him a comfort object such as a favorite toy or blanket. If he continues to cry, lie beside him with your body touching his. At any time, do your best to hold him close to you when he seems upset.

Sometimes a baby becomes upset if you can't tend to him immediately. Life happens! Simply talk to him while you finish your task, letting him know you'll be available soon. He may not clearly understand, but he will notice your presence, even if only by the sound of your voice.

Colombia: Extended Family Nurturing

In Colombia, older children and extended families play an important role by providing nurturing and stimulation to enhance a baby's development. Rather than separating the younger children from the older ones, babies are integrated into the whole family. Sara Sierra, a Colombian pediatric nurse practitioner, says, "When shopping for a house, for example, parents in Colombia don't look for a certain number of rooms. Rather, they look for a certain number of beds to ensure everyone has a place to sleep." Family ties are important for all areas of care and development. Babies learn about the world on the shoulders of their many family members.[4]

Day care is not used often in Colombia. Older children in the family often care for the babies, toddlers, and preschoolers, keeping them entertained before they go to school. Patricia Grimaldos, a dentist and artist who grew up in Colombia, notes, "Extended family plays an important role in the upbringing of the children in Colombia. There is a sense of respect as well as social involvement in their lives." Siblings learn to play with and care for their younger siblings as an expression of responsibility and unconditional love.[5]

How can you incorporate the Colombian approach into your family? Simply choose to adopt the philosophy of total family care for each other. Include the baby and younger children at functions, and consider having the younger children share bedrooms with the baby to enhance their bond. Sharing rooms often has its problems, but many people say sharing a bedroom with a sibling made them feel closer and more loving toward each other.

Achieving family unity is a deliberate choice fostered by the parents' attitude. Promoting love and unity at this stage will build a foundation for lifelong relationships among the siblings for years to come.

Chapter 5

PARENTAL BLUES AND SIBLING RIVALRY

A re parental blues real? How can a new mother be sad when she has a beautiful baby to enjoy?

Parental blues are very real, especially in the first year of life. Don't get me wrong—any parent may feel sad at any time, especially as it relates to parenting. There is so much anticipation and expectation associated with a pregnancy. When the baby comes, life feels wonderful, yet very different. You have been expecting continual baby bliss, yet you may still feel sad.

These days, you might have pressure to parent well, knowing you have only one chance to raise your children properly. Then, for reasons hard to understand, you may feel sad, unappreciated, or even unloved.

SYMPTOMS OF PARENTAL BLUES

Feeling sad, helpless, angry, and worn out are all symptoms of parental blues. If you suffer from any of these, please consult your doctor to ensure you have a "normal" parental blues condition, not a medical issue that needs to be addressed.

Similar symptoms to normal parental blues can arise from postpartum depression (PPD), a mild or severe form of depression that can follow childbirth. PPD is caused by fatigue, hormonal changes, and difficulties adjusting to motherhood. It creates discomfort and may interfere with your ability to care for your baby.

Strategies to Deal with PPD and the Blues

If you believe you have parental blues, try the following strategies to tackle the problem.

Follow a healthy diet. Sounds like a cliché, doesn't it? But it's critical. Search for information about healthy eating, which can be confusing for a mother trying to keep up with a new baby and the rest of her life. Don't think you have to make complicated changes in your eating habits. However, reducing junk food and eating more food from the earth will go a long way toward helping your mood and energy level. I suggest sticking with fruits, vegetables, dairy, meats, and grains while taking in a minimal amount of processed foods. If you choose to eat frozen entrees, look for preservative-free varieties. Eating excess carbs makes most people feel sluggish, so don't overdo the bread, rice, or pasta. If you suspect you may be addicted to carbohydrates, check with your doctor to get help.

Did you know that excessive carbohydrates can alter your mood? Ingesting carbohydrates causes a release of endorphins, which temporarily makes you feel great. Later, as your body tries to process the increased load, this overindulgence in carbohydrates may make you feel extremely tired. A new mother doesn't need any more cause for fatigue. She has a baby!

Drink water freely. Do not drink caffeinated products or any energy drinks that may alter your mood. Even mild dehydration can make you feel moody or sluggish, so make sure your body gets plenty of fluids, especially water.

Increase your exercise. "Who has time?" you may ask. Yes, new mothers are busy. You don't have to join a gym if that's not your style, but you do need to get moving. Put your baby in a stroller and go for a walk. And while you shouldn't exercise vigorously while wearing your baby, a nice stroll will be enjoyable for each of you. Babies love fresh air, and you might be pleasantly surprised by her positive response to it. Exercising in the morning invigorates you for the day. You can walk again in the evening if your schedule allows, but in my experience, finding time to exercise in the evening can be difficult. Your baby may not cooperate; you have to prepare dinner; you might feel excess fatigue from the day's activities. It happens!

Once you insert exercise into your schedule, keep it going. Exercise may improve your mood on top of many other advantages. According to Harvard Health Publications, "Besides lifting your mood, regular exercise offers other health benefits, such as lowering blood pressure, protecting against heart disease and diabetes, reducing your risk for cancer, keeping bones strong and healthy, and helping you maintain your vitality and independence in later years. How often or intensely you need to exercise to alleviate depression is not clear, but for general health, experts advise getting half an hour to an hour of moderate exercise on all or most days of the week."[1]

Get plenty of sleep. The joy and rush of having a little one at home can keep you in overdrive. The anxiety about caring for your baby may also cause you to lose sleep, not to mention the baby waking you up for feeding or changing in the night. Numerous studies have shown that sleep deprivation affects mood and overall quality of life. Even if you don't normally take a nap, figure out a good time to rest—especially while your baby is sleeping. Very little is urgent; your house doesn't have to be perfect; you can tweet your friends later. Simply rest.

Enlist support from loved ones. Do you have a best friend, sibling, or confidante who is a good listener? This is the time to activate that person's attention. Pick up the phone and call to chat, or if your confidante likes to text or email, sometimes it's nice to write out how you feel and have a caring person who listens or reads. Remind yourself that well-meaning spouses, significant others, friends, family members, and confidantes aren't always right. On the flip side, someone who knows you well may help ground you and give you good advice.

If you would like an objective, outside expert to talk to, consider consulting a psychologist or licensed counselor. If you go that route, check with your doctor for recommended professionals in your community.

Schedule time for you. Slow down and catch your breath. Each day, do something for yourself without feeling guilty. Take a long bath while your baby is asleep. Put your baby's father on baby duty while you get a pedicure. Take that walk alone. Most of all, don't feel guilty about taking time for *you*. As your baby gets older, you'll see the importance of modeling this habit.

If your sadness or moodiness is severe, if you feel you're at risk of injuring your baby, or if you have thoughts of suicide, see your doctor immediately for assessment and treatment. If you need to be on medication for postpartum depression, don't view it as a stigma. This happens to many women. Know that postpartum depression is a real disease and often cannot be prevented.

Vietnam: Family and Friends Deliver Prolonged Care

One noticeable difference about Western culture compared with many parts of Asia and other areas is that more attention is immediately placed on the baby than the mother after birth.

In the American culture, being independent is important. As a consequence, many mothers feel alone making decisions. I'm not saying women *shouldn't* be independent, but I do think we should feel comfortable asking for help and resources. Some mothers rush back to their jobs quickly and can't take time to rest and enjoy their babies. An extended maternity leave is often not available in the United States, so if you're able to get leave from your job, take advantage of this benefit.

In many cultures, extended families and friends take care of the mother postpartum while she rests. Western culture provides no distinct postpartum period when the mom is waited on hand and foot. By comparison, Vietnamese and other Asian cultures have a period of postpartum confinement for the mother. During this time, the new mother should not do anything except rest and feed and bond with her baby. Her body is supposed to be "warmed." This tradition is believed to bring the mother back to good health so she can care for her baby and prevent illness in the future.

For the mother, food intake is critical. The new mother stays in the home, does no housework, and pays particular attention to hygiene. Her visitors are limited. This elaborate family system helps take care of the baby while the mother rests. The mother can then build up her strength emotionally and physically so she can better care for her child in the long run.

In many cultures, grandmothers and aunts help with the baby for several months. This allows the mother to learn about baby rearing and breastfeeding from those who have experience. The potential negative is having people in your space, which might feel too close for comfort.

Having postpartum help from the father, family members, and friends is invaluable. This can curb a mother's worries, so she isn't constantly asking, *Is my baby fed appropriately? Is she gaining weight? Is she in the proper sleep position? Is she comfortable?* I suggest working out the details of taking a month for postpartum confinement and enjoying your new life as best you can.

WHAT IS SIBLING RIVALRY?

Oh, the bliss. Baby excitement kicks in, and your older child is happy to see this infant sibling. Or not. Either way, your older child's reaction may add stress, but a shift will occur. Sometimes, when a new baby arrives, the older sibling is thrilled until the newness wears off and she realizes someone else has grabbed her parents' attention. Or she stays thrilled with the baby but is angry with you for reasons she can't explain.

It's normal for a parent to feel guilt-ridden about adding a new baby to the family. A sibling who feels especially jealous can lead to one or both parents feeling guilty about not giving the sister or brother enough attention. This feeling is normal. The new juggling act requires figuring out how to give more than one child the attention needed. A two-parent family can often tag team, one with the baby and the other attending to the other sibling(s).

Realize that feeling jealous is a natural reaction for siblings, so don't let your guilt get the best of you. Sharing provides an important life lesson for them, one that's not easy to teach. It has to be experienced—and what better way to experience it than with a new baby?

Do realize one thing, though: *quiet doesn't mean your child is adjusting well.* Be aware of the older sibling being extremely quiet and withdrawn. That doesn't mean she doesn't need her special parent-child time. It's simply that some children hold in their emotions. So ask your child questions about how she feels. Have her role-play with her favorite toy to help her open up about her feelings concerning the change at home.

Strategies to Deal with Sibling Rivalry

Maybelline Valenti, a lovely young mother of two, was born and raised in Maracaibo, Venezuela. When asked about sibling rivalry and adjusting to a new baby in the house, Maybelline stated, "For my culture, family is everything, so fostering a positive sibling relationship is key. We usually try to create excitement for what's about to happen, and once the baby arrives, we include the older sibling in any activity that's age appropriate. If family members are visiting with baby gifts, they usually bring one for the siblings as well so they don't feel left out."[2]

To include siblings in the excitement of adding a new family member, consider these ways to help your older child deal with his swirling emotions.

Don't play favorites. It's easy to side with a small baby when an older sibling is upset or angry with him. In fact, you may feel annoyed when your toddler gets upset with the baby. But once you have dealt with the situation, move forward quickly and work toward a positive resolution for sibling jealousy.

Deal with negative behaviors. To get attention, children sometimes exhibit negative behaviors such as yelling at the baby or showing physical aggression. Often, they direct behaviors such as hitting or throwing temper tantrums at *you* as part of a phenomenon called "negative attention." They can't tell you verbally that they're lacking in attention, but indirectly, they let you know they need it.

You've heard the phrase, "Oh, she just wants attention." To that I say, "What's wrong with wanting attention? Give her some!" Don't confuse her by rewarding the negative attention, though, or she'll keep doing it. For toddlers, ignore or redirect any inappropriate behavior. Take action to stop any physical behaviors that may harm the baby. For an older child, provide appropriate consequences for negative behaviors. Spell out your expectations, and reward positive behaviors frequently.

Give extra attention. A good time to give extra attention and make your older child feel included is during loving interactions with the baby. For example, ask your child to look at the baby and note what she sees. What color are the baby's eyes? Is the hair curly or straight? How does the skin feel? Would she help put lotion on the baby? If you think your older child is too physical or doesn't know her limits, take care not to leave her alone with the baby until she learns this behavior isn't appropriate.

Take photos. Try to relax, realizing your new normal is just beginning. If the older sibling is a toddler, she won't have much memory of the birth. If the sibling is beyond the toddler years, she will likely have formed an early impression of her new sister's or brother's arrival. Either way, take a lot of photos, especially with your child or children holding the baby. This is a special moment to preserve, so even as the memories fade in a child's mind, the photos stay forever as good discussion starters. Creating good memories can help lessen the jealousy.

Schedule one-on-one time with the older child. Give the sibling who appears to need the most attention one-on-one time with you. For consistency, be sure to stick to the schedule you set. Toddlers enjoy having time carved out for activities that focus on their interests. Children four years old and older look forward to the scheduled time—ideally once a week for a couple of hours. It gives them an event to anticipate. Taking a trip to the park is nice for children, or you might do a favorite activity together. Toddlers appreciate time alone with you anywhere!

Let the child control your play together without imposing rules (other than obvious safety rules) because having the upper hand during playtime helps build confidence. I realize that two hours of alone time with the older sibling(s) might be a lot for busy families with a new baby. But with multiple siblings or difficult logistics, even fifteen minutes of one-on-one time daily is better than none.

Overwhelmed by the idea of adding one more activity to your schedule? Family and friends may help lighten the load by giving older siblings special attention.

Foster a Loving Relationship among Siblings

Follow these ideas to help your child adjust to living with siblings:

Teach your child empathy. It's good for the older sister or brother to learn to relate to the baby's emotions. One way is to ask your child what she thinks about how the baby is feeling. "Jonathan is crying a lot today. Does he seem tired to you?" This also provides a good opportunity to help your child understand the baby better. For example, if the baby is crying and you say he's sad, you can ask the older sibling what makes *her* sad. Then, talk about her feelings relating to sadness and what makes her feel better. She may come up with a good idea to comfort the baby, and this will help their relationship. Use this technique to discuss various emotions, even happiness.

Give the older sibling quality time with the baby. Just remember to be cautious about giving your child so much responsibility that she feels like the caregiver and not the sibling. Supervise all activity. Often, younger children don't know their limits with babies, especially when feeding and holding them.

One idea is to present the older sibling with a gift from the baby. Even an older child who knows the baby didn't pick out the gift will appreciate this gesture. Choose a handmade gift, a stuffed animal that provides comfort, or a small family album showing the baby and sibling in the photos.

Regard the challenge of having a new baby as an important life lesson. Don't feel guilty because you're not always having fun. The older sibling will learn to problem-solve and accept challenges, even if she's not having fun. I'm not suggesting you promote a negative atmosphere. However, know that all life challenges help your child learn to cope with future real-life situations. Provide guidance in learning these lessons.

Don't strive for perfection. It's normal to *not* love every moment of parenthood. That's day-to-day living! Maybe you feel guilty because you have to go back to work or you waited too long (or not long enough) to have another child. You may worry you aren't the perfect parent. Know this: no one is perfect, and neither is any situation. Striving for perfection only sets you up for failure.

Have your child help you with the new baby. No matter what the age, you can get your child involved in the baby's care.

Singapore: Foster a New and Loving Relationship

Mothers in Singapore constantly encourage older siblings to help out with the new baby. Fostering a "help out" attitude early inspires children to assist each other as the years march on. Mothers in Singapore thank their children frequently for the assistance. Toddlers can be your "special helper" at times, handing you things the baby might need. If the baby is crying, allow your toddler to help soothe her with loving kisses. Older children can help you feed the baby, which can be a fun caretaking task. Showing parental gratitude reinforces the positive behavior. Just like a Singapore mom, don't forget to thank your child for being a helpful sister or brother![3]

If you show your older children love, empathy, and honesty while parenting fairly, they will thrive. Over time, they'll learn to share and problem-solve in difficult situations. Having a younger sister or brother can be challenging, but growing up with a sibling to love is invaluable.

Chapter 6

SECURITY OBJECTS

Infants are born with a need to bond with their parents, siblings, friends, and family. If a security object—a fun blanket, stuffed toy, even a cloth diaper—is introduced by age six months, your baby will enjoy and be comforted by it. This security object should be soft and small. Attachment to a pacifier as a security object starts early, while attachment to other objects increases closer to nine months and may continue for years.

A baby's use of a security object doesn't mean he's naturally anxious. Because the object is mostly used for comfort, attachment to it is not psychologically harmful. In fact, its use aids in calming and soothing a baby in times of stress. Although a baby may enjoy a certain security object such as a blanket or teddy bear, don't allow him to sleep with it in the first year of life due to risk of sudden infant death syndrome (details in SIDS section).

France: Always Carry Your Baby's *DouDou*

In France, a security object that travels with French babies is called a *doudou*. Parents take the *doudou* with the child to visit friends and family as well as to child care. In fact, caregivers ask for a *doudou* when the baby arrives.

A French *doudou*—a mother's scarf, a beloved blanket, a toy or stuffed animal—can be any object that brings comfort and joy to the child in stressful situations.[1]

Your baby may feel anxious at times of separation from you, so having a security object helps alleviate his anxiety as he gains confidence being in the big new world.

STRATEGIES TO DEAL WITH SECURITY OBJECTS

Let the security object stay with your baby. Just like French babies, if your baby has a security object, it should remain with him. For example, if you're leaving town and your baby stays at his grandma's house, taking his favorite stuffed toy will remind him of home. Also, consider packing a small photo album to remind the baby of family members not present. While in a strange place, a familiar object reminds him of home. Or if he's going to a sitter's or day care, this object may help him tolerate separation or cope better with sleep or illness.

Select a security object for your baby. Some babies love security objects while others appear to reject them. Your baby may not seem interested in any object, but a child's choice of security object is not always apparent. If it's not obvious and you want to give your baby a security object, hand the chosen object to him regularly while you comfort him. That way, your baby will enjoy the touch, feel, and comfort of that particular blanket or toy.

Keep the object clean. When cleaning this object, use the same unscented, dye-free soap or detergent each time so it will keep a familiar smell. If your baby's security object can't be easily cleaned (e.g., a favorite stuffed animal that might fall apart in the washer), then use it mostly indoors to reduce wear and tear. If you purchase a security object, consider buying two so that one can be in the wash while the other is with your baby.

Also, be sure to turn to a security object in disaster situations. When your baby is used to finding comfort in his security object for little challenges, he will find the same comfort when he experiences major ones. Various types of security objects have been used for comfort and relief. Stuffed animals, quilts, and blankets are often given for emotional comfort in emergency disaster situations during times of stress. Organizations such as Project Smile collect security objects for children who are sick or injured or who have been exposed to crime or a natural disaster such as a hurricane. These objects don't replace human affection; they are supplements to human care for these children in distress.

Have a backup object in case of loss. Oh, no, it's lost! The downside of having an attachment object is the possibility of losing it. That's why I wouldn't advise taking it *everywhere.* If you notice your baby is attached to one particular toy or blanket, identify a backup object in case it gets lost. Rotate in the backup regularly so he becomes used to its touch and smell. If you're looking for a common, easy-to-replace security object, try soft cloth diapers. Many babies enjoy holding these, and they can be easily replaced.

Ensure that others respect your baby's need for the security object. Unless you live in France, sometimes you're forbidden to take the object to day care or other settings when it may be helpful. When choosing a nanny, babysitter, or day care center, consider the tolerance to your baby's security object from those involved. Some people oppose specific things for personal or cultural reasons. If your baby enjoys his security object, ensure that others in his environment respect his right to have it.

RESEARCH SUPPORTS USING A SECURITY OBJECT

People in many countries around the world do not use security objects. However, substantial research in the United States and Europe supports their use, especially in the absence of a parent.

Dr. Richard Passman, a psychologist at the University of Wisconsin in Milwaukee, studied children who had attachment blankets. He found that children who had their own blanket fared better during the stress of a medical examination without their mother present. By comparison, children who had no blankets in the absence of their mother appeared more anxious.[2]

England: Don't Leave Home without Your Teddy Bear!

Many adults had their own preferred comfort objects as children. Some had a favorite blanket, pillow, or teddy bear that provided comfort. In England, sleeping with a teddy bear is more common than you might think. A study in 2010 by Travelodge revealed that 35% of adult Britons sleep with a teddy bear, and many said they take their stuffed animals with them when they travel as a source of comfort.[3] Siobhan Louise Twissel, a nanny and graduate of University of Birmingham, England, states, "My friends sleep with loads of them. When one of them travels anywhere, she will bring her main teddy. I used to travel with thirty when I was a child. I don't sleep with my number one teddy, but he's not far away and gets to sleep with me on holiday. I normally bring him to see the children I look after, and he has a sleepover with them."[4]

DON'T WORRY ABOUT DEPENDENCY

You might worry that if your baby uses a security object, he will become too dependent on it as he gets older. Some people worry that a security object will foster feelings of dependency. However, research doesn't support this theory. When their mothers are absent, children who have security objects seem less distressed and engage in play better. Studies have also shown that learning is enhanced with children who bring a security object with them.

Do you wonder how long your baby will need to have his security object? As your child gets older and learns to cope with stress, he'll naturally give up his security object. This could be in the first year, by age two, or much later. Sometimes, it gets lost and it's given up then. I recommend allowing the child to naturally give up his object on his own. Don't push the timing. Not only does this help build his confidence, but he also doesn't feel the loss of an important part of his childhood. And, who knows? He may want to enjoy his security object into his adult years, just like many of our friends in the United Kingdom.

Chapter 7

SEPARATION AND STRANGER ANXIETY

B abies often experience separation anxiety and stranger anxiety before they develop trust with the world around them. These are two different reactions. Let's look more closely at what they mean.

WHAT IS SEPARATION ANXIETY?

Separation anxiety sounds like a diagnosis, but it's really a normal occurrence in many babies' and toddlers' lives. It usually begins around eight or nine months of age. Most of the time, your baby will outgrow separation anxiety by the time she is two-and-a-half to three years old.

You may notice that by six months, your baby looks back for you when someone else is holding her. If she drops a toy on the floor, she looks for it, and she does the same thing with you. She may cry for you. If you go into another room, she may search for you. Sometimes, she fusses as she does that. When she learns to trust that you will return, her comfort level will be restored.

Some babies who love being cuddled a certain way may not be happy if someone else holds them. That's especially true if that person doesn't hold them the way they enjoy or puts them in an uncomfortable position. But this type of discomfort is not separation anxiety, which occurs when a baby truly does not want to separate from her parent. A little one's separation anxiety may also provoke anxiety for the parent, but rest assured that it's a normal phenomenon that resolves itself as babies and toddlers learn to trust the world around them. Once your baby trusts that you'll return in a timely fashion, she'll feel more relaxed about separating from you.

Understanding Separation Anxiety

The following tips will help you deal with separation anxiety:

Know that anxiety increases with major changes in routine. For example, if your baby moves to a different room to sleep, you are away for a night, you travel with your baby, you change babysitters, or you have another new baby in the house, he may seem uneasy. The uneasiness may occur during or after the change in routine. Realize that he's trying to sort it out and wants your support while he does so.

Some babies experience anxiety later in infancy when going to sleep. You can combat this by having a steady routine and staying consistent with daily bedtime rituals. If your baby wakes up at night due to separation anxiety, make your late-night contact with him brief and boring, not playful. If he'd like his pacifier, gently place it in his mouth without a lot of fanfare. This kind of nonplayful contact will help prevent recurring nighttime awakening, which commonly happens in babies with separation anxiety.

Don't expect you can always be there. You can't live your life feeling guilty about being away from your baby. Regard that separation as an important life lesson for him. Just ensure that someone in his environment will love him and make him feel safe in your absence.

If your baby fusses, allow him to self-console. If he cries steadily and is very upset, hold and comfort him. Don't consider this overindulging him; you are simply tending to his needs.

Your emotions may vary about separation anxiety. At times you may feel sad, annoyed, overwhelmed, or guilty. Strive to see separation anxiety for what it is: your baby loves you, is attached to you, and prefers to be with you.

You can't "force" a baby to outgrow separation anxiety. Naturally, you do want your child to have less separation anxiety as he gets older, but you cannot push him to outgrow it. Sometimes, you just have to go away. And sometimes, you have to leave when he's crying. If you leave him with a person who will nurture him, most of the time he'll stop crying once you're out of his sight.

Italy: Pass the Baby—Everywhere!

In Italy, babies are welcomed enthusiastically at gathering places. In many countries such as the United States, babies are welcomed in some places and excluded in others. For example, parties and weddings may be designated "adults only."

If you talk to an Italian, though, you may hear about parents going to shopping places, restaurants, and churches with their babies who get passed around from person to person with glee. If a baby exhibits separation anxiety, her parent quickly retrieves and consoles her, but another adult or sibling is often waiting in line to give her attention. Family interaction with the baby is high with people of all ages in the room. Further, when new people come into the room, their first reactions are to engage with the baby.[1]

The Italian parenting style helps prevent separation anxiety. Whenever possible, take your little one to baby-friendly places.

Having friends and family around your baby makes it a happy, therapeutic environment for her. In addition to helping prevent separation anxiety, social immersion is a stimulating learning environment for your baby.

WHAT IS STRANGER ANXIETY?

Think of stranger anxiety as separation anxiety's cousin. They are closely related, but a few points separate them.

With stranger anxiety, your baby notices who is new to her and who is different. If she recognizes someone different, her behavior may change. I observe this painful truth at many nine-month pediatric checkups. Any baby may identify me as a stranger, and because he's not used to seeing me, he protests when I try to examine him.

Not all babies cry when approached by someone they don't know well, however. Many factors may aggravate stranger anxiety, including fatigue, an unfamiliar environment, or even the baby's mood at the time of meeting someone new.

Some babies will have stronger reactions than others. It's common for me to hear a mother say, "Liam never got as upset as his sister does when she is around someone new." Different babies, different situations.

The degree of stranger anxiety often depends on these three factors:

1. Personality: Many babies are shyer than others, and some show emotion more easily.
2. Socialization: Babies who have not been around a lot of people need more time to figure out new people.
3. Parental reaction: As a parent, if you feel stressed, your baby will pick up on your emotions and act accordingly. When a parent or caregiver is stressed, it's more difficult to pick up on the baby's cues and nonverbal language.

Stranger anxiety may elicit unusual responses in people who don't have experience with babies. Aunt Ruth, for example, may have forgotten that her own children had stranger anxiety, so then she appears huffy when your baby cries in her presence. Not to worry; stranger anxiety is nothing to be embarrassed about. Remind Aunt Ruth that it means your baby is learning about the world. If Aunt Ruth smiles, is patient, and shows she's safe to play with, your child will warm up to her in time.

Strategies for Dealing with Separation and Stranger Anxiety

The following tips can assist with your child's separation and stranger anxiety.

Practice separation. Take a tip from the Italians and pass your baby to others. From early infancy, practice separating from your baby from time to time. Usually, this comes naturally as you go to the grocery store and run errands. Many babies are in day care or with a sitter from early infancy, which allows them to explore the world with other people. If your baby isn't around people outside of the immediate family and the sitter, make sure she gets exposed to others. You can even leave the room from time to time while she plays with other children or adults, especially as she gets older.

Keep a consistent routine. No routine is perfect. Life happens. Try to prioritize bedtime at a consistent time of night and put down your baby for naps when she's tired. A fatigued baby gets cranky and likely has difficulty separating and enjoying life. With a routine, your baby learns what to expect and will gradually trust her environment. She feels safer living with that regularity.

Place other people around your baby. It's important for your baby to explore new people's personalities so she can learn to interact with them. Having both children and adults in your environment helps. Don't think it's necessary to find playmates who are exactly the age of your baby; she'll enjoy looking at people of any age!

You'll notice she's especially enchanted with babies. If you see a friendly parent with a baby in the play area, stop to say hello so your baby can get a look at him. As your baby gets older, let her socialize with other babies during a mother's day out or at day care, preschool, or play group.

Hands down, the best way to deal with separation anxiety is helping your baby build trust with others in her environment.

Stay calm. Babies pick up on any anxiety around them. If you feel nervous about leaving your baby somewhere, question why you feel that way. Get to the root of the problem. If it's solely because you think she will be upset to see you go, realize this is a normal reaction. She will eventually get through her separation anxiety. Remain friendly and upbeat while engaging in conversation with others. She will notice your reaction, and this will help her learn to trust the world.

When new people are around, reassure her and introduce her to them. Don't hand your baby to a new person immediately. If she's at the doctor's office, often the doctor will speak to you first before touching the baby. Take this opportunity to show her that *you* feel safe in the environment. To make her feel more comfortable, walk around and talk about what she sees. If there's a mirror, allow her to look at herself for entertainment, or simply take out a familiar book or toy from your bag.

In social situations, use soft, even tones when speaking to people you would like her to meet. If she appears content, pick up her hand to touch the person while you're holding her. Watch her cues, then take a step back if needed to make her feel secure.

Make sure she's not hungry when separating. Most babies will fuss if they are hungry, so put her on a regular feeding schedule. During this separation anxiety phase, most babies eat at least every three hours (three meals plus two or three healthy snacks a day).

Make sure the security object stays with the baby. If your baby has a comfort or security object, don't forget to take it with you when you go out and about. This can be reassuring for her if she gets upset.

Create a departure plan. If you move your baby to a new day care, take her with you a few times to say hello before you leave her there for the day. If you hire a babysitter, have that person arrive early on the first day. Take time to transition before you leave; don't quickly run out the door. Yes, this is easier said than done when you're in a hurry, but understand that adding a few extra minutes to the transition can go a long way to boost your little one's comfort level.

When you decide it's time to leave your baby, do so. Don't hang around and try to soothe her if she cries. Instead, distract her in an activity with the caregiver. Show her something she enjoys such as a favorite toy. If she has a security object, be sure it's available when you leave. Sure, the security object does not replace *you*, but it can help comfort her in your absence.

Most babies and toddlers show both separation and stranger anxiety. Your baby will cry and you will feel guilty when you leave— probably many times over. *This is normal.* Regard it as a backhanded compliment. *You* are her security, her life love. She misses you when she doesn't see you. But if you were with her around the clock, she wouldn't rise to the challenge of enjoying interactions with others— an important life skill for her to acquire.

Russia: Using Matryoshka Dolls to Engage

Use fun objects to engage your baby and share with others as they engage her as well. Galina Nikitina, originally from Russia, offers this example.

"Matryoshka is a wonderful nesting toy for stimulating a child's development." The toy is a set of wooden dolls of decreasing size that fit neatly inside one another. Around for more than a century, Russian matryoshka dolls are fun for all ages. They tend to have bright colors and a variety of themes. They can be used for nesting, visual stimulation, creating sound (banging), and playing hiding games such as "Where's the toy?"[2]

Tibet: Family and Community Care

In Tibet, after a baby is born, fathers take on caregiving roles to free up the newborn's mother and let her rest. They commonly continue helping after infancy too. Extended family members are also highly involved in the care of babies. A baby's contact with a variety of people in the family and community is considered important for brain development.[3] Just as in Italian families, passing the babies throughout the families and involving the fathers help babies socialize, increasing their sense of feeling secure in the world.

If your baby becomes used to being held and cared for by many people starting from a young age, it can help minimize his stranger anxiety and deal with separations from you better. While your community may look different from those in Tibet, there are plenty of people around you who will be happy to support you and nurture your little one.

Chapter 8

YOUR BABY'S SLEEP

In the first thirty days of life—the newborn period—babies tend to sleep fourteen to eighteen hours a day. They sleep so much, in fact, parents often wonder if it's normal.

If your baby is awake and alert between periods of sleeping, is feeding well, seems content, and has normal bowel movements, then, yes, all that sleeping is normal. If your baby has a fever, seems overly irritable, isn't urinating or feeding well, or is difficult to arouse, call your doctor for an immediate examination.

SLEEP PATTERNS FOR YOUR BABY

The following describes various patterns of sleep that babies experience.

Sleep deeply. Babies often sleep very deeply, so you may have to work to wake them up to feed during the newborn period. They also spend a lot of time in the rapid eye movement (REM) cycle of sleep. This deep stage is due to the rapid development of brain cell growth. It means your baby is learning new things every day. The brain stays busy from birth!

Sleep when tired. For the first one to two months of life, he will sleep when his brain and body tell him to sleep, with no particular schedule. This may challenge parents who want to set up and maintain a normal sleep regimen. I frequently hear complaints about a parent's fatigue and sleep deprivation, which can result in parental blues and even postpartum depression. My response? Your dishes can wait. Prioritize *your* sleep schedule.

Sleep when full. Various books have been written on the topic of scheduling sleep time, but the answer differs from baby to baby. Newborns sleep quite a bit. They eat, feel relaxed, and fall asleep. Some babies who are born prematurely are catching up on growth. They may not be as effective at feeding yet because their little bodies aren't as developed as full-term babies. Many times premature babies have to be awakened to feed. Babies born at a full-term size of six to nine pounds also have tremendous growth spurts requiring frequent nourishment.

In the newborn period, most full-term babies feed on demand, which might be every two to three hours. As they get older, you can space out feedings more because their tummies can hold more milk and they learn how to feed more effectively. Ask your doctor to provide guidelines for how often to feed your baby.

Sleep any time of day or night. Babies are frequently awake all night and sleep during the day—more than expected. I often hear parents say, "My baby has his days and nights mixed up!" During the first two months, a good rule of thumb is to not worry about noise. After all, your baby slept just fine in the womb with noise. He will continue to sleep fine with noise he's used to around him.

No matter where your baby is, he will get sleep when he needs it. In our world, babies sleep in a variety of places, such as a hammock, a fancy cradle, or even on their mother's back. Your baby's brain is wired to sleep when he needs sleep. That said, Meredith Small, author of *Our Babies, Ourselves: How Biology and Culture Shape the Way We Parent*, provides research that clearly shows the number of hours a baby sleeps is culturally dependent.[1] So, our lifestyles help determine how much our babies sleep.

Holland: Practical Dutch Schedules

Dutch parents are quite rigorous when it comes to sleep scheduling and, in general, scheduling their lives. A Dutch mother would ask, "If a baby is not sleeping well, then what is wrong with the daily routine?" She will then adjust things in her routine to find what works best for her baby. At age six months, Dutch babies typically sleep two hours more per day than American babies.[2] Americans are also routine focused, but busy lifestyles get in the way of keeping to a consistent plan.

As the Dutch have demonstrated, getting your baby into a consistent nap and bedtime schedule often takes setting a routine. If you have a steady work or school schedule, typically your routine will work well for you. If you have a life that requires spontaneity, routine may not come so easily.

Strategies for Napping

In the first three months of life, your baby will be on his own sleep schedule. He'll nap when he's tired and awaken when refreshed. His first month calls for a large amount of sleep. What a good time for Mom and Dad to nap too!

Many parents wonder if it's normal for their baby to catnap off and on all day. Yes, it's fine. Some babies sleep in increments of five to thirty minutes at a time. They wake up refreshed and then, anywhere from two to four hours later, nap again. This catnapping phase may last several months, but it doesn't typically last throughout childhood.

How much should a baby nap? Each baby is different. Some nap a total of two hours a day, and others, up to six hours a day. During the first six months, most babies get tired within four hours of their last nap. Look for your baby's cues. He may appear less focused and engaged. He may yawn or act fussy. He may rub his eyes or ears. His eyes may tear. Observe these actions, knowing that sleep will follow. Older babies may fight going to sleep, but they too will collapse into a restful sleep when they're exhausted.

Northern Europe: Outdoor Napping

In several European countries, including Sweden, Denmark, and Norway, it's common to sleep outdoors, even in freezing temperatures! People of the Faroe Islands, located north of Scotland and west of Norway, have been allowing their babies to nap outdoors for many centuries. In the second edition of *A World of Babies*, Mariah Schug wrote:

> Having your child nap outdoors is important for many reasons. The cool air and the sounds of the sea and wind help the infants to sleep. Your infant will take longer naps while sleeping outside, and this promotes healthy development. Being outdoors will also help protect your baby's health by reducing exposure to the many germs indoors.[3]

In the winter, babies are wrapped in warm wool clothing such as a bodysuit and a hat. Some babies who have sensitive skin need a heavy unscented emollient applied to their faces. (In America, such an emollient might be Aquaphor ointment or Eucerin Original cream.) People in Northern Europe believe the fresh air is good for these little winter babies, and they sleep especially well.

I admit that the idea of a baby napping in freezing temperatures intimidates me. I have had no exposure to this practice. Obviously, the mothers in Northern Europe have experience in wintertime outdoor napping. Their point is that napping outdoors can be refreshing and stimulating for the baby. As an alternative, I suggest supervised napping outside in the spring or fall. In the summer months, outdoor sleeping could be enjoyed in the cool parts of the day.

Be sure to feed your baby *before* letting him nap outside in the summer to prevent dehydration. Feed him again *after* the nap to ensure he's well hydrated. Placing a baby outside to nap in hot temperatures may harm him. He should never nap while in direct sunlight.

If it's quiet where you are, letting your baby nap outside is a wonderful way to have him sleep in a peaceful environment, whether in the warm or cool months. For parents, being outside relaxing is always good. Find a comfortable spot next to your napping baby to check that he's enjoying his outdoor time.

CO-SLEEPING

Talk to twenty different doctors and you will get twenty different ideas and attitudes about bed sharing or co-sleeping. Recent studies have shown that babies who co-sleep with their parents are more likely to die of SIDS (sudden infant death syndrome). However, international research disputes the overwhelming research data pointing to bed sharing having a close association with SIDS. After reading this research, I still advocate a better-safe-than-sorry approach. Why take the chance?

Strategies for Safe Co-Sleeping

Having your baby's own crib and room is a practice advocated by many health care professionals because infants will sleep more peacefully without interruption that way. On the other hand, if a parent chooses to co-sleep, this may be gratifying as long as co-sleeping is safe for the baby.

Basically, babies need a firm mattress that doesn't have extra pillows, covers, fluffy stuffed items, and parents' bodies. This ensures adequate ventilation around the baby's face, prevents the risk of suffocation, and lowers the probability of SIDS.

Co-sleeping has many advantages, including a more content baby, an enhanced bonding experience, and greater peace of mind for the parent that the baby is fine. In my clinic, I have noted a breastfeeding practice in which a baby sleeps with Mom, but in the baby's own sleep area, so that she can just roll over and feed the baby at night—easy for both parties.

There are strong opinions on letting one's baby sleep in the parents' room versus a separate room. In the engaging book *Do Parents Matter?*, anthropologists Robert and Sarah Levine wrote that the Western concept stating "co-sleeping undermines the child's independence" is largely cultural, and not backed by any particular research. Early on, babies benefit psychologically and physically by sharing a room with their parents.[4] I suggest the middle ground of coordinating room sharing with having a separate sleep area for your baby.

Japan: The Ultimate Cuddle

In Japan, many parts of Asia, and a large percentage of the world, parents co-sleep with their children for years. In fact, co-sleeping has been the world's answer to protecting infants for many centuries, although North Americans are typically discouraged from doing so. In countries around the world, however, this isn't the case.

In Japan, it's common for a baby to sleep lovingly with his mother. This is true for countries where it's common for extended family members to live in the same home. But you have to recognize as well that many countries around the globe also don't have all the fluffy soft pillows and blankets that America and parts of Europe use, so it's a safer environment for the baby, even if he is co-sleeping.

Mostly, it's important to ensure that co-sleeping is safe and enjoyable. You can choose to sleep with your baby close by, but your baby must have a separate sleep area to prevent SIDS.

During his first two months of life, it is good to have him in the same room as you for feeding purposes; it makes life easier for both of you. Many parents also want the luxury of gazing at their child and bonding through co-sleeping, especially if one or both parents are going back to work. The best timing to move your baby to his crib in the room is a personal choice. If you really want him in your room for a long time but don't want him to sleep in your bed long-term,

I suggest moving him to his crib by the time he is six months. After that age, many babies become so used to sleeping close to you that it gets harder to move them to their crib.

Types of Co-Sleepers

1. *Co-sleeper box in the bed.* A co-sleeper, or portable infant sleeper, is a small structure similar to a box that can fit next to you and isolate the baby from the suffocation hazards of pillows, blankets, and bodies. The box is typically long enough—thirty to thirty-four inches—to fit a baby comfortably for the first six months. If you choose this option, put the box on top of the covers in the middle of the bed— away from the edge of the bed—but away from pillows. Any loose pillows hanging around can inadvertently end up on top of the baby. Also, if you sleep with a loose cover on your body, you risk the blanket falling over the baby's sleep area and suffocating him. Don't put any blankets in the co-sleeper, and always ensure the mattress is firm.

2. *Co-sleeper attached to the bed.* This co-sleeper fits on the side of the bed. With this option, you don't have to worry about setting up a co-sleeper in the bed with no blankets or pillows around. You can adjust the level to the height of your bed. This option is more expensive than the co-sleeper box on the bed. In my opinion, you can get more continued use from a play yard or bassinet instead.

3. *Bassinet and/or a play yard with a removable bassinet.* A square-shaped structure with high sides, a play yard is where a baby or toddler can stay safe and enclosed. These are less expensive than a co-sleeper attached to the bed and can be used for a long time, which is why I favor this practical option. The bassinet is typically placed at the top of the play yard, and voila! You can access your baby with the roll of your body, and it's also in the best position for your baby's sleep—on his back. If you buy a play yard, you can

use it later as your baby grows. You will save more money by purchasing the play yard and the bassinet together, and it works just as well as an attached co-sleeper.

OLDER BABY SLEEPING

How long do you keep an older baby sleeping in your room? It's your choice. Many parents are ready to move their baby into her own room at six weeks, six months, or even later. However, many parents prefer to keep the baby in their room. My husband and I safely co-slept with our children through the toddler years, letting my youngest sleep in a baby box on our bed. However, some people don't feel comfortable with this because they have a hard time sleeping with their children in the room.

After six months, if your baby sleeps in the same room, she is more likely to wake up at night and want to feed or interact than if she has her own room. She knows you are in the vicinity; she can hear you in the room. If she sees you, she's likely to want to engage your attention.

As mentioned previously, as your baby reaches six months, it becomes harder to move her to a separate place of sleep. Moving her after that time is sometimes associated with sleep disturbances. It is much easier to move her sleep area when she's about four months old than at six months or older.

When should you move your baby out of a bassinet or co-sleeper? The easiest answer is when she starts to roll or outgrow a co-sleeper. Put her in a different sleep area such as a crib or play yard. Co-sleepers attached to the bed will continue to work until about six months, but once the baby pulls up on the side, she has to be moved out of that too. If you have a play yard with an attached bassinet, you can remove the bassinet and have her sleep in the bottom of the play yard.

Whatever the location, continue to place your growing baby on her back for sleep. Make sure you have no blankets, soft items, or anything else in the sleep area so she won't become tangled in objects or suffocated. This is especially important if you fall asleep or leave the room.

STRATEGIES FOR HELPING YOUR BABY SLEEP

Let's take a few tips from the Dutch—and your own touch—to get your baby to sleep better at night.

When you move your baby into a different room or sleep area, follow these tips to make the transition as easy as possible.

Set up a bed for your baby consisting of only a mattress and a fitted sheet. Times have changed. Babies should sleep on their backs with no blankets, pillows, bumper pads, or stuffed animals. That sounds harsh, right? This sleep environment doesn't sound too cozy, but it's safe. You can dress your baby in warm clothing so that she doesn't feel cold. However, avoid bundling her up when the environment is warm. If she appears uncomfortable, remove some of her clothing. If a baby is too cold or too hot, she will fuss and cry. Make your baby more comfortable by having ventilation around her face so she can breathe easily and has room to stretch.

You can also use a sleep sack or wearable blanket instead of traditional blankets. Made to replace the risk of using blankets (which may easily end up on the face and cause suffocation), sleep sacks or wearable blankets ensure your baby won't maneuver the blanket onto her face.

Stop the all-engaging play. Do your best to minimize excitement and stimulation in her environment as it gets closer to time to sleep.

Play soothing music. Typically, classical or soft music works best to calm your baby. If you use music or singing to put her to sleep, put on the same music each day so she knows it's naptime. This predictability will add consistency to her sleep schedule.

Help your baby relax, and then place her in her sleep area before she's fully asleep. Different babies often respond to different calming techniques. Calming may include rocking or laying her on her back and gently patting her tummy. If she doesn't like this, find an area of her body where she enjoys being touched.

Rock your baby to sleep—or not? There are two schools of thought on rocking your baby to sleep. One says to allow her to settle on her own, and the other says to rock and hold her until she sleeps. You may also consider a combination of both techniques.

Many Dutch mothers allow their babies to settle without a lot of rocking. If you choose not to rock or hold her to sleep, be sure she gets hands-on nurturing when you see she's getting tired. Your baby will find your hands soothing when you touch her before falling asleep.

The best way to get your baby to sleep is to place her in the crib or bassinet when she's tired. Let her fuss a bit, then gently place your hand on her belly to help her sleep. However, any out-and-out crying should get your attention. At this early stage in life as she's learning to trust you, if she cries, it's extremely important to pick her up. She may become more agitated and cry more if she is not held and cuddled when she's distressed.

Yes, it's okay to hold and rock your baby at night. Your baby will love being held and rocked to sleep. This concept is controversial in the parenting world. But consider this: Babies have been rocked to sleep for thousands of years. It nurtures them and makes them feel loved.

For early sleep training, I suggest rocking and holding your baby until she's drowsy then putting her down and letting her settle herself to sleep. Enjoy these activities as much as you like. Train her this way, especially at night, so she can learn to settle herself—a technique that will take her a long way toward learning to sleep comfortably as she grows.

If your baby cries, tend to her but keep her in the sleep area. By staying in her sleep area, she learns that it's time to sleep and not play. As babies get older, they often cry or fuss just to see you and interact. What a lovely compliment! However, you may not feel so positive about it at two o'clock in the morning! Some agitation, discomfort, or even light fussing is fine because you want your baby to learn to soothe herself. But when she's learning to trust, if she cries uncontrollably, you *know* she needs your attention. We'll address the idea of crying it out shortly, but before your baby is a year old, go ahead and soothe her when she's obviously upset.

Aim to wean off all nighttime feedings after six months. If your little one wakes up for feeding in the middle of the night after six months and your pediatrician says your baby doesn't need the nutrition, wean her off the feeding. To do that, feed her less every three nights. For example, breastfeed her for a shorter time than the other two days or give her less formula from the bottle. Every three nights, reduce the time of breastfeeding by five minutes. If she typically breastfeeds for twenty minutes, then breastfeed fifteen minutes for three nights, then ten minutes for three nights, and so on. If she bottle-feeds, reduce the amount of pumped breast milk or formula that you give by two ounces every three nights.

If you're having trouble getting your baby to go along with this technique, rethink your feeding schedule during the day. Be sure she's eating well throughout the day and at least an hour before bedtime.

However, if your baby sleeps in the same room as you, she may wake up more frequently just because she knows you are close by. This is a good reason to move her to another room, unless you don't mind feeding at night. Some people find it exhausting, but if it works for you, then continue as you think is best.

Gradually eliminate feeding your baby to sleep. Sometimes this is easier said than done. Many babies are used to falling asleep while feeding from the breast or the bottle. If this is their last memory, often they wake up again at night and cry to be fed, setting up a vicious cycle. It's better to wean babies off nipple-feeding about an hour before the desired bedtime. Babies over six months who are on solids can have a good meal of solids first and then nipple-feed. Always provide calming techniques to get your baby to unwind.

If your baby will go to sleep only during feeding, try other ways. Most babies will feed and fall asleep shortly thereafter. As the months march on, though, changing the habit of falling into a deep sleep while feeding will be helpful. The key to changing this habit is to put her in the crib or bassinet when she's drowsy and letting her settle herself. If she gets upset, pat her or sing to her to let her know it's time to sleep. It conveys a need to stay where she is, yet she can still see you are present.

Keep a routine. Babies love routine—so there's no time like the present to start one. Dutch mothers keep a consistent routine, with each day similar to the one before. You may find this impossible to set up, and that's okay. But I urge you to have a simple routine. For example, a good time to give a bath is just before sleep. Most babies enjoy music, so sing to your baby or play soft music before bedtime. As your baby gets older, you can add reading a book to your routine.

Having a daily routine can be beneficial for napping too. For example, for babies in day care, typically a two-hour period is set aside when every baby is put down to nap.

Keep a checklist for nighttime routines. For parents with different nighttime routines or work schedules, it might be helpful to make a nighttime checklist so you can keep a regular routine for your baby. It may sound trivial, but babies love predictability when they are tired. Many babies who are excessively tired can get overstimulated and will avoid sleep if their environment is altered at bedtime.

Here's an example of a nighttime routine schedule for a six-month-old baby.

6:00 p.m.—Relaxing play with parent

7:00 p.m.—Feed solids and then nipple-feed

7:30 p.m.—Warm bath, wrap up in a towel, and then cuddle

8:00 p.m.—Lights out with the usual song or music (the song or music should be consistent each night to signal it's time to sleep)

Have your baby routinely nap in the same place. Establish a napping place at home. If she's at a caregiver's home or day care during the day, request that she consistently take naps in the same place as well. This helps her learn that when she's put down in a particular area, it's time to nap.

Babies tend to sleep better in familiar areas. Sometimes this is impossible, such as when you're traveling or visiting a new place. So simply be relaxed with your routine, and your baby will learn flexibility. In general, though, know that she'll sleep better in her usual comfy environment.

Make contact with your baby at night brief and boring. If your interaction with your baby at night is enthusiastic, she will greet you with equal enthusiasm and remain alert. "Brief and boring" is your key phrase if you want your baby to go back to sleep at night.

If the house is still noisy after the baby's bedtime, use white noise in the sleep area. White noise should have a consistent noise pattern and not be too loud. If your baby is routinely awakened from sleep (perhaps by a sibling's voice), this can quickly set up a pattern for your little one. Use an air purifier or oscillating fan if needed to muffle slight noises. If you play soft music, discontinue it after about thirty minutes of sleep. A change in the music's tone and tempo can wake babies from their sleep.

Keep soft light in the room during the day. Babies can nap with light coming in from outside, so don't worry about making the room completely dark. In fact, if you're having problems getting your baby to sleep through the night, sometimes it helps to ensure the room is *not* dark during the day. Darkness creates a restful environment, but it might keep her from sleeping as deeply and as long as her nighttime sleep.

Keep the night sleep area calm. To make your baby's night environment tranquil, use minimal lighting in the room so that you can see the baby yet it's comfortable for her to sleep. If you're changing her diaper, avoid overstimulating her with too much movement. If you speak to your baby at night, keep your voice soothing and low. In time, the flip-flop of day and night sleep patterns will subside as long as her nighttime environment is calm and nonstimulating.

For extreme bedtime resistance, let a different parent put her to sleep. This works for babies about eight months old and above who are experiencing separation anxiety. I have seen many families switch parents to put a baby to sleep. When her baby was nine months old, one mother even left her house and let her husband put the baby to bed. The baby consistently cried when she saw her mother but seemed more content when the mother wasn't around. So the parents hatched a plan for the mother to simply leave the house at bedtime. Guess what? It worked. She no longer has to leave the house; she simply stays in another room. I have passed on this advice ever since and it's often met with great success.

Any method you choose to put your baby to sleep requires consistency. Babies and children learn by routine. If you're consistent with your sleep routine, your baby will start to sleep through the night. My biggest piece of advice is this: *don't provide a reason for your baby to wake up.* Wean her off feeds, stop offering her exciting activity, and put her in her own sleep area.

CRYING IT OUT (CIO)

What if your baby is more than nine months old and still not sleeping through the night? Should you let her cry it out? No, not for very long. Responding quickly to your baby's crying with holding and nurturing is more beneficial for your baby's development. This is not to say a baby should never cry; babies cry when they are upset. Prolonged crying happens for various reasons, but it should not be recurrent. If babies cry for an extended time with no attempts being made to nurture them, this can be psychologically and emotionally harmful.

Disadvantages of CIO

Some pediatricians and parents believe in the CIO system, and their babies have fared well. Maybe you are among them. But consider the following points if you are thinking about turning to the CIO method.

Age is important. Don't use the CIO method for babies younger than nine months of age. Because they're learning to trust and are still bonding, they need to be held and nurtured when they are distressed.

Understand your purpose in letting your baby cry it out. Is it your desire for her to get to sleep and have a good night's sleep? Are you exhausted? These may be valid reasons to let your child cry.

Do spot checks after five minutes. If she fusses a bit, that's okay. But if she cries persistently for more than five minutes, check on her. You can soothe her while she remains in the crib and then leave. This approach can be time consuming, but it reassures her that you're around and she hasn't been left alone for long.

If your baby's sleep problems are severe and she doesn't respond to these techniques, check with your doctor to rule out a possible medical problem. For example, some babies who are teething may have trouble sleeping during the height of their tooth's eruption. If your doctor determines this is happening, you may be instructed to give her ibuprofen or acetaminophen liquid at night to alleviate pain.

Remember, no system is perfect, so don't expect every night to be your baby's best night of sleep.

PREVENTING SUDDEN INFANT DEATH SYNDROME

I hate to bring it up. We all think about it, though—how to prevent sudden infant death syndrome (SIDS). Though a rare occurrence, SIDS is every parent's worst nightmare. In a 1983 movie called *Terms of Endearment*, a grandmother went to check on her infant granddaughter, couldn't tell if the baby was breathing, and pinched her. A loud scream from the baby followed. It was a comical scene, but those who've checked to make sure their babies are still breathing can relate.

The past two decades have seen a steady decline in the incidence of SIDS by more than 50 percent. The reported rate for 2015 was 39.4 deaths per 100,000 live births in the United States, according to the Centers for Disease Control and Prevention (CDC).[5] As health-care providers and parents, we aim to systematically reduce the risk factors. It's our job.

Research has identified risk factors for SIDS to help us prevent this terrible event. The risk of SIDS peaks for babies aged two to four months and steadily declines after the age of six months. Various reasons for this particular age range have been suggested, with many validated by research. We know that babies who co-sleep with their parents and/or lie on their stomachs are more likely to have SIDS, and breastfed babies are less likely to have SIDS. Many mothers will tell you that their babies had all the risk factors for SIDS but fared well. Pediatricians will counter with "better to be safe than sorry." I say, "Why ignore the information that current research provides?"

Strategies for Reducing the Risk of SIDS

The following recommendations can help reduce SIDS incidents and promote safe sleeping for your baby.

Babies should sleep on their backs. If you are in the room and awake, allow your baby to sleep on his side or lie on his belly. If he's in a different position other than the back, keep him in your sight. His face should be showing so that you know he's getting plenty of oxygen. If you leave the room, fall asleep, or otherwise don't watch your baby while he's sleeping, rotate him to his back and make sure to keep him there.

Mattresses should be "baby firm." Firm mattresses are available for standard cribs, portable cribs, play yards, and bassinettes. Even co-sleepers must have firm mattresses that meet the safety standards, especially if you are using a hand-me-down.

Ensure no blankets or pillows are in the crib. Unsupervised blanket and pillow use increases the risk of accidental suffocation or strangulation. You can lay your baby on a pillow or use a blanket when you're supervising him. But even during naptime, if you leave the room, your baby shouldn't have blankets or pillows in his sleep area.

If you use a Moses basket—a basket made especially for babies—enjoy your baby in the basket while watching him. Although Moses baskets are pretty and comfortable, they don't provide adequate ventilation for a sleeping baby in case he turns his face into the soft plush of the basket.

Forget bumper pads. They are history. I hope you haven't even heard of these. But if you have those cute bumper pads to line the bottom of the crib, get rid of them. Your baby can roll on them or get caught in them, possibly causing strangulation. Also, bumper pads restrict air ventilation in the crib, thus increasing the risk of suffocating.

Never sleep on a sofa or chair with your baby in your arms. If your baby is asleep in your arms, you must stay awake. If you sense you might fall asleep, take a moment to put your baby in his secure sleeping area on a flat mattress.

Waterbeds are a no-no. Your baby shouldn't sleep on one, and neither should you with your baby present. Because a waterbed mattress moves, it doesn't give your baby enough support. Also, it's soft enough that a baby could be smothered if his face is even minimally embedded in the mattress. Save the fun waterbed for the toddler years.

Use oscillating fans to create good ventilation. An oscillating fan to stir the air is a wonderful asset to your nursery. A study in 2008 by the Kaiser Permanente Division of Research showed that infants who slept in a bedroom with a fan moving the air had a 72 percent lower risk of SIDS compared to infants who slept in a bedroom without a fan.[6] Face the fan away from the baby so he doesn't get too cool. Also, don't let your baby get too hot or bundle him in too many clothes.

Are you getting the point? **Ventilation.** As mentioned previously, babies should have plenty of airflow around their faces.

Don't let your baby sleep in a swing. If your baby falls asleep in a swing, he should be moved to a firm mattress and placed on his back for continued sleeping. Some car seats and baby bouncers are used for babies who have excessive gas or gastroesophageal reflux (spitting up recurrently) because an angled position can alleviate some of their symptoms. If he falls asleep in a baby bouncer or car seat, make sure he is in the same room so you can keep an eye on him. Also, ensure he is at an approximate thirty-degree angle, strapped in, and unable to slump forward. When you are leaving the room or going to sleep at night, move him out and onto a firm mattress. Ask your pediatrician if your baby can sleep in his car seat or baby bouncer; most are designed well enough for supervised babies to sleep in.

Breastfeed to reduce SIDS risk. If you are able to breastfeed on an ongoing basis, do so. The American Academy of Pediatrics recommends exclusive breastfeeding until your baby has reached six months, followed by continued breastfeeding as complementary foods are introduced (with continuation of breastfeeding for one year or longer as mutually desired by mother and infant).[7] If you aren't able to or prefer not to, this does not mean your baby will have SIDS. It's a very rare occurrence. But research shows infants being breastfed are less likely to have SIDS than those who aren't breastfed.

Pacifiers are a plus. Once your baby has learned to nipple-feed in the first two days of life, it's okay to use a pacifier. Some parents prefer no pacifier, but I find (and studies confirm) that they help soothe babies and assist with fussiness. In addition, a 2005 meta-analysis research study concluded that "published case-control studies demonstrate a significant reduced risk of SIDS with pacifier use, particularly when placed for sleep." The reason for the protective effect of a pacifier is unclear. It is possible that babies who use a pacifier are more easily aroused, breathe easier, or are in a more beneficial sleep position.[8]

Parents may worry about the side effects from pacifier use after a baby is one year old. Two rare side effects of late pacifier use are decreased speech due to overdependence and a slightly increased risk of ear infections.[9]

The goal in the America is to wean your baby from his pacifier before age one. If a baby is speaking fine and healthy, I usually don't push too hard after age one year to wean. By comparison, in some countries such as Sweden, mothers wean their babies from a pacifier as late as three years of age.[10] (See the section on pacifiers in Chapter 10 for more discussion.)

Immunize your baby. Immunizations help build your baby's fragile immune system to fight potentially fatal diseases. This helps your little one develop and grow in the healthiest way possible, reducing SIDS risk factors.

I know some parents worry for the opposite reason: that vaccines could become a factor in causing SIDS. However, the CDC notes, "Studies have found that vaccines do not cause and are not linked to SIDS."[11]

Don't smoke. If you are on baby duty, never smoke. Pregnancy is the best time to quit smoking. If you are a parent and smoke, having a baby at home provides a good opportunity to quit smoking. In fact, *just being around smoke increases your baby's risk of SIDS.* If a mother smokes and shares the bed with her infant, the risk increases. A 2009 study from the University of Sydney concluded that 81 percent of babies who died of SIDS had been exposed to smoke. Of those who died, 32 percent of the babies were bed with a parent when the sad event occurred.[12]

Don't drink or use drugs while on baby duty. When people drink, their judgment is impaired, their muscle tone is altered, and their sleep cycle deepens. This environment doesn't support routine baby care. In addition, a parent using certain prescription or over-the-counter medications, alcohol, or drugs can more easily roll over on the baby unaware and cause suffocation.

The risk of SIDS increases dramatically if a parent has been drinking or using drugs. A 2009 study from the *British Medical Journal* concluded that a higher incidence of SIDS deaths observed in a co-sleeping environment was noted with parents who had recently used drugs or alcohol.[13]

If you plan to consume heavy amounts of alcohol or use drugs that may change the way you think, have someone else care for your baby. If you are breastfeeding and consuming alcohol, pump and discard your breast milk for twenty-four hours after you drink. If you use prescribed medicine, check with your doctor to be sure you can still effectively care for your baby during its use or if there's any problem with breastfeeding while taking the medication. If you take illegal drugs, seek help from your doctor or local hospital to stop. It's clear: if you are drinking alcohol or using mind-altering drugs while taking care of your baby, you're endangering your child's health.

Finland: Baby in a Box

In Finland, parents are given a "maternity package" in a baby box that contains items to care for infants. This package comes from the government—taxpayers' money at work. Inside are clothes, diapers, blankets, sheets, bathing products, teething toys, and more.

According to the CDC, Finland has one of the world's lowest infant mortality rates.[14] Could the baby box itself have something to do with the low rate of infant deaths in Finland? Made for a baby to sleep in, it has a small mattress, short walls for ventilation, and nothing else. No blankets or stuffed toys are placed in the box, and the mattress is firm. The box meets SIDS prevention criteria and has for many years. Further, the baby and box can be placed anywhere to sleep.

I think of this sleeping box with all its contents as a gift—in fact, it would make a great baby shower gift! Several states in America have recently worked to promote safe sleep by implementing a variation of the Finnish program, giving a filled baby box to new mothers. The box can be picked up at a distribution center or, in some cases, mailed to the new parents. How delightful for those mothers who receive essential items at the time of their baby's birth plus a sleeping box that reduces the risk of SIDS!

This baby-in-a-box concept is akin to a bassinet. What Finnish people have known long before SIDS research is that sleeping babies need a firm mattress, an isolated, well-ventilated area, and nothing else. If you use a baby box, ensure the box is not too tall and has good ventilation. (You can find photos and information about the Finnish maternity package at http://www.kela.fi/web/en/maternitypackage.)

PART 2

Decisions to Make

Children are human beings to whom respect is due, superior to us by reason of their innocence and of the greater possibilities of their future.

—Dr. Maria Montessori

Chapter 9

NAMING YOUR BABY

Megan and Steven are having their third child. They have decided not to find out the gender of the baby. Their previous pregnancies resulted in two gorgeous boys, Lucas and Jacob. Acknowledging that these names are traditional, they wonder if they should go with a trendier name for their third child. Megan is concerned because they have to pick out two names—female and male—and can't agree on any name both parents like. Steven says, "Oh, Megan, stop worrying so much. When the right name comes to both of us, we'll know." Megan doesn't feel so sure, and she's twenty-four weeks pregnant. The clock is ticking to make a decision.

Have you ever pondered baby names? The majority of parents know what they will name their baby before birth. But with so many choices, it's no wonder some parents wait until *after* the birth to make a final decision.

A baby's name is a personal decision, one that should be evaluated by both parents. Occasionally, one parent readily accepts the choice the other parent has settled on. More often than not, like Megan and Steven, parents toss names back and forth until both approve the final name.

If you are naming your baby, here are types of names and baby name tactics to consider before making your final decision.

FAMILY NAMES

Some parents stay with traditional family names that have been passed down generation after generation. For example, in the British royal family, consider Prince William and Princess Catherine's choice for their first child, George. The name George has been used multiple times before, including Queen Elizabeth's father, King George VI.

In France, it's common to use both sets of grandparents' names for a new baby. If the baby is a girl, she might receive two names, one from each grandmother (for example, Sofia Pauline). Similarly, a boy might have two names and be named after both grandfathers.[1] Honoring a favorite family member or revered ancestor is a lovely tribute to your new baby's family. The shared name is a permanent connection between your baby and family namesake.

TRENDY NAMES

What's popular these days? You can find long lists of names online and in books or just check the roster at a day care or kindergarten to get ideas. Although many traditional names have become popular, it's also common to see variations of traditional names in trends. Ask yourself the following questions.

Do you want to use original names or spellings? Some parents choose to come up with original names for their babies. For example, actors Gwyneth Paltrow and Chris Martin named their baby Apple. Then there's Irish songwriter Bob Geldof and his wife, Paula Yates, who named their baby Fifi Trixibelle.

However, I'd advise you to do some soul searching before you choose an original name. Remember, babies will be called that name for their entire lives. Will they appreciate it? The lovely name Quinton sounds very urban, but remember, your son will have to spell his name out for most people his whole life.

How does the baby's name sound? When you choose a name, say it out loud many times and listen to how it sounds. Are there too many or not enough syllables? Will the name be easy or difficult to pronounce? Does correct pronunciation matter? If you choose a middle name, state that name out loud as well. Say both the first and the middle names with the last name to hear how the whole name sounds together. For instance, if your daughter will be named Emily Grace Moore, say all three names out loud several times to see how it sounds.

Will you use a nickname in place of the given name? For example, some parents name their baby Benjamin and called him Ben. Many people who move to another country choose a name that represents their heritage, reminding everyone of the family's background. If you're choosing a name in another language, consider having a nickname in English for people who have trouble remembering. For example, a lovely name in Italy is Matteo, and the nickname in English could be Matt.

It's important to look ahead into the child's life. If you give your son a name but primarily refer to him by a nickname, other people might not know that unless you tell them. They'll make mistakes that could be embarrassing. So be ready to feel okay about naming your child one name and calling him another.

As an example, our son's name is Wesley John, and we call him Jack. On his birthday, I didn't bat an eye when I walked past the scrolling marquee at his school that said "Happy birthday, Wesley!" Not everyone knows or remembers his nickname.

What about initials? Don't forget to think about how your child's initials sound or look. For example, Susan Ivy King will be monogrammed SIK. How about Billy Alexander Davis? Similarly, don't choose a name that could cause your child to be easily teased. For example, I have met a boy named Elvis Presley.

Bangladesh: Naming Ceremonies

In Bangladesh, a ceremony is used to name the baby in a formal way. This helps establish the identity of the newborn and present her to the community. Traditionally, naming ceremonies in Bangladesh take place before the first birthday. Depending on the region of the country, a naming ceremony might be on the eleventh or twelfth day of life. Both Hindus and Muslims in Bangladesh perform them, with some similarities and differences in each ceremony.

A naming ceremony could be performed in a mosque or temple, or simply at the home of the baby's family. In Bangladesh, the ceremony begins with a bath and new clothes for the baby. A prayer is then said for the baby.

After religious rites are given, the mother or father whispers the baby's name in her ear. After the ceremony, the name is announced for the first time to the group of family and friends. When the naming ceremony is complete, a feast is provided for friends and family, who offer blessings and gifts for the baby.

Jewish Culture: Naming Traditions

Within the Jewish culture, naming traditions depend on family background and custom. Specifically, a boy is named on the eighth day after birth and a girl within three weeks of birth. The process is symbolic; the babies are given a traditional Hebrew name that will be used for the rest of their lives. During the ceremony, the baby receives a blessing and the parents have the opportunity to explain the significance of the name they chose. As with naming ceremonies in Bangladesh and other parts of the world, Jewish naming ceremonies commonly end with a celebratory feast or buffet.[2]

Often, Americans announce the name of their baby by word of mouth and birth announcements. Naming ceremonies are not as common in the United States, but a proclamation for the new life that has just arrived enchants me. You can adapt the idea of a naming ceremony to any religious, cultural, or spiritual preference.

Chapter 10

ITEMS FOR YOUR NEW BABY

E very parent's needs are different. Some like a lot of baby "stuff"; others want to minimize; the rest fall somewhere in between.

This chapter is built to address the needs of parents, whichever style they prefer. The first section includes a brief list of the necessities. The rest of the chapter describes optional purchases that can make your life easier but aren't necessary for your baby's health or safety. As you read through the optional lists, you can decide for yourself what your family needs.

BABY'S SHOPPING LISTS

If you'd like to save money plus hassle, a few absolute essentials are all that is needed for a new baby in the first year of life. These items include:

- Food (breast, bottle, and, subsequently, solid foods)
- Clothing
- Diapers
- Wipes
- Car seat
- Sleep area (described in Chapter 8)

If you want more than these essentials, here's a more comprehensive list.

Changing and Sleeping

Changing pad. This can be a standard changing pad or just an easily cleaned or washable blanket or pad that you place on the floor or table.

Changing table. Again, you can buy a changing table with great organization for holding diapers, wipes, and other supplies, or you can use the top of a dresser, the floor, a table, or whatever else you are most comfortable with.

Sleep area. We've discussed sleeping areas a lot, but the basic options would be a crib, bassinet, play yard, or co-sleeper box.

Feeding

While it might seem excessive, there are several feeding tools that you should consider having on hand.

Bottles. Even if you plan to breastfeed exclusively, it's good to have bottles available. You could use them if you leave the home or for supplementation purposes. If your baby is ill, bottles can also be used to give Pedialyte, an electrolyte solution to rehydrate.

Breast pump. This helpful device will pump extra breast milk in between or after feedings. Also, breast pumps are beneficial to relieve engorged (extra full) breasts. For more information on pumping breasts, see Chapter 17.

Bottle nipples. Buy nipples for newborns only. Initially, I recommend purchasing only slow-flow nipples. This type of nipple will ensure the baby doesn't get too much milk through the bottle at once. Stick to one brand only; it's confusing to your baby to have to learn several nipples at once.

Baby bowls. These are made specifically for babies. Some mount to a table or high chair to prevent an easy fall to the floor.

Formula. Plan to have formula on hand. Even if you decide to breastfeed, you never know if you might need it for emergency purposes—for example, if you leave home and have a flat tire and no pumped breast milk. Check to see if you can get samples at the hospital or from your pediatrician. (Two cans are sufficient at first.) Don't stock too much formula for your baby; sometimes, the type of formula changes due to the baby's different needs. However, once your baby has learned to tolerate the formula well, then buy it in bulk by the case or look online for multiple-can coupons for cost effectiveness.

High chair. If you purchase a high chair or get a used one, ensure the chair itself is stable and the straps work properly. Don't use an antique or unstable high chair. If buying a high chair is out of your budget, find other ways to sit with your baby and feed her.

Around the world, high chairs are much less common than you'd think. Many parents hold their babies while spoon-feeding or have a second helper. Joanna Goddard, a blogger at *A Cup of Jo*, interviewed freelance writer Adrienne, who lives in Spain. Adrienne said this about high chairs: "My friend went to a restaurant in the south of Spain and asked for a high chair, and the waiter said, 'That's what grandparents are for.' He wasn't kidding; he was totally serious."[1]

Although high chairs are convenient, if you're inclined, you can revert to the era of pre–high chair days. An alternative is holding the baby on your lap or having someone else hold her while you feed.

Sippy cup. If you buy a sippy cup, get one soft-tip cup to start early. A soft-tip sippy cup helps the baby learn to drink from a cup starting at age six months. Your goal is to eventually move to a harder-tip sippy cup or straw cup, which tends to be accomplished between ages nine and twelve months.

Baby spoons. A baby spoon should be used when starting to feed your baby pureed foods because adult-size spoons are too large for your baby's little mouth. After age one year, your baby can try using the spoon herself. Most toddlers don't use spoons and forks independently until around age eighteen months.

Safety

Cabinet and door latches. These are important to keep babies and toddlers away from choking hazards. Place any toxic chemicals in high, locked cabinets.

Rear-facing car seat. Ensure your baby's car seat remains rear facing until your child is two years old. Any car seat you purchase today should be a rear-facing variety. After age two, your child will move to a forward-facing booster seat.

Outlet covers. Place covers on all electrical outlets to prevent accidental electrocution.

Safety gates. Keep pets out of the baby area and secure the area your baby is enjoying. As your child gets older, safety gates also help keep him away from stairs and out of areas that haven't been safety proofed.

Sun shields for the car. Sun shields will make your baby more comfortable when sleeping in the car during the day and also help prevent sunburn.

Entertainment

Board books. Research shows that reading to your baby early in life can promote lifelong literacy. Baby board books are a good choice. They expose babies to pictures and words, and they're durable for ongoing play.

Rattles and other toys. There's no need to overstock rattles or toys, but it's nice to have a few for entertainment. Be sure these toys are made for infants. And be careful not to attach items your baby can choke on.

Teething toys. Babies love to chew on toys made specifically for teething. It's not mandatory to buy specific toys; seek inexpensive items your baby can chew on, including a burp cloth or a frozen banana. Here's a tip from the Middle East: place a piece of fruit or vegetable in cheesecloth. Hold the end to ensure your baby doesn't get a chunk of food in his mouth. You now have a homemade way to combat teething and introduce your baby to different tastes!

Extras

Baby book or scrapbook. A scrapbook full of photos and information makes a nice keepsake for your child when he is an adult. You can easily make your own or purchase a premade one.

Baby bathtub. Babies can be bathed anywhere, including the sink. You can find various bathtubs for small infants that can be placed inside the bathtub. Some have a seat so your baby won't stand and slip. Get a bathtub that's easy for you to use for bathing your baby and prevents slippage.

Diaper bag. Any bag with several pockets usually suffices. If you plan to carry bottles, diaper bags typically have the best pockets for transporting them.

Diaper pail and liners. Use these in your changing area for quick and easy disposal of dirty diapers.

Baby monitor. Purchase a monitor with a minimum of two receivers; one often breaks or gets lost.

Infant body carrier or sling. If you plan to wear your baby, make sure he fits well on your body. (For more on babywearing, refer to Chapter 1.)

Stroller. If you plan to wear your infant quite a bit, take your time deciding if you need a stroller. Most babies are easily carried in the first six months before they become mobile. If you decide later to get a stroller, you will have had time to figure out which type of stroller you'd like to have or find an affordable used one.

WHAT TO DO BEFORE BABY ARRIVES

You have much preparation time before your baby arrives. Here's a list of things you can do ahead of time.

Decide where to store toys, clothes, and other things. It's important to find a place to store baby things and put them there. If you're buying furniture (especially expensive furniture), think about what your baby can use throughout childhood. For example, if you're buying a chest, think about what might look nice and be useful for both a toddler and an older child. Baby furniture that's used for only a year or two gets in the way; you'll want to avoid that.

Wash your baby's clothes. Any clothes you buy should be washed in dye-free, perfume-free detergent before your baby wears them. A baby's skin tends to react to new things. Because she's been in the womb and not exposed to environmental products, her skin may be sensitive. Washing a baby's clothes before she arrives can even be fun. Pack them away and wait in anticipation for the right time.

Instead of expensive baby detergent, use dye-free, perfume-free detergent made for the whole family. If your baby has sensitive skin (many do), she could react to the detergent used to clean your clothing. Many brands of dye-free, perfume-free detergents available are less expensive than baby detergents on the market. Use this kind of detergent for at least the first nine months until you feel assured your baby doesn't have sensitive skin.

Install the baby's car seat. Make it easy on yourself: install your baby's car seat before she's born. Then have it checked by a safety inspector or someone you trust who knows car seat safety. Car seat safety inspectors can be found in your community or at the local children's hospital. If you don't know where to find one, contact the National Highway Traffic Safety Administration at https://www.nhtsa.gov/equipment/car-seats-and-booster-seats.

BABY'S CLOTHING

Clothing choices are personal in many ways. Some parents have a certain style they'd like for their child, while others want clothing that's strictly functional. Although it's fun to dress your baby in a variety of outfits, I wouldn't recommend spending a large amount of money on clothes in the first year. Babies outgrow them so quickly!

What to Look For

A good fit. Infant clothes in the first year should fit the baby—but not too tightly. Conversely, wearing loose clothing is okay in the first six months, but once your baby becomes mobile and if the clothes are too large, he will have difficulty getting around.

    Cotton. When buying clothes, look for mostly 100 percent cotton because it's a breathable, natural fiber. Synthetic fibers sometimes aggravate sensitive baby skin. Often, the item feels comfortable to touch, but synthetic fibers can trap moisture, causing rashes and discomfort.

China: A Baby Garment for Prosperity

Historically in China, traditional parents made a multicolored garment for their baby from small fabric pieces requested from one hundred prosperous families. Because of this custom, they believe their baby has a better chance of success in life.

    Speaking with acquaintances from China, I learned this traditional practice is less common now due to restraints on time and today's fast-paced lifestyle. Still, Western parents might enjoy having a multicolored handmade garment from multiple families as a keepsake as well.

Inventory for the First Three Months

- Gowns or one-piece sleepers—four to six
- Shirts—four to six

- Pants—three or four pairs
- Onesies—four to six
- Small cotton hat—one
- Diapers—three dozen initially (stock up on various sizes)
- Socks—four to six pairs
- Receiving blankets—three or four
- Jacket—one, if seasonally required

Blankets

Always supervise your baby while she's in a blanket because it can easily cover her face and cause inadequate ventilation. Blankets used while babies are sleeping in cribs are linked to sudden infant death syndrome (SIDS) and shouldn't be placed in the baby's sleep area when the baby is unsupervised. Instead, use blankets while attending to your baby. Part of the joy of snuggling and cuddling is to warm your baby in a blanket.

Blankets in the crib. Babies under age four months can sleep safely in a swaddling type of blanket while in the crib. A swaddling blanket fits over your baby like an outfit; it can't loosen and ride up over the face and cause suffocation. To keep the blanket's material from contact with the baby's face, the blanket typically fastens with hook-and-loop fasteners or snaps.

After age four months, you won't need receiving blankets. Your baby will outgrow these and become more mobile, even kicking them off. By nine months, she might attach to a particular blanket. If so, have a backup blanket in case you lose the first one.

Clothing

Use clothing that gives you easy access to the diapers, with no bulky seams. Count on your baby wearing at least two different outfits a day—or more—due to drooling or spitting. Always ask yourself, *Do these clothes look comfortable?* The neck should not be so loose that it catches on things when the baby is crawling, but it should be comfortable enough to pull on and off the head. Pants should fit comfortably over the diaper, but not so loose it's difficult for your baby to crawl and pull up to stand.

Whenever possible, avoid elastic bands, zippers, and collars on your baby's clothing. Also, they should never have buttons, which babies readily put in the mouth, risking choking. Look instead for snaps or hook-and-loop fasteners.

Most baby clothing is labeled by age. While shopping, don't buy a lot of clothing sized for 0–3 months, because your baby will outgrow them very quickly.

Shoes

It's not necessary to buy shoes for your baby before she walks unless providing protection from the weather is needed. If any, shoes should fit comfortably and socks shouldn't be tight. Many families enjoy putting a variety of styles of shoes on their children.

Greece: Christening Tradition

In Greece, the godparents are required to buy the first pair of shoes for a baby's christening. They also often buy items such as christening clothing, sheets, and a baptismal cross and chain. Whether or not the sentiment is religious, having special keepsakes from family or loved ones can be a great tradition. Ask grandparents to make or buy a special blanket, or have your aunt who knits make a pair of booties.

DIAPERS

Two types of diapers are available for commercial use: cloth and disposable. Each has advantages and disadvantages. If you interview a number of parents, you will hear a variety of opinions. Which type of diaper will work for you and your baby?

Cloth or Not?

Cloth diapers. Lovers of cloth diapers are a growing community. These diapers are environmentally friendly—with nothing to throw away except poop! In addition, they are more cost efficient than disposables. If you have enough diapers to wash one load a day, the cost of buying and laundering cloth diapers is still significantly less than for disposable diapers, hands down. However, unless they are changed in a timely manner after being soiled, you increase the likely incidence of diaper rash associated with cloth diapers. And changing them frequently means more laundry.

In my parents' day, cloth diapers were a piece of absorbent cloth folded into a square or rectangle and fastened with safety pins. That was tricky! Ladies pricked their fingers and their babies, and the pins unfastened easily. Then along came better diaper-fastening devices such as hooks and loops or snaps. These hold on the diaper material and keep its contents from leaking. A good-fitting cloth diaper will not leak if changed regularly. However, if you can't get to changing it quickly, the moisture soaks through, which can also happen with disposable diapers. Every diaper has a maximum saturation point!

Cloth diapers come in various shapes and sizes. If you plan to use them, study them first to figure out which kind is right for you. But whatever style you choose, buy cotton. It's a lighter, more natural fiber and holds more moisture when wet than synthetic fibers. A good starting point to visualize and read about different types of cloth diapers is The Natural Baby Company at www. thenaturalbabyco.com/guides/cd-guide/five-major-styles.html.

Disposable diapers. Made of chemicals and material that absorb liquid, disposable diapers are not reusable. The disposable diaper is made of three layers.

1. The outside—made of polyethylene.
2. The central area that absorbs the moisture—sodium polyacrylate, which is highly absorbent. It helps keep the liquid off the baby's skin. Sometimes, if the central portion is soaked fully or left for a long time, crystals form on the

baby's bottom. This is normal and easily rinsed away. The most likely time to find these crystals is after a full night's sleep without changing the diaper.

3. The inside layer that touches the baby's skin—polypropylene. Some diaper companies add other agents such as aloe, petrolatum, and vitamin E.

Various designs made with dye are typically placed on the outside of the diaper where the dye doesn't touch the baby's skin.

Chlorine-free diapers are free of dioxins—known carcinogens in humans. From my reading, we allegedly receive more dioxins from our environment than a baby does in his diaper. Thus, there aren't enough dioxins in the diaper to cause a problem. That said, if you're a purist, chlorine-free diapers appear to be a good choice of diaper.

Any of the chemicals mentioned could cause allergic reactions, but true allergic reactions to diapers are rare. Some parents feel that a baby gets fewer rashes with a particular brand of diaper, but this comes down to trial and error.

The sides are resealable, and typically the waist and legs have elastic bands. The elastic areas help seal in moisture, urine, and baby poop. Most are sealed with tape or hook-and-loop fasteners and can be adjusted by tightening the diaper according to the baby's waist size. After you use a disposable diaper, be sure to throw it away.

Wetness indicators. Many diapers have a wetness indicator—a strip on the front of the diaper that can change color when the baby urinates. This avoids having the parent open the diaper frequently to check for wetness. In the baby's first two months, these might not work well because, at that young age, babies tend to have small amounts of urine that aren't enough to wet the strip.

Added scents. Most diapers are unscented. Avoid purchasing the scented variety, because scented diapers, especially when combined with moisture, can cause skin irritation.

Diaper covers. Whether you buy cloth or disposable diapers, using diaper covers can help prevent leakage, but they tend to hold in more moisture. Diaper covers are most useful at night when the baby sleeps or on a long trip when you can't always do a quick change. However, if they're used with every diaper, they can trap too much moisture and increase the risk of diaper rash.

PACIFIERS

Pacifiers, in some form or another, have been around for thousands of years. They have been called "soothers," "binkies," "artificial teats," "dummies," and various terms of endearment.

Pacifier use has recently been controversial. Certainly, it's a personal decision to use one. One mom recently told me she felt her breast was her baby's best pacifier. I can't argue with that. Another mom said that with three kids, she can't keep her infant on her breast between feeding times, so she uses a pacifier to soothe her baby. I can't argue with that either.

The Canadian Dental Association points out that a soother (pacifier) is better than sucking the thumb. That's because a baby can get rid of a pacifier at any time—but not a thumb.[2]

Loving Form of Nurturing

A pacifier combined with holding, cuddling, rocking, and kind words creates a loving form of nurturing for your baby. Infants have a need to suck; it's a reflex from birth created by a signal from the brain to help babies eat and soothe themselves.

Pacifiers can soothe your baby during times of distress. If babies like sucking on pacifiers to feel content, the pacifier is also a friend. And while holding your baby, using a pacifier often helps him fall asleep.

Sudden infant death syndrome (SIDS) is seen less commonly in babies who are pacifier users. The American Academy of Pediatrics (AAP) states, "Although the mechanism is not known, the reduced risk of SIDS associated with pacifier use during sleep is compelling."[3] For this reason, your doctor will likely promote using one.

Should Your Baby Be Fed Rather Than Pacified?

Before using a pacifier to quiet a crying baby, think about when your baby was last fed and how much he ate. Maybe your baby is hungry. In the first six weeks when it's not easy to read hunger signals, pacifiers might inadvertently replace a meal, even with the most attentive parents. Generally, babies older than about one month of age continue to cry if they're hungry and a pacifier is offered. Younger babies can suck, enjoy, and miss out on a nutritious feeding.

Is Your Baby Feeding Well?

Newborns should be made to wait until they're feeding well on the breast or bottle before you introduce a pacifier. If you plan to breast-feed, pacifiers should be held back until your baby is latching and has adjusted to breastfeeding. It helps your baby avoid nipple confusion. Once he has fed well for at least four feeds, it's okay to introduce a pacifier.

Here are a few simple pacifier tips.

Choose a pacifier with a similar appearance to a breast nipple, and stay with your choice for at least one month. This early decision helps avoid nipple confusion.

Use single-piece pacifiers. Two-piece pacifiers have a risk of breaking, and the broken part can become a choking hazard. Avoid attaching the pacifier to a cord, as this could cause strangulation in a baby.

If you prefer using a pacifier, diligently keep giving one to him. Many babies initially appear uninterested. If your baby loves his pacifier, he might wake up in the middle of the night crying for it. Not all babies do this, but it's a potential drawback to pacifier use.

Keep pacifiers clean. To sterilize pacifiers, put them in a hot, steamy dishwasher or boil them for two minutes. Change out your pacifiers three times a day or as needed, such as when one gets dropped in a dirty or soiled area. Never sweeten the pacifier with food or syrup, as this can create a sugar-dependent, cavity-prone baby.

Use pacifiers for soothing only. Babies like to use a pacifier for most forms of soothing. Although this is not a problem during the first six months of life, using it a long time for soothing will likely create a dependency. As your baby gets into the second six months of life, instead of taking away the pacifier, introduce other forms of soothing for your infant when distressed.

Prevent dependency on a pacifier. Typically, around age one, it's easiest to reduce or stop using the pacifier because toddlers might become overly dependent on it. They need to learn other techniques for self-comfort.

To summarize, use a pacifier liberally in your baby's first six months. Whenever you feel your child needs it to calm down, be distracted, or feel content, enjoy the benefit of pacifier nurturing. Then, between six to nine months, adjust your baby's pacifier habits to get him ready to wean off the pacifier by age one. Use it only for significant calming or assisting him to sleep. Instead, use other methods to calm your baby, such as a calming touch, soothing words, soft music, a warm bath, baby massage, and babywearing.

From nine to twelve months, use the pacifier no more than two hours a day. When it's not in use, keep it hidden in a handy place. If the pacifier is not in sight, your baby won't think about it. Continue to use other forms of soothing, even adding a security object such as a small blanket or a soft, favorite toy he loves holding.

Ireland: A Pacifier Tradition

In Ireland, it's socially acceptable to have a soother (pacifier) well after age one year. A large percentage of Irish parents wean their babies off the pacifier more slowly and gradually than in some other countries. A slow wean is a gentle alternative to weaning the pacifier abruptly. As you consult with your pediatrician, go ahead and find the right timing and use for a pacifier.

Earlier, we talked about Sweden having a similar tradition of allowing children to have a pacifier up until their third year. This is the extreme end of the spectrum, but again, there is no perfect formula for weaning a child. If your baby needs more time with a pacifier, it's okay to ease off slowly. Between you, there's a balance between soothing and preparing to wean.

MEDICAL ITEMS

Moms who like to plan ahead may make a nestling kit for their babies. A nestling kit contains medical items that might be necessary in a pinch or contain items used frequently.

Nestling Kit

For your nestling kit, get a box or plastic container and put these items in it:

- Baby nail scissors
- Emery board and nail file
- Adhesive bandages
- Box of 4 x 4 gauze
- Medical tape
- Diapers
- Diaper covers (if using cloth diapers)
- Ice pack
- Baby lotion (unscented only)
- Antibiotic ointment
- Pacifiers
- Tweezers
- Bulb syringe
- Thermometer
- Small scissors
- Baby shampoo
- Baby sunscreen (oxybenzone- and retinyl palmitate–free)
- Baby wipes
- Diphenhydramine (Benadryl)
- Ibuprofen (Advil, Motrin)
- Acetaminophen (Tylenol)

- Saline nose drops
- Simethicone drops (Mylicon—used for excessive gas)
- Diaper rash cream
- Pedialyte

Note: Use medicines only under the supervision of your doctor.

A FEW ITEMS FOR MOM

In addition to the basics for baby, it's helpful to have these extra items on hand after the baby arrives to increase Mom's comfort.

Comfortable clothing with easy breast access for nursing. The easiest piece of clothing for nursing is a large shirt you can lift to place the baby on your breast. Shirts made specifically for nursing mothers have snaps to access the breast. Clothing should be comfortable, enabling you to get into any position you like to breastfeed and lounge with your baby.

Lanolin ointment for sore nipples. If you're breastfeeding, the hospital where you deliver may give mothers lanolin. Get an extra tube, since you're likely to use it even as the baby grows.

Nursing bras. Your breasts should be released easily from your bra for your baby to breastfeed. Nursing bras have special snaps or hook-and-loop fasteners for easy access. Some breastfeeding mothers also use loose sports bras for nursing. However, bras made specifically for nursing tend to allow quicker access and be more comfortable for a breastfeeding mother.

Nursing pads. Nursing pads are placed in front of the nipples to prevent breast milk from leaking before breastfeeding or between feeds. Typically, breast milk leakage occurs in the first couple of months of breastfeeding and then slows down as the baby gets into a regular schedule and rhythm of feeding. Some mothers leak quite a bit, while others don't leak much at all. Cloth nursing pads are more comfortable and absorb more liquid than the disposable type.

Norway and Parts of Northern Europe: Wool Breast Pads

In Norway and many parts of northern Europe, mothers use wool breast pads to soak up excess leaking breast milk. Because wool is a sturdy fiber, these breast pads are quite durable. And wool is a natural fiber, so it keeps the breasts warm and comfortable. The pads are available in different sizes and can be easily laundered.

To wash wool breast pads, soak them in warm water and wool-specific detergent for ten minutes or more. After soaking, wash them by hand, squeezing the pads to loosen the wool. Rinse them well in warm water and hang dry. For mothers who are breast-feeding in the winter, wool pads are a great way to cope comfortably with leaky breasts.

Chapter 11

CIRCUMCISION

Faced with a tough decision, Sadie wasn't sure if she'd have her son, Samuel, circumcised. He was due any time and she still hadn't decided, despite her discussions with her mother, grandmother, and even coworkers. Samuel's father had chosen not to be involved with his son, so this decision was hers alone. She consulted her pediatrician, who told her that circumcision was a personal choice but that the procedure wasn't entirely necessary. That made her even more bewildered about how to decide.

Circumcision has been around for centuries, dating back as far as the ancient Egyptians. It's estimated that one-third of all males worldwide are circumcised. It's a surgical procedure performed on baby boys to remove the top portion of the skin covering the penis, called the foreskin. Circumcision is usually performed within a few days of being born. Many people choose to circumcise because their fathers and grandfathers have been circumcised. But no law in the United States mandates circumcision, thus circumcision is a personal choice. Parents can choose to circumcise a boy based on health or personal reasons, cultural beliefs, or religious suggestions.

In a 2012 policy statement, the American Academy of Pediatrics stated that the health benefits of circumcision are not great enough to recommend it.[1] However, research shows that circumcised individuals have a decreased risk of penile malignancy and urinary tract infections. Circumcised males also have a lower risk of HIV and sexually transmitted diseases (STDs) than those who aren't.[2]

Circumcision in Religious Groups around the World

Many people around the world circumcise male babies to honor their religion and God. Circumcision is most common in people who are Jewish or Islamic. A *mohel* is an official in the Jewish religion—a doctor, rabbi, or cantor—trained to perform *brit milah*, the covenant of circumcision. The circumcision is performed on the eighth day after birth, although it can be postponed if health problems factor in. Family members are typically present for the delicate procedure, and they enjoy a celebratory meal afterward.

Islamic circumcision tends to vary from country to country. Dr. Ovais Mohiuddin, a Muslim and practicing pediatrician in Dallas, Texas, states, "There is some cultural variation in the practice. The person performing a circumcision on a baby does not have to be a Muslim. There is no ritual associated with the procedure. There is no set time when it is done, although it is usually done before one year of age. In some countries, such as India and Pakistan, a circumcision might be performed when the child is a little older, but this is a waning practice."[3]

Coptic Christians are a religious group in Egypt and the Middle East that circumcise as a rite of passage. Many Christians believe the Bible doesn't mandate them to circumcise, but they might circumcise for other reasons.

Buddhists, Hindus, and Pagans do not circumcise but perform other rituals for newborn babies.

PERFORMING CIRCUMCISIONS

Most circumcisions employ a local anesthetic to reduce pain from the procedure. Usually, a drug called lidocaine is administered in either a dorsal penile nerve block or a ring block. In both of these procedures, a numbing agent is injected prior to the circumcision procedure.

To ensure it's performed safely and accurately, the baby is strapped in so he can't move. It's best to have a nurse stand by to soothe the baby. The nurse might speak or sing lovingly and use a gentle touch or a pacifier. In some cases, such as when it's performed by a *mohel*, the parents are allowed to watch and even photograph the circumcision.

During the procedure, part of the foreskin (the skin that surrounds the penis) is removed, although the foreskin is never completely removed. The procedure requires a cut just at the glans (the tip that looks like a bulb) of the penis, exposing it after the foreskin is cut.

Types of Devices Used

Three types of devices are used to circumcise: a Plastibell, a Mogen clamp, and a Gomco clamp. A *mohel* traditionally uses a Mogen clamp. Doctors or surgeons use any of the three in an office or in a hospital.

Plastibell. The foreskin is stretched to fit on top of a plastic "bell," tied with a string, and removed. The Plastibell protects the penis underneath the foreskin, which enables the doctor to remove the foreskin with ease. The plastic piece is left on the penis and will fall off in seven to ten days.

Mogen clamp. This device is used to remove the foreskin with no bell covering the penis. The foreskin is stretched beyond the tip of the penis and removed.

Gomco clamp. A bell fits over the penis while the foreskin is cut. This bell is removed at the end of the circumcision, leaving the circumcised penis without the plastic piece.

It's best to trust the judgment of the person performing the procedure concerning which surgical device is used. If you prefer a specific procedure, find a surgeon who will perform it for you in their office. For example, you don't want to ask a doctor who is used to the Gomco to use a Plastibell.

All babies are watched to ensure no excess bleeding occurs. A Plastibell leaves a piece of plastic behind that falls off in time. After a Gomco or a Mogen clamp is used, the residual foreskin might swell.

Best Time to Circumcise

If you want to circumcise your son, don't wait too long. The best time is when your baby is more than one day old but less than one month old. If the circumcision is performed later in infancy, a general anesthetic is required. Sometimes, you have to wait if he has a structural problem that needs correcting, if he has a health problem such as an infection, or if he was born prematurely. If you are pondering circumcision, carefully research and weigh the pros and cons.

POST-CIRCUMCISION CARE

Using the Plastibell requires no particular care except to keep the area clean and dry. This is typically not difficult, since urine is sterile and will not harm the circumcision. If feces accidentally soil the Plastibell, it's easy to rinse the device with warm water and dry it with a soft towel.

Use of the Mogen or Gomco clamp may require some type of clotting or sealing substance applied afterward to reduce bleeding. The penis will look swollen after the procedure. However, this doesn't mean the Plastibell is a superior procedure. Some doctors prefer the Gomco or Mogen because they can view the circumcision immediately to assess the result. Others prefer the Plastibell due to less swelling and bleeding after the procedure than with the Mogen or Gomco.

If the penis is bandaged, the doctor or *mohel* should instruct you on how often to change the bandage at home. If a Mogen or Gomco clamp was used, you'll see swelling at the site where the foreskin was partially removed. A thin, yellow, crusty coating will start to appear after twenty-four hours. This crusty area, called *granulation tissue*, is part of normal circumcision healing. To prevent granulation tissue from sticking to your baby's diaper, put a thin film of a petroleum jelly on the circumcision site when you change his diaper.

Most circumcisions need no care after they are healed. Approximately one month after circumcision, your doctor will tell you if you need to gently retract the healing areas of foreskin to prevent adhesions. Adhesions are unnecessary accumulations of healing tissue and, sometimes, can cause the foreskin to adhere to the glans. In most boys, retracting the foreskin is not necessary.

Signs to Look For

After circumcision, call the doctor if:
- There's excessive bleeding around the glans.
- The baby produces no urine in more than eight hours.
- The penis becomes increasingly red after forty-eight hours.
- The penis becomes tender to the touch after forty-eight hours.
- There's foul-smelling discharge or oozing from the wound site.
- The baby has a temperature of more than 100.4 degrees Fahrenheit (38 degrees Celsius).
- The baby's eating habits are abnormal.

CARE OF THE PENIS IN UNCIRCUMCISED BOYS

Uncircumcised boys have a penis with foreskin covering the glans all the way to the tip. That foreskin should never be forced back. It will retract naturally on its own in time, typically over a period of several years.

Bath time is the best time to clean the foreskin in a boy who has not been circumcised. Gently pull back the tip of the foreskin (the area where urine comes out) and rinse that area well. At some point in childhood or early adolescence, the glans (the bulb-shaped top portion of the penis) will appear.

It's possible you won't see the glans until your baby is older and the foreskin loosens, although in some cases, the glans can be seen under the foreskin as early as birth. Once the foreskin loosens and the glans appears, gently clean the glans. Use a soft washcloth, unscented soap, and water, rinsing well before the foreskin goes back to its normal position. Be careful: trapped soap underneath the foreskin can cause irritation.

PROS AND CONS OF CIRCUMCISING YOUR SON

Pros for Circumcision

- Easier care of the penis—no need to teach your son to retract and clean his foreskin
- Less irritation to the penis
- Decreased incidence of urinary tract infections (UTIs)
- Lower incidence of HIV and STDs
- Lower risk of penile cancer
- Lower risk of phimosis—having a tight foreskin that's difficult to retract in uncircumcised males
- Religious practice and ceremony
- Social—fulfills a need to look like his dad, brother, or other males who are also circumcised

Cons against Circumcision

- Not a required or routine medical procedure
- Painful procedure—requires injected pain medicine

- Risk of complications—infection, scar tissue, and excessive bleeding
- Altered cosmetic result—circumcision might not look exactly as the parents wish
- Social—fulfills a need to look like his dad, brother, or other males who are not circumcised

Sadie decided not to circumcise her son based on the statement by the American Academy of Pediatrics that circumcisions aren't medically routine procedures. Being a single parent, she felt more comfortable not having to take care of a surgical wound after birth. After interviewing her pediatrician, she felt comfortable she'd get good information to learn about foreskin care.

Circumcision is a personal choice, but new parents can certainly find guidance from family, their pediatrician, or their religious or cultural leaders.

d by your state, babysit privately for payment, or even ex-
absysitting (for example, you babysit one day, she babysits
r). Some friends babysit in exchange for favors. If you are a
m friend of your sitter, you have the benefit of knowing her
l parenting style and integrity. If she hasn't had children of
, her child-rearing practices might be surprising in a good or
ay. A conscientious solo babysitter or nanny often takes care
child at a time or a group of siblings, providing one-on-one
r your baby.

ily Members Caring for Children
nd the World

y members as babysitters usually bring with them the element
st, especially if you enlist a grandparent, aunt, or uncle. A family
ber happily providing child care is a common practice in Latin,
an, and Asian cultures, where extended families frequently live
by. It can be applicable for many families in North America and
pe too. This can be of particular comfort, as a family member is
known to the parents and generally understands their preferred
e of parenting.

In Laos, it is not uncommon for grandparents to live with their
ildren and, subsequently, take on a caretaking role. Grandchildren
e encouraged to associate with their elders from an early age so
at they acquire good personal and social skills.[1] The advantages
f having a family member caretaker is similar to those of a solo
abysitter—individual attention and a lot of nurturing. A disad-
antage could be lack of respect for your own parenting style—a
ommon complaint with enlisting grandparents as caregivers.
Laotian grandparents are respected and typically have the "final
say" in their caretaking role. They love big and mean well. But, having been through parenting themselves, grandparents hold strong
opinions.

Although the obvious benefits of having a family member care for
your baby are vast, considerations for the wishes of you, the parent,

Chapter 1

CHILD CAR
WORKING PA

M any parents have to work and must pu
baby in the hands of someone else. Th
is a time when the baby can't report
home, so it's important for parents to choose careg
The choices for child care in the United States and
are a nanny, babysitter, family member, or day care.
according to their schedule, philosophy, and financia

IN-HOME BABYSITTER OR
NANNY

A babysitter or a nanny is a person who stays with yo
sitter typically works out of her own home, whereas a
come to your home. A babysitter or in-home babysittii
commonly cares for more than one child at a time. The si

are important. A classic example can show up at feeding time. You might have one way to introduce solids, but the grandparent has a totally different idea and doesn't respect your directions. Often, it's hard for your own parents to see you as anything other than their child, and they believe they know best.

Communicating clearly with your child's caregiver is important. If you can come to an agreement, it's likely that a babysitting grandmother will respect your nurturing style and give your baby a lot of one-on-one attention. Of course, this is not the case with all grandparents; some believe a child needs to fend for himself. As with any babysitter, it's important to decide what you want and clearly state your expectations.

DAY CARE CENTERS

Day care centers can be more affordable than hiring an individual nanny or babysitter. There is plenty of supervision by state agencies to reduce the risk of accidents or abuse. Babies gain social skills while in day care, and the staff is generally well trained to help them get along with other children. In some cases, babies are able to enter day care as young as two months of age, provided they have received their appropriate vaccines. It's best not to place a premature infant or chronically ill baby in day care until the baby's doctor has approved. These babies may have a weakened immune system and thus be more likely to pick up an illness than a full-term baby who does not have health problems.

QUESTIONS TO ASK

Ask these questions of a prospective nanny, babysitter, family member, or day care provider:

What is your experience with babies? Babysitting a five-year-old child is much different than babysitting an infant. Do you want to entrust your baby's care to a person who has never taken care of a baby? A person who has cared for babies (whether her own or someone else's) is more likely to understand baby behavior than one who hasn't.

What would you do when my baby cries? If the answer is "Let him cry it out," reconsider choosing this person or attempt to re-educate. Generally, the "cry it out" answer is due to lack of education in a baby's psychological welfare. Of course, it's not always realistic that a caregiver can get to the baby immediately, but every attempt should be made to console a baby who's crying. Babies are learning to trust the world, and if significant crying is overlooked, they are more likely to be chronically unhappy. (For more on baby crying, see the section "Spoiling Babies When They Cry Is Impossible" in Chapter 3.)

Will you take care of my baby if he is sick? If your child is attending day care, expect the answer to be no. Have a backup plan for the days your baby is sick. If you get a call from the day care employees saying your baby is ill, be prepared to pick up your child right away. State regulations dictate that sick children must be sent home so other children are protected. Babysitters who aren't caring for other children are free to attend to a sick baby if they don't mind risking illness for themselves.

If your child is sick and you are able to stay home with him, it's probably best for all. After all, a babysitter who gets sick can't easily care for your child, and those who care for more than one child typically won't care for a sick child.

If your child goes to the home of another child who is sick, know that your child is at risk of picking up the same illness. Granted, being around other children means your child will sometimes get sick anyway. That's part of building up the immune system, which must happen sooner or later.

Benefits of Day Care Centers

Toddlers who attend day care at early ages may be less likely to have asthma later in life. It's believed that's true because of a child's persistent exposure to immune system challenges.[2] So, if you feel guilty about leaving your baby in day care, know that a benefit is building the baby's immune system.

Another benefit of day care or a home with other children is exposure to other people. Babies love to look at other babies and children; it's part of their developmental curiosity. They are interested in seeing themselves and observing other children. Babies in day care or with a sitter or nanny tend to have less separation anxiety later when they start school because they have built more confidence with separation.

An additional benefit of day care is meeting other families and networking. It's nice to know various families for your own personal socialization and your baby's enjoyable interaction with other people as he grows.

What type of routine do you have? If the babysitters have no routine, are they willing to keep one for your baby? Babies love routine and enjoy the harmony that results. Eat, sleep, play, enjoy.

Day cares are often able to provide a more consistent routine than a babysitter can because their days have to be structured. That said, a good sitter or family member can *create* a routine, so don't discount them just because it's easier to get that structure at a day care.

What type of activities do you provide during the day? You want to ensure your baby is not sitting in the crib playing on his own during the day. Look at the area where the babies are fed. Ask what happens while they are awake. Examine the toys. The caregiver should speak to and read to your baby. Older babies can engage in many floor activities. They should be encouraged to interact with one another, but not placed with toddlers, who might inadvertently cause injuries.

Can you give me references or proof of good service? Day care centers and licensed home day cares usually have to answer to the state; babysitters, nannies, and family members usually report only to you. Good references and reviews are important for all of these, but when choosing a babysitter or nanny, be sure to obtain credible references before hiring.

Is my baby at risk of being physically or emotionally abused? This is a question you must ask yourself. Is your baby high maintenance, chronically ill, or a formerly premature baby? Babies who are born premature, have a chronic medical problem, or cry a lot are more likely to be abused.

In a day care setting with other caregivers around, if your baby cries, you generally don't have to worry about abuse. The workers are kept accountable. However, a person is more likely to lose patience when alone in your home. If you choose a nanny, consider placing a "nanny cam" camera in your home to check in visually. Let your caregiver know the cam is in the home. Handle your caregiver fairly *and* ensure your baby is treated with respect.

What happens if you can't watch my child one day? If you use a private sitter, nanny, or family member, you must have a backup person in case of illness, vacation, or other issues. In general, day care centers don't have this problem if they're well staffed.

What is the ratio of adults to babies in your center? A day care should have a ratio of one worker to three or four babies to ensure that your baby gets plenty of nurturing and attention. Higher ratios of children to caregivers might not necessarily mean your baby won't get enough attention, but the lower the ratio, the more time a worker has to spend with your baby.

What is the staff turnover rate in your center? As babies get older, they're likely to attach to a certain day care worker. Even very young babies show signs of attachment to those who care for them outside of the home. A person who consistently stays with your baby is a plus for your baby's ability to attach. Moving your child from one person to another can create feelings of irritability and insecurity. Plus, it takes time to get to know a particular baby's routine. It's best to request the attention of one or two people who will get to know your baby well.

Italy: Montessori Method Learning

Choosing an early Montessori Center could be in keeping with your parenting philosophy. The Montessori Method was created in the late 1800s by an Italian physician, Dr. Maria Montessori, who believed children should learn through respect, observation, and promotion of independence. Dr. Montessori created a number of hands-on learning tools, many of which can be used as early as infancy.

She identified babies as having an "absorbent mind" and believed that with appropriate and respectful guidance, their minds will gain the knowledge and experience they need. Many books have been written on the Montessori Method, one of my favorites being *The Absorbent Mind* by Maria Montessori.[3] In this book, the discussion of the Montessori Method is truest to her original teaching.

If you're choosing a Montessori school and want to be a Montessori "purist," check the background, training, and accreditation for the school you choose. On the other hand, many fabulous day cares and schools use some aspects of the Montessori Method, and one of these might be just right for you and your child.

I am an advocate for Montessori since I have seen it work well on multiple children for many years. The philosophies of Maria Montessori were well ahead of child development research, which fully backs Montessori training. For example, Dr. Montessori believed children should be spoken to kindly and not yelled at—a form of verbal abuse that can negatively alter brain function.

Realize that verbal abuse is long lasting and potentially damaging. Many parents make this mistake. Raising your voice in frustration is not shouting, but babies do *not* understand or process shouting or rude tones of voice in a positive way. Stern reprimands intimidate babies; they don't teach them appropriate behavior.

PART 3

Diet and Nutrition

You are the butter to my bread, and the breath to my life.

—Julia Child

Chapter 13

ALLERGIES TO FOOD

The prevalence of food and skin allergies in children has increased over the past two decades. Food allergy is a topic within the pediatric community that raises a variety of opinions regarding diagnosis and treatment. However, one opinion is not debated: *Food allergy is a real diagnosis.* Many food allergies in children resolve as the child gets older, but some plague a child for life.

Babies who are at higher risk of food allergies are those with a family history of allergy, asthma, or food allergies.

FOOD ALLERGY VERSUS FOOD INTOLERANCE

"Food allergy" and an "intolerance" to a certain food are two different problems as explained here, along with additional factors.

Food allergy is a response by the body rejecting the offending substance in the food that triggered the response. When children eat a food they're allergic to, an immunoglobulin in the blood called IgE is activated. The IgE identifies the substance as foreign to the body and attaches itself to cells in the body. This attachment in different areas causes the symptoms to show up.

Food allergies typically happen suddenly, and even a small amount of the food can trigger an allergic reaction.

Food intolerance tends to be a gradual process that often has milder symptoms and is commonly outgrown. Typically, food intolerance is noted with increased quantities of a certain food. For example, some babies who eat too many prunes will have diarrhea. Food intolerance could also cause vomiting, excessive gas, fussiness, or crankiness. Intolerance can occur if the food is overeaten, but it's rarely life threatening.

Severe food allergy is rare. Life-threatening food allergy symptoms might include lip or tongue swelling, shortness of breath, difficulty breathing, wheezing, and loss of consciousness with respiratory collapse. Although these symptoms are feared, this type of reaction is very rare. If your child eats a food and starts having difficulty breathing, gets swollen lips, or becomes lethargic, seek urgent medical treatment; call 911 immediately. Medicines can be given to your child to help reverse an allergic reaction.

If your child has had an allergic reaction to a certain food, work with your doctor or an allergist to discuss avoidance factors for the future. Avoidance includes medication for emergencies and learning how to detect the food in anything your child eats. For example, many nut products are found in foods. Children with severe fish allergy can even react to vitamins that include DHA (docosahexaenoic acid), made from marine byproducts. Parents of babies with severe allergies have to watch their baby's diet closely. They are also instructed to carry an injectable medication, called an EpiPen, to use in case of exposure with symptoms.

Some food allergy can cause symptoms that are difficult to detect. Food allergy in infants might appear in the form of a rash that looks like eczema, vomiting, or diarrhea. Many babies with food allergy are likely to have skin symptoms such as eczema. Older children with food allergy tend to have respiratory symptoms such as congestion, cough, or even asthma, although babies could have respiratory symptoms as well.

Common Allergenic Foods

Those marked with * are most likely to cause a severe food allergy.
- Eggs*
- Fish, shellfish*
- Milk
- Peanuts*
- Soy
- Tree nuts*
- Wheat

Food allergy tests in babies are often inconclusive. For example, a baby might be truly allergic to a certain food such as eggs but still test negative for eggs. This is because the immune system is not mature. As children get older, allergy testing becomes easier to interpret because they will test positive as their immune system develops.

Research has shown a strong correlation between starting solids too early (before age 4 months) and a tendency toward developing allergies.[1] When your baby is between four and six months of age, you can start giving him solid foods—but not before four months.

ALLERGIES AND BEING BORN OUTSIDE THE UNITED STATES

A 2013 study in the *Journal of the American Medical Association* (*JAMA*) showed that children born outside the United States have fewer atopic disorders (allergies) than those born in the country.[2] Further, if the children are born elsewhere but reside for ten years or more in the United States, their tendency to have allergies increases.

Why is this so? The concept is currently being studied, and answers vary. Some researchers believe parents raised outside the United States follow a healthier diet and eat less processed foods, which are widely known to be allergenic. Another theory is that many other cultures use spices—like ginger, cinnamon, and turmeric—in baby food, which can help reduce allergy and inflammation. In addition, each baby's environment, genetic makeup, immune system, and exposure are different.

South Asia: Use of Turmeric in Baby Food

Is there a way to prevent allergies? Not definitively, but you can aim to reduce their incidence. One of the best-known ways to build a good immune system is healthy eating. Turmeric is a tasty spice with known anti-inflammatory properties.[3] Turmeric is used in most curry dishes, adding a rich yellow color. Although some studies feel the "superpower" benefits of turmeric are overrated, research has left no doubt turmeric can help reduce inflammation in the body. If you are making a large portion of pureed vegetables for your baby, add a small pinch of turmeric. It's a strong-tasting spice, and a little bit goes a long way. For a baby food recipe using turmeric, see "Baby Food Recipes from around the World" in the Appendix.

WAYS TO REDUCE ALLERGIC REACTIONS IN BABIES

The following tips are useful to reduce allergies in babies and children.

Give your baby nuts and fish. Soft fish can be given when a baby starts chunky foods. Many scientists and physicians recommend you feed pureed nuts and shellfish to babies as early as age six months.

Children are more likely to enjoy a variety of foods and flavors if you start them early. How does this tie into food allergy? Infants who become allergic to certain foods will be allergic whether you give them that food at six months or eighteen months. As they start on solid foods, their palates are developing, so the earlier you start feeding them tasty foods, the better. For example, if you live in India, where an abundance of spices are available, your baby is likely to grow into a toddler who eats an assortment of flavors. Your baby's taste buds will "adjust" to the food you provide. In other words, a baby's diet doesn't have to be bland because of food allergy concerns.

Wait until age four to six months to start solids. As mentioned above, starting to feed babies solids earlier than four months has been linked to developing allergies in children.

To check for a food allergy, wait three days between each new food you introduce. That way, you can more easily identify the particular food that's causing a reaction. Look for symptoms such as a rash on the body, vomiting, or diarrhea. If no new symptoms develop, continue that food. If the baby has one or two loose stools or spits up, continue the food and see what happens. If the food is pureed and your baby gags or spits the food up immediately, that's not an allergic reaction; he or she simply doesn't like the taste or texture. Wait a month and try again. Maybe his palate will mature some in that time.

Know your family history of food allergy. Always mention any family history to your pediatrician to clarify the advisability of adding any new foods or otherwise modifying the diet. Life-threatening food reactions in a parent often prompt the pediatrician to wait before suggesting the addition of a particular food to a child's diet. Your pediatrician may consult an allergist to see if the baby has inherited the food allergy from the affected parent or how to proceed to introduce the food.

Breastfeed to build the immune system. Receiving breast milk helps your baby build a strong immune system. If infants at risk of allergies are breastfed *exclusively* for at least three months, they are less likely to have any allergies or wheezing. You can eat what you want while breastfeeding; there's no current evidence showing that foods you eat cause any type of allergy in your baby.

Should I use a hypoallergenic formula? These formulas may help babies at risk of allergies avoid the symptoms. Hypoallergenic formulas have proteins that are partially broken down for easier digestion of the protein. Many pediatricians use hypoallergenic formulas to treat babies with eczema. Soy formulas typically don't help allergy symptoms. There is no evidence that switching a baby from cow's milk protein to a soy formula helps or hinders development of allergies.

The presence of triggers of allergies in our food and environment continues to warrant research to help families prevent and treat potential health problems. If you suspect a food or environmental allergy in your baby, discuss your concerns with your doctor.

Chapter 14

FEEDING YOUR BABY

Feeding your newborn baby is a one-of-a-kind experience to form a bond with your new baby. Relaxed feeding in a calm atmosphere will go a long way to reduce stress for both you and your little one. A flexible feeding schedule will help keep your baby calm and content. The following advice is useful to know when feeding your baby.

NIPPLE-FEEDING YOUR BABY

Nipple-feeding includes the choice of breast, bottle, or a combination of both. Nipple-feeding is the preferred method for all babies because they enjoy the suckling sensation.

Bottle-feeding only. Some mothers strictly bottle-feed with either pumped breast milk or formula, depending on their preference or necessity. At times, breastfeeding doesn't work out for a mom and baby. Perhaps the mom has been ill or feels uncomfortable placing the baby on her breast. Some members of society can make a mother feel guilty if she chooses not to breastfeed. This is because people know the benefits of breastfeeding and have opinions about how a mother should feed her baby. I believe breastfeeding your baby is a personal decision, period. Using the same type of nipple, however, is recommended to prevent confusion for your little one.

Breastfeeding. If you are breastfeeding, it's best to feed "on demand" because it will enhance quicker milk production. "On demand" means to feed when your baby is hungry or wants to suckle. This can make your nipples painful or sore at first, but they will get used to the persistent suckling. At times, you might feel like you're a pacifier substitute. This is normal while you and your baby figure out the best feeding schedule for proper nourishment. Bottle-fed babies can often appear more content in the first week of life since they're not waiting for the mom's breast milk to come in.

If you plan to breastfeed, avoid using a bottle until your baby has learned to latch on well. Your baby could get accustomed to the bottle's faster flow, making it difficult (but not impossible) to reattach to the breast. The exception to this would be when a baby isn't gaining weight or is getting dehydrated. The doctor may think your baby needs supplementation of formula or pumped breast milk. If you're asked to supplement and are also breastfeeding, attach your baby to the breast first before giving her a bottle.

Breast milk has approximately twenty-two calories per ounce. Breast milk calories may change according to the time of day, feeding frequency, and how long a mom has been breastfeeding. Nutritional value of breast milk for the baby, however, stays fairly constant. Race and age do not affect the calories of breast milk, but drinking plenty of fluids does help increase production.

Formulas have twenty to twenty-four calories per ounce, and the calories vary depending on the formula prescribed. Babies who are premature or small for gestational age tend to need more calories per ounce early on. This can be accomplished by using a formula that has more calories per ounce or by adding a prescribed fortifier to pumped breast milk.

Frequency of Feeding

Consider the following points about how frequently to feed your baby.

The newborn period (birth to one month). Newborn feeding should be frequent and on demand. Allow your baby to sleep as long as he likes and eat any time. If you are bottle-feeding, your baby should take one to three ounces for every feeding.

Even though we say "on demand," most doctors recommend waking the baby up to feed if more than three hours have passed without feeding. After a few weeks, your baby will "demand" more at a time, and the feeding routine gets easy.

If you're breastfeeding, remember that your store of milk is building and you shouldn't exceed three hours without pumping or feeding. Frequent feeding will increase your milk supply. If you'd like to pump, wait until your baby is two weeks old. Let your baby drink as much milk as he wants from your breast. Do the pumping after the breastfeeding is finished.

Age one month and up. At the one-month checkup, your doctor could say your baby's weight is appropriate and she can be left to sleep longer at night without being awakened for a feed. Your baby is old enough to let you know by vigorous crying if she is truly hungry. As the one-month mark approaches, continue to feed every two to three hours during the day. If at one month your baby is still feeding every two to three hours overnight, then feed her every two hours during the hours approaching bedtime.

Frequent feeding before bedtime is not considered excessive; you are giving your baby what she would naturally eat at night upon waking up. Many parents have found that feeding more frequently through the evening can help their baby sleep more contentedly at night. Ask your doctor to reevaluate at the two-month checkup to see how weight gain is coming along and help you further stretch the time your baby sleeps at night.

Make sure your baby gets adequate feedings during the day. If she isn't latching onto the breast for fifteen to twenty minutes or eating two to three ounces of formula per feeding at one month, she may not be ready to sleep more hours at night.

Africa: Advice from Breastfeeding Mothers

In my clinic, I've taken care of many children who have immigrated from other countries. From conversations over the past two decades, I've noted that breastfeeding mothers from Africa offer this advice: "Put your babies on the breast when they're hungry, no matter how often." While this is sometimes hard advice to follow, breastfeeding on demand strengthens a baby's sense of trust in you, not to mention helps calm him and bond with you. With that thought in mind, try to adopt this African practice as much as is possible for you.

And, hey, if you pump, enlist your husband or other family members to take a turn feeding your baby and give you a break! As long as your baby is fed in whatever manner works for your family, she'll grow and thrive.

SCHEDULING FEEDINGS

Typically, when breastfed babies in Africa cry, they're put on the breast promptly, even if they've just been fed. This contradicts the belief that breastfeeding mothers should schedule feedings. I find the practice quite interesting, as many African mothers come to the office and don't complain much about excessive baby crying. Are African babies more satisfied? Less hungry? Have less gas? Or are the mothers providing nourishment *and* acting as pacifiers for their babies? It's a good discussion to have with a group of friends and/or your pediatrician.

Remarkably, babies who breastfeed whenever they like don't tend to have a problem with obesity. In America and many parts of

Europe, we often hear, "Let's get him scheduled!" In fact, there's a tendency to worry too much about schedules, when true scheduling with a baby is often impossible.

During the first two months, simply relax with any attempts to schedule feeding. Babies have their own agenda and ability to suck. Your baby's feeding demand might be vigorous, laid back, or somewhere in between. Plus, each breast has its own milk production quantity.

Bottle-fed babies, just like breastfed babies, are individuals who grow at different rates. Yes, feed them on demand. If your baby doesn't seem satisfied after feeding and it's only one hour later, put him on the breast or give an extra ounce or two. We can learn a lot from the women of Africa.

For mothers who prefer to work out a schedule, know that's okay also. Scheduling helps foster predictability. It is easier to work from an "on demand" type of schedule at first. However, babies do love routine, and if given the opportunity, most babies gradually schedule themselves.

Chapter 15

BURPING, GAS, AND HICCUPS

To have a comfortable baby tummy requires air to be released in the form of a burp. Burps could be loud and adorable or soft and difficult to hear. Regardless of the sound, air takes up excess space in the baby's stomach and can cause discomfort during or after feeding.

BURPING AND GAS

How can you tell if your baby needs to be burped? First, if she doesn't seem happy or is fussy during a feeding, consider burping her. When she's continually fussy throughout feeds despite burping, talk to your doctor to be sure she has no medical problem.

Breastfed babies will need less burping than babies who aren't breastfed. Babies who breastfeed tend to eat more slowly and with greater effort, thus causing less air to build in the tummy. Babies who drink formula or expressed breast milk from a bottle eat more quickly and tend to suck in more air than breastfed infants. Therefore, they require more frequent burping.

Burp your breastfed baby when she detaches from the breast or as needed. Bottle-fed newborn babies should be burped after each ounce of formula or expressed milk. After one month, most babies do well to be burped after taking in two ounces of formula or expressed breast milk.

After the newborn period, your baby will give cues that she's ready to burp. Specifically, she'll become fussy and agitated or squirm during feeding. When she requires burping after feeding, she will often exhibit the same symptoms of overall discomfort. You might not always hear a burp after every feed. Try for up to five minutes. If your baby seems content, you could continue feeding or stop if you are finished. If your baby seems less content later, repeat the process of burping.

To combat gravity and prevent air accumulation, babies should not be fed while lying flat. During feeding, position your baby at an angle of about forty-five degrees. If you have trouble picturing forty-five degrees, visualize the angle of the car seat while your baby is resting. And if this position is difficult to maintain through a full feeding, use pillows to support your arm or your baby. If you use pillows, watch to make sure your baby's face is not too close to a pillow, ensuring she has good ventilation. When you are both comfortable, your baby's mealtimes can become wonderful bonding moments. (For more information on nurturing to enhance bonding, see Chapters 1 through 3.)

How to Burp a Baby

Have a burp cloth handy because sudden movements can cause the baby to spit up. Know that a burp makes room for the digestion of more milk. Just remember that, regardless of positioning, burping should be a gentle maneuver.

1. *Best position: upright, over the shoulder.* To start the process, place your baby in an upright position. Gently change the baby's position from the feeding angle to a position on your shoulder. If she isn't burping well, try gently rocking her while patting her on the back.

2. *A good upright position is Indonesian vertical baby rocking,* described in Chapter 3. Gently rock your baby in an up-and-down motion to help release the air. After feeding, the key is very gently, since too much motion can cause the unwanted side effect of spitting up.

3. *Gentle leg movements.* Another helpful technique is laying your baby on her back and gently moving her legs back and forth in a bicycle maneuver. Gentle movement helps decrease the risk of spitting up after feeding, which happens commonly. The movement of your baby's muscles and the change in position help gas pass more easily. If this doesn't work, try the bicycle maneuver first in the process of burping. Then, after using the bicycle maneuver, move her to the upright over-the-shoulder burp position. This also helps work out a stubborn gas bubble.

4. *The football hold.* A popular tried-and-true technique for treating gas (and soothing a crying baby) is the football hold. Place your baby face down, her chin in your hand and her legs hanging toward your elbow. To ensure she can breathe easily, ease her chin into your hand. Hold the top of her body at a slight incline, then gently pat her back. You can also move her back and forth in a gentle rocking motion.

5. *Position change.* Think about how air moves if trapped in an enclosed area. Typically, a change must occur for the air to escape, right? Sometimes, changing positions from flat to upright can help move out a gas bubble. Essentially, any change in the way you position your baby can help bring your baby to a burp.

6. *Reduction of air intake.* To reduce the amount of air your baby ingests, make sure she's getting a good seal around the breast nipple or bottle nipple. This helps prevent air seepage. Do you hear smacking during feeding? If so, your baby is sucking in air. Both bottle-fed and breastfed babies can get into awkward feeding positions, and smacking means they need to be rearranged to get a good seal on the nipple.

If your baby is bottle-fed, your choice of bottle and nipple will help reduce air in the tummy. In the first three months, choose a slow-airflow nipple and a bottle that minimizes air intake. Many slow-flow nipples have an internal system to help reduce gulping and minimize your baby's air consumption. Some bottles come with collapsible inserts to ensure air reduction. The goal is a more comfortable tummy with less spit-up and discomfort from gas.

All babies create some gas. Their intestines are immature, and their bodies are learning to digest. This is normal because the stomach isn't used to digesting breast milk or formula. Typically, by four months of age, gas and excess air is not much of a problem. Luckily, at this milestone, your baby's swallowing muscles are better developed and intestines more mature. As the months march on, gas becomes less and less of a problem.

HICCUPS

Hiccups in babies are very common, both during pregnancy and after birth. They're caused by an irritation to the diaphragm, a muscle that sits just below the lungs and above the belly. Hiccups can occur for any reason, such as a change of position, a temperature shift in the environment, a distended stomach after feeding, the need to burp, or a recent crying spell.

Babies hiccup in the womb, causing excitement for all to enjoy. It's easy to visualize a tiny baby having a sweet little hiccup. Baby hiccups during pregnancy are typically of no consequence—except to keep the mother, who's awake, thinking about her baby hiccupping.

Hiccups continue on after birth when hiccupping becomes more noticeable and common. Usually, it's hard to figure out why your baby is hiccupping and probably not necessary to do so. Parents often worry about hiccups, but most babies who hiccup hardly notice it happening. Babies who spit up frequently or have gastroesophageal reflux disease (GERD) tend to hiccup more because they swallow more air and their stomachs tend to become more distended than other babies. Similarly, babies who cry a lot tend to hiccup more.

Latin Folk Remedy for Hiccups: Wet Red Thread

Several Latin parents and grandparents insist that using a red thread can help cure hiccups. This is too fun of a superstition not to pass on. Here's how to do it. Get a small piece of red thread. Wet the thread with your saliva. No, not water; your saliva. Place the red thread on your baby's forehead. Wait. At some point, the hiccups will go away. (They will disappear anyway, but at least you did something!)

Other old folk remedies that don't work include pressing down on the eyeballs, pulling a baby's tongue, or pressing the fontanel (soft spot on head). You never want to startle your baby. That action can make him cry, can cause him to suck in more air, and will probably make him hiccup more. If your baby seems uncomfortable with hiccups, consider the following remedies.

Work to reduce gas. Babies who hiccup several times a day might also have excess production of gas, leading to more fussiness. Your treatment is aimed at reducing gas and soothing your baby.

Nipple-feed or use a pacifier. Hiccups are difficult to stop, but a pacifier soothes the baby and relaxes his diaphragm. Breastfeeding or bottle-feeding could help if it's close to the time to feed. Feeding can also help calm your baby and relax his diaphragm muscle.

Change the feeding position. To reduce excess air swallowing, try feeding him before he becomes frantic. Ensure that your baby is at a thirty-degree or higher angle while feeding to help him expel air. After feeding, position him at an inclined angle to reduce air. A helpful after-feeding position is baby-over-the-shoulder while burping. Be sure to hold your baby at the inclined angle and rub his back. These soothing mechanisms to reduce crying not only enhance bonding and nurturing but reduce hiccups as well.

Make burps more effective and more frequent. Try to get your baby to burp well. Also, burp him frequently to reduce air and increase your burping time to reduce the number of hiccups. If all else fails, give him a warm bath to relax him, which will potentially reduce his hiccups.

Hiccups generally don't cause any pain but can occasionally keep a baby awake. They're basically benign. However, if the hiccups occur all day long or result in a lot of spitting up or crying, notify your doctor.

Most babies get hiccups frequently, often daily, in the first year of life. As they approach their first birthdays, though, regular hiccups will likely become a faint memory.

Chapter 16

BREASTFEEDING

T he American Academy of Pediatrics recommends exclusively breastfeeding all infants, if possible, until age six months, followed by continued breastfeeding as complementary foods are introduced, with continuation of breastfeeding for one year or longer as mutually desired by mother and infant.[1] However, you are the final decision maker concerning whether or not to breastfeed your baby.

COMPARING BREASTFEEDING TO FORMULA-FEEDING

Breastfeeding has more health benefits than formula feeding, according to the *Journal of the American Medical Association (JAMA)*. A Harvard University study in September 2013 followed 1,312 expectant mothers. The results showed that babies who were breastfed longer had higher language skills at age three and intelligence at age seven than those who weren't.[2]

Further, the AAP cites studies to back the claims of numerous breastfeeding benefits, including fewer infections, a lower rate of SIDS (sudden infant death syndrome), a more normal weight, and less asthma than formula-fed babies.[3]

According to a study published in February 2013 in the journal *Pediatric Clinics of North America*, a breastfeeding mother might enjoy easier weight loss after pregnancy. Breastfeeding lowers the risk of breast cancer and ovarian cancer, has positive cardiovascular (heart) health effects, and reduces the risk of type 2 diabetes. If that's not enough to prompt a smile, breastfeeding also decreases the risk of uterine bleeding after delivery.[4]

The sooner your baby latches to the breast, the easier breastfeeding will be. Breastfeeding should begin within the first twenty-four hours of the infant's birth. To obtain good production, it's best if the baby attaches to the breast promptly. Most lactation specialists recommend exclusive breastfeeding without introducing the bottle unless medically necessary.

Place your baby directly on the breast right after birth to enhance milk production. The later a mother starts, the more difficult the process of breastfeeding becomes. This is because early stimulation of the breast by breastfeeding helps provide good milk production. If the breasts aren't stimulated within forty-eight hours of delivery, milk production decreases. A mother will likely produce significantly less milk (or even no milk) if her breasts are stimulated on or after the third day of delivery.

Breastfeeding for two or more? If you are breastfeeding twins or multiples, you will likely get more breast milk production. Because of the frequent demands of more than one baby, a twin's mom will naturally produce enough milk for two babies. If you have trouble keeping up with two or more babies, the doctor will ask you to supplement additional calories with pumped breast milk or formula.

Whether you have one baby or multiples, a lactation specialist can help. A first-time breastfeeding mother will benefit from having a lactation specialist help her and the new baby learn to breastfeed.

Some babies need little assistance; they are placed on the breast and immediately begin to latch and feed. Others are more "relaxed" and don't breastfeed as easily. These little ones need the help of an experienced lactation specialist or mom who has previously breastfed.

If you have a baby who doesn't latch easily or started a bottle and needs to get reattached, don't give up. It's rare for a full-term infant to refuse to attach to the breast if given the time and support to do so.

Make sure both mother and baby are comfortable because it's almost impossible for an upset baby to latch. To get your baby calm and relaxed, hold your breast in one hand and rub your nipple against your baby's lower lip. As your baby's mouth opens, gently insert your nipple into it while supporting the back of his head with your hand. Insert as much of your nipple as possible.

Nipples and areolae (the darker part around your nipple) are different sizes, and most infants will take the entire nipple extending to the areola. In time, you will experience a comfortable rhythm with breastfeeding. If your baby doesn't suck instinctively, gently insert a pinky finger into the mouth to stimulate sucking, then reposition your body.

At first, your nipples could be sore, which is normal. You could feel pressure and discomfort with early breastfeeding, but before long, your breast will get used to the feeling.

Most pediatricians recommend allowing full-term, breastfed babies to feed on demand. "On demand" means whenever they want to feed. In the first month, some babies are aggressive feeders, and some are more relaxed. Slow-feeding babies often have to be stimulated to get their full feed. Most infants in the first month take in one to two ounces of formula per feed, or they feed fifteen to twenty minutes on the breast. Again, this varies.

Newborn babies love to sleep. It might seem like your baby is sleeping all the time. Sometimes in the first two weeks, infants sleep so much that you have to wake them up to feed them. In the first month, a breastfeeding baby should feed on demand and not go more than four hours at night without a feed. Preferably during the day in the first month, they should feed a minimum of every two to three hours. If your baby seems tired and it's time to feed, wake her from sleep by undressing her. You could also use a warm washcloth to wipe down her body.

Before your milk fully comes in, your infant might latch for more than twenty minutes. If so, move her to the other breast. Usually, babies will latch longer while waiting for the milk to come in. Sometimes early on, they don't latch well at all, so be patient. An experienced breastfeeding mom or family member can help get the baby attached to the breast. If you have the good fortune to have a lactation nurse, access her expertise. If your baby is still having trouble, contact your doctor, who will give you advice or refer you to the appropriate resource.

Don't be afraid to ask for instructions if needed. Given these criteria, "on demand" can seem confusing. Doctors often give instructions based on the baby's overall weight and health. For example, in the clinic, I've seen newborn babies with weight loss. I instruct the parents to wake the baby more frequently and work to keep her on the breast longer than usual.

Don't worry; by age one month, most babies are "demanding" their feeds without extra help from you.

Milk production may start out slow, especially at the very beginning. Keep feeding regularly to enhance your breast milk production. During the first three to five days of your baby's life while waiting for milk to arrive, your baby receives *colostrum* from your breast. Colostrum is immune-boosting early breast milk that also allows your baby to remain relatively content while waiting for your milk to come in. Colostrum prepares the infant's digestive tract for the nourishing flow of your breast milk.

Latching begins at birth, but breast milk production can take three to five days for a first-time breastfeeding mom or a mom whose body is under stress. The goal is for breastfeeding moms to produce breast milk for the baby as much as possible and for a long time.

Sometimes, breast milk has to be supplemented with formula, especially if the baby is premature, becoming dehydrated or jaundiced, or has lost an excessive amount of weight. If your doctor says your baby must have additional calories or fluid for medical reasons, don't worry. In time, as breast milk comes in, supplementation can usually be discontinued. Sometimes, supplementation with formula is needed for the duration of breastfeeding, and that's okay too. The baby still gets full benefits from the breast milk consumed.

As you get used to your baby's patterns and expressions, you'll become aware of signs that your baby is hungry. When babies are hungry, they make suckling noises. This is often difficult to interpret right after a feed, as babies like to suckle to soothe. If a baby is hungry, a pacifier won't be soothing, and she will move toward the breast to feed. Often, frantic crying follows. In this instance, soothe your little one so she can attach to the breast in a calm state.

You'll also learn to recognize that frequent wet diapers and increases in weight let you know your baby is getting enough breast milk. In their first six months of life, babies wet their diapers at least once every three to four hours. During the newborn period, once your milk is in, your baby will also produce stools frequently. As the months pass, the frequency of poopy diapers tends to lessen. Knowing your baby wets her diapers frequently and having regular weight checks with your doctor assures you she's getting plenty of breast milk.

Make breastfeeding a comfortable, serene experience. Stay calm and get yourself comfy. You will experience better *letdown* if you are in a relaxed state. What does that mean? The letdown reflex usually happens in the first five minutes of breastfeeding. That's when the hormone oxytocin is released, sending a signal to the breast to release milk. Some mothers feel the letdown reflex as increased breast fullness, a tingling, or warmth; others don't feel their letdown at all.

About the time letdown occurs, babies change their swallowing patterns. You can actually hear your baby swallowing. Sometimes, letdown occurs when your baby cries or when you're holding him. That's why many breastfeeding moms wear breast pads. They absorb the extra breast milk that can flow at letdown.

Comfortable Positions for Breastfeeding

In the first two weeks of breastfeeding, it's helpful to find a position that's most comfortable for your baby. Any position the baby finds comfortable and can breathe easily in is good. The following are common positions breastfeeding mothers use.

Cradle position. This is a common position used for comfort and ease for breastfeeding while sitting up. Your baby's head is in the crook of your elbow with her whole body facing you. Your arm supports the baby's head and neck.

Football position. Your baby's back is lying on your forearm (hence the term "football position"), and you support her head and neck in your palm. This takes pressure off your abdomen if you've had a Cesarean section.

Side-lying position. Lie on your side with your baby on his side. Use a pillow to get comfortable. Cozy up to your baby and use your free hand to lift your breast and nipple into his mouth. Support your baby's head and neck with your free hand. For more more information and illustrations of comfortable breastfeeding positions, visit www.lisalewismd.com/breastfeeding-positions.

What If You're Unable to Breastfeed?

Some medical conditions exclude breastfeeding from your baby's diet. For example, a mother can't breastfeed if she has active HIV or tuberculosis, if she uses illegal drugs, or if she's on a medicine that could harm the infant. Some illnesses also do not permit breastfeeding. And, sadly, some women who want to breastfeed simply can't produce breast milk or produce it only in small quantities.

If you aren't able to breastfeed, you might search for a breast milk donor. Ask your doctor about a local breast milk donation resource or check with your local La Leche League, an international organization that promotes healthy breastfeeding. It provides support and educational resources for breastfeeding mothers (http://www.llli.org). You can search for local support resources online as well.

You could also contact the Human Milk Banking Association of North America for information on obtaining donated breast milk at www.hmbana.org.

The good news: even if you're sick, you can still breastfeed most of the time. For most illnesses, feeding while you're sick will strengthen your infant's immune system. Your breast milk responds to your illness by producing the "fighting cells" of the immune system called antibodies. When these antibodies are secreted in your breast milk, they help protect your baby from serious illness.

Your doctor can advise you if you need to temporarily or permanently stop breastfeeding for any reason. If you stop, you can continue to pump to keep your breast milk production optimal until you're able to breastfeed again.

Iceland: Relaxed, Nonjudgmental Breastfeeding

I wanted to hear what parents in Iceland would say about parenting practices, so I put out feelers on Facebook. I went to an Icelandic parenting page named *Góða systir* and told the readers I was writing a book. Within five hours, sixty-eight people responded, offering to give information. What struck me was the overall relaxed and non-judgmental attitude the Icelandic people have toward their parenting styles. In particular, with breastfeeding, while they acknowledge that "breastfeeding is healthy," they didn't have any taboos about formulas if needed. For example, Heiddis Gudnadottir, a mother of three girls and one stepson from Akranes, Iceland, wrote, "In Iceland, you breastfeed your kid wherever you are. It is normal to see a mother feeding her baby. I would say if you can and are able to breastfeed, you should at least try it. But if it does not work, then you are not a bad mother at all." Well said, Heiddis.

Should I Breastfeed after My Baby's First Birthday?

There's no requirement to breastfeed after age one, but if it feels like the right thing to do, keep breastfeeding as long as you and your baby like the experience. There's no set age to stop breastfeeding, despite what societal norms have taught you.

Breastfeeding after age one is considered late in Western cultures where women are trained to stop breastfeeding between six months and one year. If a woman breastfeeds longer than that, she could feel frowned upon by her family and peers. Thus, breastfeeding after age one year is not as common, although some babies benefit from extended breastfeeding.

Some babies are more fussy or anxious, and breastfeeding continues to soothe them beyond age one. Others might have had a major life change such as a move or illness, and for them, one more change would be stressful. Similarly, at age six months, your baby transitions to solids. During this time, you may notice that your baby makes a slow transition with more of a preference to continue breastfeeding. Or your baby may quickly gobble down the new purees! No baby is the same, and every mother's situation is different.

The Philippines: Prolonged Breastfeeding

In the Philippines, breastfeeding is so strongly advocated that the country has legislation called "Implementing Rules and Regulations of the Milk Code" that promotes breastfeeding for the first two years of life.[5] Kimmy Ramos, a mother of one in the Philippines, outlined compelling reasons to practice prolonged breastfeeding. Kimmy stated, "I am very close to my son. Breastfeeding was my bonding time. He doesn't like anything sweet or salty, in general, since breast milk is not as sweet as formula. And breastfeeding encouraged me to eat healthy since I was basically eating for both of us. It's normal here."[6] To accomplish her goal to bond with her baby and keep both of them on a healthy diet, Kimmy said she was able to lean on her family for support.

Kris Pua Posadas, a stay-at-home mom from the Philippines, also enjoyed the benefits of prolonged breastfeeding with her son. Kris adds, "I directly breastfed my first child until he was about thirty-seven months. My son's milk was available to him everywhere we were, all the time, at absolutely no cost. I also believe that it soothed many stressful moments for both my child and me." Kris felt that prolonged breastfeeding was practical and convenient for both her and her son's needs.[7]

Breastfeeding for a Long Time

Want to prolong breastfeeding and avoid obstacles along the way? Here's how you can breastfeed as long as you'd like.

Ensure you have a feeding and pumping plan in place. One problem with prolonged breastfeeding is the lack of a plan for life's circumstances. For example, if you're breastfeeding and have to leave town for a family emergency, does your baby come with you? If not, ensure your pump goes with you, or you risk having reduced milk supply or total cessation.

Is your employment environment "pumping friendly"? If you're working while your baby is breastfeeding and your baby's caretaker is giving pumped milk in your absence, make sure you have a quiet, private place to pump while you're at work.

Plan what to do if your baby gets hungry in a public place. In America, breastfeeding in public—although legal in most states—remains culturally taboo. Many countries in Europe and all over the world have laws to protect women who want to breastfeed in public. I doubt attitudes toward breastfeeding in public will change overnight, but it would be helpful for mothers to be able to feed in public with no judgment. With that in mind, your plan might include carrying a nursing cover or finding out ahead of time if there's a mother's room wherever you end up going. Some moms drop the concept of "breastfeed on demand" and feed their baby before they leave the house. Another convenient option is to carry pumped breast milk in a cooler to use when your baby is ready to feed.

For babies less than one year in age, make their bottles or sippy cups available when you're not home. If you don't have enough pumped breast milk, your baby can drink formula from a bottle in your absence. Formula supplementation when needed is a good form of nutrition.

Is your doctor breastfeeding-friendly? Although many health care providers promote breastfeeding at birth, they may, unknowingly, not take time to discuss the support you need for breastfeeding long term. If you ever get an idea that your doctor thinks you are breastfeeding too long, it's time to re-educate your doctor. Pediatricians can learn from their patients, but remember, you can catch more flies with honey than vinegar.

A supportive family is important. If you feel any members of your family aren't on board with your extended breastfeeding plan, determine what's holding back their support. Do they have a preconceived notion the baby might become too dependent on you? Don't feel you "must" have everyone on board with your plan, but those who are involved in the care of your baby should understand the importance of your decision for extended breastfeeding. Open the lines of communication, but, in the long run, the decision is yours.

Supplement with foods for babies six months and older. Babies who are breastfed after age nine months continue to require a well-balanced diet to develop a taste for various healthy foods. Babies who don't receive solids in the first year of life can have texture sensitivity due to their lack of exposure to the foods. If babies are not given solids in the first year of life and beyond, they might not learn to eat solids properly. Their brain is developing and needs an opportunity to experience the textures and tastes of various foods. Babies exclusively breastfed, taking in no food in the second half of the first year, could experience malnourishment and anemia. Breast milk remains the perfect food, but babies who breastfeed for extended periods of time need a variety of solid foods.

Timing duration for breastfeeding. The American Academy of Pediatrics states it's best to breastfeed from birth to six months. Any breastfeeding beyond this time is a bonus for your baby. What if you are only able to breastfeed for a month or two? Pat yourself on the back for accomplishing breastfeeding, then move forward choosing formula wisely.

Ultimately, however you determine to feed your baby is up to you, your pediatrician, and your baby. There are certainly proven benefits for breastfeeding, but if that's not feasible, feeling guilty about feeding your little one formula doesn't help either of you! Recognize, like moms in Iceland, that you do what you can and that so long as you are both fed and healthy, there's no wrong answer.

Chapter 17

PUMPING BREAST MILK FOR YOUR BABY

T here are a variety of reasons to pump breast milk. Whether working or staying at home with your baby, having pumped breast milk saved in the freezer can provide peace of mind when you aren't with your baby. Pumping breast milk before going back to work may help reduce stress. Learning to pump your breasts before you start back at work can be helpful once you return to your job.

ADVICE ON PUMPING MILK

Pumping breast milk after breastfeeding or between breastfeeding can help free you up later. Pumping provides an extra supply of milk for use while you're gone from home. This also allows others (such as Dad or Grandma) to enjoy the experience of feeding your baby.

However, when your baby is in early infancy and you're getting to know his feeding schedule, pumping between feedings isn't recommended. When and if you do pump your breasts, pump off the excess milk left over after your baby feeds so he gets the required calories first. You might notice your baby feeds frequently in the first two to six weeks. This is normal and not considered overfeeding. Because it's difficult to detect exactly how much your baby is getting, visits to your doctor or health care provider are helpful to determine how well he is growing.

Pumping helps relieve engorgement and saves breast milk for your baby. You can pump breast milk manually or by using an electric pump. If you pump and feed frequently, your breasts will make extra milk. You might find yourself engorged again, but if you want an extra supply of milk, you can keep pumping.

Manual versus Electric Pumping

Electric or battery-operated pumps. These devices tend to pump faster than you can do it manually. Battery-operated pumps are smaller and easier to take with you than electric pumps. If you purchase a double pump, your breasts are emptied simultaneously, which obviously saves time.

When purchasing a pump, look for one that's easy to use and clean. Having a hassle-free situation makes you more motivated to pump. Read reviews and ask friends and family for their recommendations. If you have the opportunity, look at various pumps and check their assembly and use. Determine if it's lightweight. You will have a lot of items to carry once the baby arrives, so it's easier to have a lightweight pump for use outside the home.

Be sure you have a shoulder bag to go with your pump and keep pumping supplies in the same place or bag for easier access.

Consider a pump that uses more than one size of breast shield and a funnel that fits over the breast and attaches to a collecting pouch. Then you can change breast shield sizes easily if needed. The comfort level of your shield could vary as your breasts fill and their size changes.

While some mothers love breast pumping, it's not easy for others. Effective pumping requires a relaxed state, and relaxation can be difficult to achieve. Make a plan to relax in advance. Think about your baby and imagine him on your breast. Carry a photo of your baby breastfeeding. It's even helpful to hold a blanket or an item that reminds you of him.

Hand or manual expression. Learning hand expression could be helpful if your pump malfunctions, you're caught without it, or you simply find that buying a pump is too expensive. This means manually pumping using both hands with the benefit of skin-to-skin contact instead of skin to plastic. Hand expression is also considered a form of exercise.

The disadvantage of manual expression is that it takes a lot of time. Also, milk can spray in all directions while pumping, and extra physical energy is required. (Some consider the latter "disadvantage" a perk!) Various manual devices are available. Some companies make a funnel to move hand-expressed milk into a storage container. Alternatively, you can make your own with a standard funnel and a storage bag attached. The Marmet Technique of self-expression has been used worldwide by women to successfully hand-express their milk. (For step-by-step instructions, see http://www.medelabreastfeedingus.com/tips-and-solutions/130/ how-to-manually-express-breastmilk---the-marmet-technique.)

Princess Grace of Monaco was a strong advocate of breastfeeding. In Monaco, the Princess Grace Hospital holds weekly breastfeeding support group gatherings. The hospital also hosts half-day breastfeeding education events to give advice on breastfeeding, positions, and even hand expression.[1]

However you decide you want to pump, you can find support groups and other sources of education to make the process easier. In America, breastfeeding support for pumping is most often provided by lactation consultants, family members, and/or members of La Leche League (http://www.llli.org).

STORING BREAST MILK

Breast milk can be stored in a regular freezer up to three months and a deep freezer for up to six months. A deep freezer cools the milk faster and can store it for longer periods than a refrigerator because of its lower temperature. The breast milk should be labeled by date. Use your oldest breast milk first.

To thaw breast milk, take out a bag and leave it in the refrigerator or at room temperature. Once a frozen bag has thawed in the refrigerator, use the milk within twenty-four hours. If a bag has thawed at room temperature, use it within two hours of complete thawing. Once frozen breast milk is thawed, don't refreeze it. You can store fresh breast milk in the refrigerator for up to two days before using it.

Avoid overheating the milk when warming it, and don't use a microwave. Always check the temperature. If you forget to check the temperature and it's too hot, you risk burning your baby's mouth. In addition, overheating breast milk could inactivate some of the immune system benefits and enzymes (substances that help the breast milk remain fresh and digestible). The best way to heat breast milk is to place a bag of it in warm water for five minutes. Alternately, breast milk could be left to thaw until reaching room temperature and then given to your baby.

Breast milk that's been pumped and placed in the refrigerator should be used within forty-eight hours. If breast milk is taken out of the freezer and placed in the refrigerator, then use it within twenty-four hours. Breast milk can spoil, which can be harmful to your baby's digestive tract. Label any breast milk in the refrigerator with the date and time it was placed there. Also, note if the breast milk was freshly pumped or from the freezer.

COMMON SIDE EFFECTS OF BREASTFEEDING

Engorged breasts. If more milk is produced than your baby drinks, engorgement will occur. Engorged breasts are full of milk and, therefore, painful. If your baby isn't emptying your breasts and your breasts are engorging, simply pump the excess milk.

A warm shower or warm compress can help as well. The warmth will increase blood flow to your breast. Engorgement is more likely to happen early on in breastfeeding. During this time, you'll likely produce excess breast milk until your body knows the right amount for your baby. Once your baby is consuming the milk more vigorously and his quantity increases, the engorging will typically subside.

Blocked ducts in the breast. A small, light red, warm, or hard spot on the breast could be a clogged duct. These blocks can occur when the breast isn't emptied on a regular basis, and they can be painful. Clogged ducts should be treated the same as an engorged breast, with warm compresses and more milk expression. Yes, *more* milk expression. To work out the block, feed more on the side of the clogged duct (yes, I know—ouch!) and pump the breast as well. Then gently massage the area for relief. If it's intensely painful or associated with fever, call your doctor to ensure you don't have a skin infection or other condition.

Sore or cracked nipples. When you first breastfeed, nipples often become sore and crack easily. To alleviate this problem, you can apply lanolin (an emollient commonly used to soothe the surface of the nipple) after breastfeeding. Before your next breastfeeding session, gently wash off the lanolin with warm water and a washcloth. After your baby feeds, apply the lanolin again, even if the soreness is better. Frequent application of lanolin can help prevent the nipple soreness from returning.

Avoid any substances such as perfumed products or harsh lotion that might irritate your nipples. Also, wet nipples can harbor skin irritations and cause external skin infection. Keep your nipples dry by using nursing pads. They have absorbent material and can be placed in the bra to keep your nipples dry. To stay in place, some have adhesive material on the opposite side.

INCREASING YOUR BREAST MILK, IF NECESSARY

Feed your baby frequently. If you're not producing enough breast milk, the best way to produce more is to feed frequently. Pumping after feeding can also increase production due to the extra stimulation of the breasts.

Eat natural foods. If you read various reports on galactagogues (substances that potentially increase a woman's production of breastmilk), you'll notice that most are natural foods, such as garam masala. A popular galactagogue, fenugreek, is an ingredient in the spice mix garam masala. Garam masala is a blend of spices used in India. Just note that if taken during pregnancy, fenugreek can stimulate contractions of the uterus. Although widely used, the safety of fenugreek use is not well studied. Cook with garam masala instead of taking it as high doses in supplements. You can buy garam masala at specialty stores or use the easy-to-mix recipe in the Appendix.

Take care of yourself to enhance your milk production. Eat a variety of foods, including fresh fruits and vegetables, nuts, dairy products, and grains. Use natural spices, but hold off on hot spices and mouth-burning peppers such as jalapenos or Thai peppers. They won't harm your baby but certainly can cause your little one intestinal discomfort. Drink a lot of water and avoid processed foods. Nap when you are tired. Exercise when you have the energy to do so. Also, take your prenatal vitamins and always get good nutrition.

Asia: Increasing Breast Milk with Ginger

In addition to garam masala, various other spices and foods have been associated with assisting increased production of breastmilk. In Laos and Thailand, ginger is popularly used as a galactagogue.

A study in 2016 by the National Institutes of Health showed that women who ate ginger in the early period of breastfeeding produced more breast milk than a control group without ginger consumption. No side effects in the ginger group of breastfeeding moms were noted.[2] Cooking with ginger could well be a plus during your breastfeeding days! Ginger cookies, anyone?

Chapter 18

DECIDING TO FEED YOUR BABY FORMULA

F ormulas have the nutrients to help your baby grow and get his digestive tract ready for the addition of pureed foods between ages four and six months. The wide choice of formulas can seem overwhelming, but, really, providing formula for your little sweetie is quite simple.

CHOOSING A FORMULA

Choosing a formula for ongoing feeding or for supplementing breast milk typically begins in the hospital or later and generally involves your pediatrician. Some families have definite ideas concerning which formula to choose based on experience within the family or advice from friends.

Most standard formulas contain twenty or twenty-two calories per ounce. Breast milk is also approximately twenty-two calories per ounce. Formulas for premature babies tend to be twenty-two to twenty-four calories an ounce because these babies require more calories early on. Formulas also contain a variety of essential vitamins and minerals, including supplemental iron and DHA.

On average, most babies drink two to three ounces at every feeding in their first month. Between one month and four months, babies typically drink three to four ounces for each feeding. By four to six months, babies take in anywhere from four to eight ounces per feeding, totaling an average of twenty-four (or possibly more) ounces in a twenty-four-hour period. After age six months, when babies are eating solids, most drink twenty-four to thirty ounces of formula a day.

Some babies want more formula at each feeding, while others will have smaller quantities during one feeding, but they should both achieve the overall goal for the day. Some spit up or have a fast metabolism, so they require more formula; others require a bit less. By measuring growth, your pediatrician can help you determine the correct quantity of formula to ensure your baby is gaining weight appropriately.

Types of Formula

Cow's milk protein formula (also called a whey or casein protein formula) is typically advised by pediatricians as the first formula you try. While processed for consumption, the protein in the formula is broken down so your baby can tolerate the milk component.

If your baby is placed on a cow's milk protein formula and you think he needs a different one, change formulas only after discussing it with your pediatrician. Any change can cause tummy upset, spitting up, diarrhea, constipation, or gas. If your baby shows symptoms that suggest a possible change is warranted, your pediatrician can help you choose the best formula for your baby's needs. Other possible types of formula are noted here.

Protein hydrolysate formulas are typically made from cow's milk protein that has been partially broken down. Protein hydrolysate formula is prescribed for babies with cow's milk protein allergy and excessive gas and sometimes as a last resort for babies with colic. Partially broken-down milk protein formula is easier to digest than regular formula and often well tolerated by babies. This type of formula is often less tasty than regular formula and quite expensive. Plus, babies who spit up will tend to spit up more on these formulas because of a thinner consistency than regular formula. As with all formulas, a protein hydrolysate formula should be used only if recommended by your doctor.

Occasionally, a baby is allergic to cow's milk formula and develops eczema, an allergic skin condition. Pediatricians will sometimes prescribe a protein hydrolysate formula for these babies.

Lactose-free formula is a formula in which the commonly used sugar, lactose, has been removed. Lactose intolerance in infants is extremely rare. Babies who don't tolerate cow's milk formula are typically reacting to the protein, not the lactose. However, some babies do have sensitivity to lactose. Many parents with a gassy baby who switched to lactose-free formula with positive results can testify to this reality. Therefore, if your baby is fussy with excess gas, ask your pediatrician about a lactose-free formula.

Reflux formula is a special formula thickened with rice that can help reduce spitting up. Pediatricians sometimes prescribe a formula thickened with rice cereal for babies with gastroesophageal reflux disease (GERD), which causes them to spit up a lot. This thicker formula might reduce GERD symptoms, but the increased starch component could also cause constipation.

Amino acid formula is used in cases of true cow's milk allergy. These doctor-prescribed formulas are for babies with true milk protein allergy who don't respond well to a protein hydrolysate formula. Like the protein hydrolysate type, these formulas are expensive and not very tasty. However, they provide a nutritionally balanced diet for babies with a milk protein allergy.

Soy formula is a non-cow's-milk formula made from soy protein. As an alternative to other lactose-free formulas, some families prefer soy formula. Healthcare professionals may switch babies with gas or colic to a soy formula; others believe it's not helpful.

The American Academy of Pediatrics does not routinely recommend soy formula. Approximately 10 to 35 percent of babies who are allergic or intolerant to formula based on cow's milk don't tolerate soy formula either. In addition, soy protein may have estrogen-like effects, which can cause hormonal imbalance. Cow's milk is more prevalent in the Western diet, so the current thinking is that, for those intolerant of cow's milk protein, amino acid formulas are better than soy formulas.[1, 2]

Forms of Baby Formula

No matter which type of formula you choose to try, they come in powdered, ready-to-feed, or liquid concentrate forms. Which is the best for your baby? All three types give the same nutritional content and calories. The choice of one over the others is typically based on convenience and cost. Subtle differences in consistency are usually apparent only to the mother, not the baby.

Powdered formula is the most convenient and cost-effective method. The most popular choice by far, powdered formula is easy to transport on the go and won't spoil in your bag. Powdered formula requires mixing, but this is easy to do.

Once a can is opened, the contents must be used within a month. Breastfeeding moms who supplement only occasionally or moms with formula-fed babies who want the convenience of a smaller amount to transport can buy individual packets. These are more expensive but take up less space in the diaper bag. Also, if unopened, they can be stored until the expiration date, which is typically many months or even a year away.

Ready-to-feed formula is convenient but more expensive than formula you mix. Once opened, it has to be used within forty-eight hours. Ready-to-feed formula cannot be carried in a bag for more than an hour or the formula is at risk of spoiling. Once a can is opened, any extra formula should be placed in a refrigerator.

Liquid concentrate formula, like powdered formula, requires mixing. Some parents like it better than the powdered formula because of its consistency. Once your can is opened, mix it all at once. Store any mixed, unused portion in the refrigerator and either use it within forty-eight hours or discard it.

TIPS FOR PREPARING AND STORING FORMULA

Keep all containers of formula inside, away from heat and freezing temperatures. Formula should never be stored outside or exposed to heat. This will keep your formula fresh for your baby. Make sure that your storage area is away from your stove, oven, window, or appliances that generate heat. Containers exposed to heat can break down the components of formula, decreasing the nutrition and health benefits for your baby. Similarly, unopened formula containers should not be stored at freezing temperatures; room temperature is best.

Warm the formula in the baby's newborn period. After a few months, babies can easily tolerate room-temperature formula, but most babies enjoy a warm bottle in the early months. To warm your formula, place the bottle under warm running water or in a bowl with warm water. Special bottle warmers are sold commercially but aren't necessary. Don't warm the bottle in the microwave. Liquids put in a microwave can be unevenly heated and cause burns in a baby's mouth. To test the formula for a comfortably warm temperature, squeeze a couple of drops out of the nipple. The drops should feel lukewarm, not hot.

It's okay to try giving your baby cool formula at age nine months and up (or even a few sips of cow's milk to get your baby used to the taste). Prior to nine months, it's not harmful, but most babies won't like cool or cold formula.

Check the expiration date of your formula. Ensure that the formula hasn't expired. Expired formula usually doesn't harm the baby, but it could be less nutritious and potentially contaminated over time, so don't use it.

Don't use dented cans. A dent in the can means a potential crack, which could cause the formula to spoil. Also, it's possible that rust from the can could leak into the formula.

Before preparing your formula, wash your hands in warm, soapy water. The best defense against illness is hand washing. The area where you prepare the formula should be clean and free of potential food contaminants as well. An example of such a contaminant is food that's not cooked, such as raw chicken. Babies' immune systems aren't well developed, and exposure to food contaminants in the environment can make them sick.

Clean the formula container before opening it. Use soap and water to wash the container and dry it with a clean towel.

Sterilize bottle nipples and bottles. Boil nipples for two minutes or clean them in a hot, steamy dishwasher. Each time you feed your baby, put a clean nipple on the bottle. Never use the same nipple for the next feeding. Bottles, too, should be washed in hot water or preferably in the dishwasher.

Prepare your formula according to package directions. It's important to use the ratio of formula to water given on the formula package. Too little water will cause tummy upset, and too much water will decrease the nutrition your baby needs.

Sterilize the water used to mix formula. Use bottled water or boiled and cooled water. Tap water from the sink can be risky because, occasionally, it harbors organisms that could be harmful to a baby's immune system. If you have good quality tap water, you can likely use it after age six months. Ask your doctor about the water quality in your area to get recommendations for what to mix in your baby's bottle.

Use all bottles that have been warmed within one hour of heating. Bacteria and other germs grow in warm fluid. If your baby doesn't finish a warmed bottle after an hour, toss the remaining formula even though it's cooled.

Check for recalled formula. Formula is typically manufactured in a safe environment, and recalls aren't common. Formula that's been recalled for potential problems or contamination is usually removed from the grocery shelves. To be safe, you can check with the Food and Drug Administration (FDA) at www.fda.gov to determine if your formula has any recall concerns.

Japan: Custom of *Sayu*

In Japan, most homes and restaurants keep a tea kettle readily available and boil the water several times a day for tea. One simply has to ask for *sayu*, and it's quickly understood that sterile water is wanted. *Sayu* is boiled water cooled to a warm temperature for drinking. The background of *sayu* dates back many centuries and has roots to the practice of traditional Ayurvedic medicine.

There is no need for expensive bottled water for your baby's formula. Instead, incorporate the Japanese custom of *sayu* into your baby's life by keeping a tea kettle handy. Making and using *sayu* for your baby's formula is uncomplicated. Boil the water, let it cool, and place it in a container in your refrigerator for use within twenty-four hours. As a second option, you can keep hot *sayu* in a thermos for use later in the day.

Remember to use *sayu* only for formula mixing. Babies don't need water; too much water can cause electrolyte imbalances, which may be harmful to your baby.

Chapter 19

NIPPLE-WEANING– BOTTLE OR BREAST

Weaning is the process of reducing and eventually stopping breastfeeding and bottle-feeding. A child who is weaned no longer feeds from the breast or bottle and gets nutrition from a variety of foods in the diet.

If you're breastfeeding and attempting to wean the baby off your breast, you can wean her to a bottle or a cup. Introducing a cup early, no later than nine months, helps your baby wean off the breast or bottle when you are both ready.

WHEN TO WEAN YOUR INFANT

Most pediatricians recommend weaning babies off the bottle at age one year. When to wean a baby from breastfeeding is a matter of personal choice. Often, though, babies simply wean themselves as they get more nutrition from solid foods.

Some mothers prefer to bottle- or breastfeed after age one. If you plan to do this, gently brush your baby's teeth after each bottle- or breastfeeding session to prevent cavities. To effectively brush your baby's teeth, use a tiny amount of non-fluorinated toothpaste on a small, soft toothbrush. Brush fully erupted teeth only. If teeth are partially erupted, the brushing will be painful for your baby.

Moms wean their babies from the breast early for various reasons, the most common being a return to work and difficulty pumping. Also, some babies bite after their teeth come in, and that serves as motivation for many moms to decide to wean at that point.

Scenarios for Weaning

Here are possible scenarios for weaning from the nipple, whether breast or bottle.

Scenario 1: Weaning when breastfeeding and producing a full supply of milk. If you are breastfeeding and making a lot of milk, weaning quickly will cause engorgement. To minimize engorgement, cut out one breastfeed every five days. That means if you're breastfeeding six times a day, breastfeed five times a day for five days, then breastfeed four times a day for five days, and so on. This produces a slow wean. If you engorge, then pump or express the excess breast milk until the pressure is relieved.

If you're returning to work, the easiest feeding sessions to drop first would be those during the day. You can continue to feed at night until you wean your baby off the morning and evening/night-time feedings.

For babies six months of age and older, wean to a sippy cup. Sippy-cup training can best be accomplished while your baby is alert and relaxed. Get a sippy cup with a valve or a soft tip that resembles a nipple. With a soft tip, your baby can be trained to suck on the tip. If your cup has a valve, you can remove the valve and gently pour sips into your baby's mouth as training to suck the cup. (See the information that follows on sippy cup choices.) Either way, if you continue to offer the cup regularly, your baby will gradually learn to use the cup.

Although babies can drink from a sippy cup quite early, you might find weaning easier if you give a bottle when your baby is tired. Older babies still like to suck. When she's tired, use a bottle with a nipple for soothing. In this way, you can alternate back and forth between the bottle and the sippy cup. Later, when she's approaching one year of age, you can gradually take the bottle away without causing much distress.

Scenario 2: Weaning when breastfeeding with formula supplementation. This scenario is typical for either a mother who's not producing enough milk and whose baby needs more calories or a mother who chooses to breastfeed and supplement formula while breastfeeding because it's convenient. This is usually an easier wean off the breast than if only breastfeeding.

If your breasts are producing less milk for any reason and you'd like to wean, you can drop one breastfeeding session every three days. So if you're breastfeeding six times a day, switch to breastfeeding five times a day for three days, then four times a day for three days, and so on. If you engorge between feedings, you can pump off the excess breast milk, but pump only enough to relieve the engorgement.

Scenario 3: Weaning when your baby is bottle-feeding only. Whether your baby is on formula or breast milk in a bottle, wean her to a sippy cup. The best time to start the sippy cup is at age six months, and no later than nine months. Give your baby formula or breast milk in a soft-tip cup. She can wean off the bottle once she has accomplished drinking from a sippy cup. To help her be motivated and engaged while trying the sippy cup, ensure she's ready to drink and not already full when you experiment.

Spain: Slow Weaning Process

Dr. Blanca Santos Ruiz, a pediatrician in Spain, points out that a slow weaning from the breast is common in her country. Dr. Ruiz states, "Most mothers transition to bottles little by little. Mothers who breastfeed for longer than one year, however, usually let the babies wean themselves."

Dr. Ruiz also points out that sippy cups in Spain are not very popular. Most moms in Spain like to wean their babies to a bottle.[1] If you choose the wean-to-a-bottle method after age one year, protect the teeth with brushing after each bottle as described above.

A more gradual weaning process is doable with patience. You may adhere to the schedule previously suggested or drop one feed per day whenever you choose. Give a sippy cup (or bottle if age six months or less) instead. This type of weaning process is likely to cause less stress on you and your baby.

Types of Sippy Cups

Standard sippy cup with valve. Try a regular sippy cup with a valve first. You can take the valve out and gently pour a little bit of the drink in your baby's mouth. Once you see her start sucking on the cup, put the valve back in. The valve helps to slow the flow of fluid so that she's less likely to choke. If she still doesn't seem to get the hang of it, try again. A good place to do this persistently is in the bathtub. That way, while she's still adjusting to drinking out of the cup, she can initially spit some of the milk out and not leave you a lot of mess to clean up. Don't buy too many of these cups, as you have to keep the valves clean. They're also pricier than standard sippy cups. Keep a few on hand for training purposes only and then move to a sippy cup with a straw or a standard cup without a valve.

Standard sippy cup with no valve. These cups are cheaper, work as well as the cups with a valve, and are easier to clean. They're great cups to use once your baby gets the hang of a soft-tip sippy cup or a standard sippy cup with a valve.

Straw sippy cup. Some babies immediately sip from a straw cup or are quickly trained to use them. Easy to use and carry, they don't leak as easily as the ones with a valve. Straw cups are better for the teeth, too, because you don't have to worry about a backwash of fluid onto the upper teeth. In the first year of life, the backwash is not a problem because the upper teeth are just coming in, but it becomes a consideration as your baby gets older.

Soft-tip sippy cup. These work well for babies who resist using a standard sippy cup or a straw cup. They're more expensive, and the tip isn't as durable, so these cups are best used for weaning only. When your baby starts using sippy cups exclusively, the cups with the firmer tip or straw sippy cups are more long-lasting than the soft-tip cups. However, in the first year of life, the soft tips work just fine to teach your baby to sip from a cup. So if your baby prefers them, they can help wean her to a firmer tip or straw cup later.

Taiwan: Weaning with a Regular Cup

Many countries give their babies a drink directly out of a cup without a transitional sippy cup. In Taiwan, it's common to fill a small cup with fresh water and give the baby a sip. The baby sits in the parent's or grandparent's lap while a small amount of water is gently poured into the mouth. This introduces the child to the concept of drinking directly from a cup.

To try this, use water that you've boiled and cooled, using the Japanese custom of *sayu* as described in Chapter 18. You can also use bottled or filtered water. Hold and control the cup yourself. (If you hand your baby the cup, you'll be changing clothes immediately!)

The cup technique is best used in a baby seven months and older. Just a sip or two works; you still shouldn't let your baby drink too much water. If you want to provide extra feeding in a cup beyond a sip or two, consider giving your baby pumped breast milk or formula.

GETTING YOUR BABY TO SLEEP WHILE WEANING

When your baby goes to sleep at night, it's easier to wean him off the bottle if you put him to bed without a bottle early on. Many infants fall asleep during a feed and get into the habit of falling asleep only with the breast or bottle. For this reason, it's fine to put your baby to bed with a bottle or after falling asleep at the breast if he prefers it in the first six months.

At age six months, however, find other ways to get your baby to sleep. Let him get drowsy, then put him in his sleep area before he's fully asleep. In this way, he learns to settle himself to sleep but still has the comfort and memory of you putting him down. If he seems fidgety or upset, pat his little tummy while he's still lying in his sleep area. Alternatively, stay close by so he knows you're present.

If your baby uses a sippy cup and still takes the bottle, try a slow wean off the bottle to sleep. There are two possible scenarios for babies who don't want to take a sippy cup before sleep: one wants his formula or breast milk only in the bottle; the other doesn't sleep without drinking from the bottle.

Here's a tip for babies who by age one won't take a sippy cup before sleep or refuse to go to sleep without drinking formula, cow's milk, or breast milk. For one week, put half water and half formula or breast milk in each bottle you give. After one week, mix three-fourths water and one-fourth breast milk or formula. Then, after another week (two weeks total), give water bottles only and start giving breast milk or formula only in a sippy cup. Again, this technique is only for babies who have the sippy cup down and have reached a year of age. In the first year, water intake for babies should be minimal, since they need the majority of their fluids from breast milk, formula, and food. You needn't rush to wean your baby off the water bottle. You can continue to give water bottles at bedtime because they aren't harmful to the teeth.

If your baby will drink only milk from the breast or bottle, continue to put breast milk or formula in the cup four times per day, whether she drinks it or not. Initially, start with an ounce or two to avoid wasting. Try giving the sippy cup with breast milk or formula when you know she's thirsty, such as after an energetic play session.

A baby who will only fall asleep breastfeeding typically won't transition to bottles or a cup easily, so try breastfeeding more through the evening before he's sleepy. Then, when it's time for him to sleep, minimize the number of minutes he breastfeeds. Give him what he wants, of course, but work to have as short a session as possible. The goal is to give most of his calories early in the evening so he's not ravenous at bedtime. He enjoys cuddling, so continue to hold him close. Again, place him in his sleep area when he's drowsy but not fully asleep so he can learn to settle himself to a slumber.

If your baby remains resistant to weaning off the bottle or breast at bedtime, talk to your doctor about his routine. Rest assured all babies eventually wean off the bottle—and yours will too.

Chapter 20

STARTING FOODS FOR YOUR BABY

I t's best to start all babies on solid (but pureed) food by age six months. Getting used to the texture and taste of solid foods is important to brain development during the first year of life. In addition, babies who don't start solids or eat solids minimally in their first year miss out on the nutritional benefits and are more likely to be picky eaters in their toddler years.

If your baby is formula-feeding and your pediatrician approves, start solids between ages four and six months. If your baby is breast-feeding, breastfeed exclusively until age six months and then start solids. Starting solids before age four months could increase the risk of allergies and asthma. Any baby starting pureed food should be able to sit up with support and hold his head up well.

INTRODUCING SOLIDS

Your baby's first foods should be in the form of pureed fruits and vegetables. Some parents prefer to start with vegetables to prevent a "sweet tooth" in their baby. Although not supported by research, I pass on the tip from many parents who are certain that starting with vegetables helped keep their baby eating vegetables consistently. This is logical because the taste buds develop and adjust to the foods your baby eats.

We can't change genetics, however, and the tendency to love sweets is inherited. Luckily, we have fruits to supplement the vegetables for babies and children with a sweet tooth.

Baby food brands such as Gerber make preservative-free foods that are prepackaged and easy to feed to your baby. You can also make your own baby food by pureeing simple fruits and vegetables to the consistency of what's called a *stage one* food for ages four to six months and *stage two* food for ages six to eight months. Stage one food is a thin puree; when the baby reaches six months of age, her stage two puree can be slightly thicker. As your baby grows and her head control improves, her pureed food can be given in thicker and thicker consistencies.

Your baby may eat any pureed cereal you choose. If you like warm cereal, share yours with her. If it's a chunky cereal, use a blender to make a puree. If you choose rice cereal, select brown rice instead of white rice. Oatmeal is a good heart-healthy choice, and it can be pureed with fruit if desired.

To start on pureed foods, consider having the following items:

- a place for your baby to sit, such as a special chair with a tray or a high chair
- a comfortable place for you to sit in front of her
- a soft-tip spoon made especially for babies
- a baby bowl or dish
- a soft towel or napkin
- a splash mat under the chair to capture any food that drops (optional)

Initially, a good time to feed is when your baby is getting hungry but isn't yet ravenous. It's best for her to be in a relaxed state for this new feeding adventure. At first, feed your baby purees one to two times a day. Between seven and nine months of age, most babies can eat pureed foods three times a day.

Because most babies won't like their food cold, you can warm the food slightly or give it at room temperature. To warm your baby's food, place the food in a small container inside a warm bowl of water for ten minutes. As with bottles, refrain from heating baby food in the microwave because uneven heating can burn your baby's mouth.

Place the stage one pureed food on your baby's spoon and let her smell it to stimulate her taste buds. Move the spoon gently toward her mouth. She will likely open her mouth as the spoon approaches so you can feed her the food. Voila!

ADJUSTING TO THE NEW WAY OF EATING

Some babies take to the spoon and pureed foods quickly. Other babies appear disgusted by the taste or texture of the food. They might even gag. If this happens, stop the feeding and try the same food again the next day. If he cries or seems unhappy during feeding, hold off giving that particular food for a month and try again. It's surprising how well a baby will eat as the taste buds develop.

Start out with one to two ounces of pureed fruit or vegetable each feeding. Some babies who are getting used to food want only a tablespoon or two at first. The quantity of fruits and vegetables babies eat in the first couple of months of feeding varies quite a bit, so don't let the amount worry you. At this point, most of the baby's calories still come from breast milk or formula. Too much cereal can cause constipation or excessive weight gain, so give cereal only once a day.

Watch for cues that your baby is full. If he doesn't open his mouth, seems distracted and not interested, or relaxes in his chair, he's probably had enough. When babies are starting to eat, the meal doesn't replace a bottle or breastfeeding. Once your baby is eating enough food to feel full, though, you'll notice he won't drink much formula or breast milk afterward.

Wait three days between each new food you introduce to check for possible food allergies. Typically, these allergies appear in the form of a rash, diarrhea, or vomiting. Rarely, a severe food allergy can cause respiratory difficulty, a swollen face or lips, and wheezing. A little spitting up, a light rash around the mouth, or one loose stool doesn't mean you should stop giving a particular solid. If you notice multiple loose stools, persistent vomiting, or a red rash on the body, though, stop. Check with your doctor for the best time to restart it. For more information and reading on food allergies, see Chapter 13.

Don't save food that's been warmed or in which you've dipped your baby's feeding spoon. Once the food is warmed or your baby's saliva is in the puree, harmful bacteria could grow. Instead, put the amount you think your baby might eat in a bowl and save the rest.

Stools will change color and consistency with new foods. The color can be brown, yellow, green, or perhaps the same color as the food you have given him. The thickness of the stools will vary, which is normal since the digestive system isn't used to processing food. Consider any changes in stool consistency to be an adjustment to the new foods. However, if you notice persistent diarrhea or constipation, check with your doctor.

At ages six months and up, your baby may eat any pureed food except honey. Anything else! Honey can cause infant botulism, which is a type of severe food poisoning that can be fatal. The AAP recommends starting all foods except honey before age one year.[1]

Uganda: Baby's First Foods

In rural Uganda, pumpkin and papaya are common first foods for a baby to eat when weaning from breast milk. Although malnutrition is strikingly high in Uganda, these two foods are quite plentiful and nutritious.[2] Pumpkin is high in fiber and has an antioxidant called beta-carotene, which is converted to vitamin A in the body. Vitamin

A is important for your baby's brain, skin, immunity, and eye health. Also high in fiber, papaya is loaded in vitamin C. Vitamin C helps boost immunity plus keeps skin, tissues, and bones healthy.

If you want to add extra nutritional benefits for your baby, an easy pureed pumpkin recipe is available in the "Baby Food Recipes from Around the World" section of the Appendix.

ADDING SOFT, CHUNKY "FINGER FOODS"

When your baby is pulling up to stand at approximately nine months, start giving her soft, chunky foods. Eating by hand is a great way for your baby to practice fine motor skills, enjoy a variety of textures, and get used to various consistencies and tastes. Check with your pediatrician prior to starting soft, chunky foods to be sure your child is ready. If she's not already sitting at the table with the family, put her there and eat together. In Middle Eastern communities, sharing a meal with families and loved ones is an essential element of the Arab culture. Family meals are an important part of sharing quality time, and the habit is best started early.

Safely prepare finger foods for your baby. Finger foods should be soft, finely chopped, easily broken between two fingers, and approximately one inch (the size of your thumbnail). Give all finger foods one piece at a time to avoid the risk of choking if she stuffs several pieces of food in her mouth at once. Similar to the soft pureed foods, wait three days between each new food you introduce. This is to get your baby's mouth used to the taste and texture of the food. Three days later, you can add another food, and so on. Once she has eaten finger foods for a month, you don't have to wait three days in between each new food.

Your baby can eat finger foods without teeth. You could be uneasy because your baby has no teeth, or at least no teeth around the back of the mouth (molar area). Your baby's sturdy gums will take care of any chewing concerns. Babies have hard ridges especially made for chewing soft foods.

The most nutritious finger foods to offer are fruits, vegetables, and legumes. Dairy products such as small pieces of grated cheese are nutritious and can be added as well. Give your baby crackers and other complex carbohydrate foods no more than three times a day unless directed by your pediatrician. Carbohydrate foods are necessary in the diet, and these foods are fun for your baby to enjoy while learning to eat, but don't let your baby eat them in excess. Excessive carbohydrates can reduce the appetite for healthier foods and increase the risk of childhood obesity.

If your baby has allergic tendencies or you have a strong family history of allergies, talk to your pediatrician about the best order for starting new foods.

Maintain formula or breast milk as the predominant source of protein for your baby until her first birthday. She should drink twenty-four to thirty ounces a day of breast milk or formula. Depending on breast milk production, this is equivalent to breastfeeding four to six times a day. You can use cow's milk for cooking or to give your baby in small sips. (You'll find the list "Finger Foods and Healthy Food Ingredients for Purees" in the Appendix.)

Wash and rinse all fruits and vegetables well and cook meats thoroughly. Washing your fruits and vegetables under running water removes excess chemicals or pesticides. Cooking meats well will prevent bacterial growth. The pieces of meat need to be soft enough that your baby doesn't choke.

If you use canned foods, be sure they are free of preservatives. Most commercial baby foods are soft, well cooked, and preservative-free. Many other foods in the store are marked as preservative-free, so look for them. In particular, steer clear of nitrites, which are used to preserve meat and have been found to be carcinogenic (cancer causing).

When choosing fruits that aren't fresh, select fruits with no added sugar or artificial sweeteners. Frozen fruits and vegetables have better nutritional value than jarred or canned foods. Better yet are fresh fruits and vegetables in their natural state, which are the most nutritious. But when you do purchase canned or frozen, make sure that there are no additives.

Don't give your baby small, round, hard food that can lodge in her throat. Finger foods should be small and soft. Don't give large pieces of fruits or vegetables. Also, provide meat that's boneless and soft, perhaps cooked in a slow cooker. Again, ensure that your child eats only one piece at a time.

Avoid the following foods at all times through the first five years: large chunks of food, raw vegetables, pieces of food that are hard, large pieces of cheese, popcorn kernels, pretzels, marshmallows, hot dogs, large chunks of meat, whole nuts or nut pieces, hard candy, gum, dried fruit, and seeds.

What If Your Child Chokes?

Take a CPR (cardiopulmonary resuscitation) course that teaches what to do in the event your child chokes on food. The course can typically be completed in one day. Hopefully, you will never need to help your child or someone else's in an emergency situation, but it's good to be prepared.

Contact your local hospital, American Red Cross, or American Heart Association to find infant and child CPR courses near you. Once you have completed the course, keep a handout nearby to remind you what to do in the event your child chokes. A good informational guide is available from the American Red Cross at http://www.redcross.org/take-a-class/cpr/perfoming-cpr/child-baby-cpr.

Refined sweets have no nutritional value, so totally avoid giving them in the first year. Resist the temptation to give your baby bites of cookie, ice cream, and other sweets. On his or her first birthday, the birthday cake is a rite of passage for many babies, but don't make cake an everyday habit. After all, habits learned young become life-long patterns. You don't have to be as restrictive as your child gets older, but remember: the key to introducing sweets is moderation. Model good eating for your baby.

Some babies enjoy the pleasure of finger foods quickly, and others take to them more slowly. Once your baby is eating all food groups of finger foods, you can discontinue most pureed foods. Many babies naturally reject pureed food as they learn to enjoy the various flavors, textures, and varieties of finger foods.

China: *Congee*, the Versatile, Basic Soup

In many parts of Asia, babies start their diet with a watery rice soup. In China, this soup is called *congee*. Over time, mothers make the congee with less and less water for their babies. They add a variety of mashed vegetables into the congee. When their babies are close to one year of age, they add mashed meats as well. (You'll find the recipe for rice congee in the section "Baby Food Recipes from Around the World" in the Appendix.)

Around the World: Spices, Herbs, and Natural Extra Flavors

Don't be afraid to use spices, herbs, and natural extra flavors. Babies in Mexico and Central America often eat foods that contain cilantro, mild peppers, and chili powder. Moms in many countries such as China cook with garlic for their babies, even early on when the children are about age six months. The health applications of garlic have been reported for centuries, including promoting heart health and reducing infection.

Initially, use any herbs and spices in a relatively small quantity. The quantity tolerated by babies is unclear, but they generally don't like strong flavors. You can increase the amount as your baby moves into the toddler years. This allows him to get used to the taste and also experience positive health effects as he grows. The goal? To diversify his taste buds so he'll continue to enjoy the health benefits of a variety of foods and ultimately grow into an adult with a healthy diet.

HEALTHY AND SAFE EATING AND DRINKING

Give your baby healthy foods that your family would ordinarily eat. The goal is for her to eat the same food you do and enjoy dining with the family. Presenting new foods entails repeating foods the baby didn't want to eat at a different meal. If you try a food and she doesn't like it, there's no harm in offering the food again and again. Your goal is to ensure your child gets used to all food groups, with emphasis on fruits and vegetables. However, formula or breast milk should remain the child's chief source of protein. Meat isn't mandatory, but it's good to introduce it and get her used to the taste.

Clare Monson, a blogger, artist, and mother of two in central Portugal, gives her baby foods her family would ordinarily eat as finger foods—bread dipped in olive oil, olives cut in half, and chorizo or sausage. According to Clare, eating chorizo (a type of pork sausage) in small pieces is helpful for teething symptoms.[3]

While sharing what you are eating with your little one is great, it's best not to give your baby additives, preservatives, or much processed food. Read labels and look for preservative-free foods. Fresh food that's grown from the earth is healthier than processed food, and it gives your baby the needed vitamins and essential nutrients.

Some babies gag easily when solid foods are introduced. Be alert for consistent gagging. This is a normal reflex to help prevent them from choking. When starting solids, if your baby gags consistently, spits up recurrently, has difficulty swallowing, or refuses to eat, talk to your doctor to ensure your baby has no medical problems causing the difficulty with solids.

Water is okay to add to a baby's diet in the first year of life, but provide water in limited quantity. Early introduction of water can help get your baby used to drinking water as a habit. Many Latin parents give their babies water daily to hydrate them. I advise them to use only one or two ounces a day. If babies drink water in large quantities, the result can cause electrolyte disturbances and severe illness. Electrolytes are minerals and salts that keep the body healthy.

As mentioned previously, most of your baby's fluid intake should be from formula or breast milk. If you would like to add water, do so in very small quantities (sips!). If approved by your doctor, use the following regimen to introduce water:

- Age four to six months: one ounce of water twice a day
- Age six to nine months: two ounces of water twice a day
- Age nine to twelve months: three ounces of water twice a day

In the baby's first four months, boil, cool, and save the water. After four months, if your community has treated water that's good for drinking, it's okay to use filtered water from the tap. You can warm the water slightly or give it to her at room temperature. Babies over six months of age can enjoy their water cold, but test it first. Offer a small sip and see how your baby likes it.

Even when you add water to your baby's regimen, continue to give her the normal amount of formula or breast milk each day. Pay attention during this time to the amount of formula or breast milk she ingests. Aim to get her used to water without letting it suppress her appetite. You want her to continue to eat solid foods and nipple-feed normally. During warmer months, your baby might be extra thirsty. If this is true, give her additional formula or breast milk. If your baby has been in a prolonged period of heat, with your doctor's approval, you can give her Pedialyte (or a generic equivalent), which is an electrolyte solution that helps prevent dehydration.

Drinking Juice—Good or Bad?

Juice is typically not recommended for babies because its nutritional content is negligible. Juice helps relieve constipation, but it shouldn't be consumed in excess by anyone of any age. Pieces of fruit naturally provide more fiber and nutrients than juice alone.

Many families, including parents in New Zealand, enjoy giving their babies juice as a treat. Juice in limited quantities is not harmful. So, if you would like to give your child juice, use 100 percent natural juice (not concentrate) occasionally (no more than twice a week) for ages six months and older. The rest of the day should be your baby's usual diet of solid foods, breast milk, formula, and small amounts of water.

If you think your baby needs juice to combat constipation, check with your doctor. If the doctor agrees, use the following dosage guidelines:

Age two to four months: Mix one ounce of baby apple or baby pear juice with one ounce of bottled or filtered water in equal parts. Give two ounces twice a day. If there are no results, you can give two ounces three times a day.

Age four months and beyond: If your baby is on solids, give him pureed fruits and vegetables two to four times a day. Avoid bananas, which could be constipating. If your baby becomes constipated, mix 100 percent natural juice with water (half water and half juice). Start with two ounces a day. If you don't see relief from the constipation, increase to four ounces a day, up to a maximum of six ounces a day. During this time, continue giving pureed solids to babies four to eight months of age and small pieces of fruits and vegetables to babies nine months and beyond.

Chapter 21

PREVENTING OVEREATING AND OBESITY

I t's important to start early to prevent obesity. Although this might seem like a daunting task, it's manageable with a few simple suggestions.

Obesity in babies can cause a decrease in motor development, breathing problems, reflux, and, most important, a risk of remaining obese and developing complications. Obese children are more likely to have joint problems, an increased risk of diabetes, and social isolation than those who aren't obese. Many obese children stay overweight into adulthood, causing a host of medical problems.

DANGERS OF OVEREATING

An overeating baby takes in a large amount at every feed, appears hungry between feeds, and gains extra weight. You can determine if your baby is an overeater by having your doctor monitor her weight and growth.

If your baby is breastfeeding, it's not easy to overfeed; therefore, breastfed infants tend to be less obese than formula-fed infants. Babies who breastfeed eat slowly and naturally regulate their eating, and they tend to stop when full or the breast is empty. By comparison, a bottle-fed baby is likely to quickly finish the bottle and might not feel as satisfied.

How to Prevent Obesity through Healthy Eating

If you choose to bottle-feed, that doesn't mean your baby will be obese. You can prevent obesity in your baby.

Work to determine if your baby is truly hungry. In the first two months, pay attention to your baby's cries and learn to figure out if she's hungry or crying for another reason. During those months, allow your baby to eat on demand. Don't force her to stick to a schedule; let her respond to her natural hunger cues. After two months, most babies will eat every three to four hours. The exception to this is a baby who's catching up on growth or one who spits up frequently and needs smaller, more frequent feeds.

Use a slower-flow nipple for a longer time. Newborns to age two months use slow-flow nipples. They naturally tend to eat more slowly, regardless of the nipple, because they're working out the process of sucking and swallowing. If your baby is more than two months and finishing a bottle in less than fifteen minutes, change the nipple to one with slower flow. Slowing down your baby's eating pattern can help reduce any excess intake of formula. A baby who eats more slowly from the bottle than the breast notices she's full and stops when she's finished.

For bottle-fed babies, pay attention to the quantity of formula your doctor has recommended. The goal is for your baby to eat at a normal pace and not gulp formula too quickly. However, be careful not to slow your baby down too much! It could frustrate her or cause her to tire while feeding.

Use the following guide for how long your baby should take to finish a bottle. As mentioned above, if you find your baby is taking less time, try a slower-flow nipple.

- Newborn to two months: on demand; times could vary
- Two to four months: fifteen to thirty minutes
- Four months and beyond: fifteen to twenty minutes

Load up on fruits and vegetables. If you determine that your child eats too much, when it's time to start solids, focus on fruits and vegetables. These safe foods don't add a large number of extra calories to your baby's diet.

Once your baby can finger-feed, let her feed herself until she's full. Don't spoon-feed her extra food to get her to eat more. Avoid working extra hard to get her to finish her meal; let her eat the amount she wants. Trust that she can decide when she's finished eating.

Teaching your child to stop when she's full will serve her well as a lifelong habit. The only exception is if your child is gaining weight too slowly. In this case, work closely with your pediatrician to find a cause and treatment. If the cause is nutritional, your pediatrician or nutritionist will help you find ways to increase calories.

Don't give finger-fed babies large quantities of foods that are high in carbohydrates. Your baby shouldn't eat crackers, dry cereal, or bread products at each snack. These taste yummy, but healthier snacks to eat come straight from the earth—fruits, vegetables, dairy products, and legumes (beans). Refrain from giving cake, cookies, or any other junk food. Instead, plan ahead so you have foods ready when she's typically hungry.

Throughout this book, you'll note an emphasis on fruits and vegetables because they help build the immune system and come with numerous other health benefits. Fruits and vegetables make wonderful snacks and are great to add to meals along with forms of protein and grains.

Make sure family members, sitters, or caregivers know how to feed your child. Educate all caretakers to follow your philosophy of healthy feeding. Many people aren't aware that a nine-month-old infant should not be eating cookies and refined sweets, because they were trained to eat them as a child.

How to Prevent Obesity through Activities

Eliminate electronics. The AAP recommends that babies don't watch television or play on electronic devices. Watching television and using electronics devices in the first year of life can have negative effects on an infant's brain development.[1] Instead, encourage your baby's natural engagement in physical activity from an early age.

Promote plenty of exercise. Yes, exercise. Some babies like to observe and don't move around as much early on. Once he's moving, he should be up and active. Babies instinctively start moving on their own, but keep play and stimulation going from birth and after they are mobile.

Put your four-month-old infant down on a mat and let him move around. Once your baby is crawling, follow him, encouraging the behavior. When he's pulling up to stand and starting to walk, keep encouraging physical activity. If the weather is good, take him outside to get fresh air and activity. These lifelong healthy habits set babies up well into the toddler years, childhood, and, ultimately, adulthood.

Encourage lots of sleep. Obesity and sleep deprivation are related because a lack of sleep interrupts the hormones that control the appetite. Also, babies who are tired become irritable and may want to eat more to soothe themselves. You can't force your baby to sleep or nap, but you certainly can ensure you set the stage for a good sleep schedule.

Japan: Celebrating a First Meal with *Okuizome*

If you talk to a Japanese parent, you will typically find a Japanese child has quite a diverse diet. In fact, according to the World Health Organization, Japanese people have the highest life expectancy in the world.[2] They focus on healthy, unprocessed food for their babies and children.

In Japan, a one-hundredth-day-of-life celebration focusing on a family's wish for their baby's "good health life" is called *okuizome*, or "first meal." At this celebration, healthy foods are prepared and offered to the baby. An assortment of traditional foods such as rice, fish, and soup are placed in front of the baby. Parents and grandparents each use chopsticks and press the foods against the baby's lips, as if the baby is actually eating the food. At this early age, Japanese babies don't usually eat the foods, so *okuizome* is more of a symbolic event.[3] The dishes and tray are small and gender specific for the baby girl or boy. Friends and family join in and model eating foods from the earth. Use your own special baby dishes and traditional family foods for your baby's first celebration meal—any day you choose!

Chapter 22

YOUR BABY'S NUTRITIONAL NEEDS

I f you study recipes from around the world, you'll see a variety of ingredients are used to prepare baby food. It's no secret that breast milk is best for the baby to drink, and a mother may choose to breastfeed for a prolonged period. Nutritionists don't always agree on food content, but we do know that in addition to breast milk or formula, babies thrive on a diet heavy in fruits, vegetables, legumes, and grains. But what about vitamins and other food sources?

VITAMIN SUPPLEMENTATION FOR BREASTFED BABIES

Vitamins that are appropriately dosed have many health advantages for your baby. Formula-fed babies already receive vitamins in their formula and typically don't need extra vitamin supplementation. Vitamin D is important to supplement in exclusively breastfed babies. According to the AAP, breastfed babies should take 400 IU of vitamin D daily in the first year of life.[1] (IU is a measurement of dosing called International Units).

Babies can easily become deficient in vitamin D, especially those who are breastfed. Babies on formula do not need vitamin D supplementation because vitamin D is added to the formula. According to the AAP, "Infants who are exclusively breastfed but who do not receive supplemental vitamin D or adequate sunlight exposure are at increased risk of developing vitamin D deficiency." Vitamin D is passed through the breast milk, but many mothers who breastfeed might not get enough vitamin D to pass along to their babies.[2]

In fact, vitamin D deficiency is common in all ages due to lack of exposure to sunrays rich in vitamin D and low intake through diet. Natural sunlight is an excellent source of vitamin D. Little sun exposure, especially in the winter, increases the risk of vitamin D deficiency. Plus, babies are kept from exposure to direct sunlight in early months at any time of year, and later, sunscreen is applied to prevent sunburn. Unfortunately, this necessary practice decreases the absorption of vitamin D.

Vitamin D deficiency can result in a bone disorder called rickets. In turn, rickets can cause bones to not grow straight and weaken a child's strength. Vitamin D deficiency is also linked to asthma,[3] cancer, and the development of type 1 diabetes.[4] It's important to ensure vitamin D is taken with breast milk or food to promote its absorption.

Multivitamins for Infants

An infant multivitamin, such as Poly-Vi-Sol with Iron, gives an extra boost of vitamins to breastfed babies. The vitamin content is similar to that of most formulas. In addition to vitamin D, the liquid vitamin Poly-Vi-Sol provides vitamins A, C, D, E, B1 (thiamin), B2 (riboflavin), B3 (niacin), B6, and B12. (All doctors might not agree the extra boost of vitamins is necessary, however.)

When your baby is six months of age, if your doctor approves, you have the option to discontinue the vitamin D supplements and start Poly-Vi-Sol with Iron (1 ml daily). Poly-Vi-Sol and other baby vitamins are given in liquid form. The best way to administer infant liquid vitamins is to use a dropper, gently squeezing the vitamin liquid into your baby's mouth.

According to the CDC, iron-deficiency anemia is the most common nutritional deficiency worldwide.[5] Anemia is a blood disease that can impair brain development and health in babies. Most doctors check for anemia at the nine-month checkup, which indirectly provides information on your baby's iron status. If a baby is deficient in iron, he will likely become anemic if iron is not supplemented in the diet or through vitamins.

For this reason, many breastfeeding mothers take a vitamin themselves that contains iron to supplement their baby's diet. Sometimes, extra iron supplementation has side effects, especially if your baby isn't eating enough fruits and vegetables. If you find your child is having constipation or gastrointestinal disturbances due to the iron, greatly increase his fruits and vegetables to combat these annoying side effects. However, the supplement of iron in babies over age six months is not meant to replace the need for fresh fruits and vegetables. If your child eats red meat, green vegetables, and iron-enriched products such as iron-fortified cereal, he may be just fine skipping iron supplementation.

Should you include zinc-enriched foods in his diet? Yes. Most breastfed and formula-fed babies need additional zinc in their diet as they grow into the eating solids phase. Standard formulas do contain zinc, although not a large amount. Zinc is highest in meat (chicken and red meat) and beans, plus some baby cereals are zinc fortified.

Few doctors will tell you *not* to give your breastfed baby vitamin supplementation in some form. Recognize the importance of ensuring your baby gets the vitamins he needs and discuss any use of vitamin-enriched foods and supplementation with your doctor.

Middle East: Hummus for Babies

Garbanzo beans, also known as chickpeas, are a good source of protein, fiber, iron, and zinc. They're also reported to act as a galactagogue (a substance that helps produce breast milk).

In the Middle East, garbanzo beans are reported to have existed in the Mediterranean area as early as 3,000 BC. They have been consumed just as long for the nutritional benefits. In Lebanon and much of the Middle East, a popular garbanzo bean dish is hummus. Because the flavor of hummus can be strong for babies initially, a good way to get them used to eating it is to start with a mild recipe and gradually add ingredients over time. (In the Appendix, you'll find a recipe for a mild form of hummus that's an example of how a Lebanese mom gives her baby garbanzo beans.)

To help your baby get the vitamins he needs, go ahead and feed the baby hummus! It's something that you'll both enjoy snacking on.

MEAT (OR NOT) IN YOUR BABY'S DIET

During the first year of life, meat is not mandatory since breast milk or formula is your baby's main form of protein. Meat is an acquired taste, so if you plan to make meat a staple in your family's diet, it's best to get your baby used to its taste in the first year.

Note: Plenty of vegetarians never eat meat, and they live and grow just fine by getting their protein from other sources.

If you plan to feed your baby a meat-free diet, consult your doctor as your baby begins eating solid food to ensure you are giving alternate sources of protein as well as essential vitamins. See the section "Vegetarian Diet" in this chapter for more.

Seafood Consumption and Supplementation of ARA and DHA

Arachidonic acid (ARA or AA) and docosahexaenoic acid (DHA) are fatty acids derived from algae and fungi. DHA and ARA are important for developing the brain and eyes. Preterm infants are at greater risk of DHA and ARA deficiency than full-term babies since these fatty acids are passed from the mother to the baby until the end of pregnancy. If the pregnancy is shorter than usual, less DHA and ARA will pass from the mother to child.[6]

ARA and DHA are found to be higher in individuals whose diets are high in seafood consumption than those whose diets are not. They can be supplemented during pregnancy and through the breastfeeding or nipple-feeding period. Breastfeeding mothers on prenatal vitamins that contain DHA and ARA don't have to worry about supplementation of DHA and ARA; they are naturally excreted in the breast milk.[7]

Most women do not get enough DHA and ARA in their diets.[8] Some fish contain mercury, and doctors and the FDA recommend "swimming away" from fish with mercury while pregnant and breastfeeding.[9, 10, 11] (King mackerel, marlin, orange roughy, shark, swordfish, tilefish, and tuna all contain high levels of mercury.)[12] For babies whose diets are supplemented with formula, should mothers use DHA- and ARA-based formulas? Yes. The FDA has determined that DHA and ARA are safe to add to infant formulas as well as foods such as infant cereal.

Although concentrations have been measured in breast milk, more studies are needed to determine dosing of DHA and ARA for infants and children. No recommended minimum or maximum dose of DHA and ARA has been established. A 2002 study in *The Journal of Pediatrics* showed no adverse events in pre-term infants who consumed formula with DHA and ARA.[13] However, more studies are needed to assist doctors with dosing protocols to ensure that overdose of DHA and ARA in babies doesn't lead to toxic effects.

Vegetarian Diet

Vegetarians have practiced meat-free eating for centuries. Vegetarian diets have been embraced worldwide, with children faring well as long as care is taken to provide them with a diverse, healthy diet. With one of the highest rates of vegetarians in Europe, England promotes good old-fashioned fruits, nuts, vegetables, and other food from the earth. In most cities in England and the United States, vegetarians can easily find foods made without meat. Over the past two decades, America has seen a rise in vegetarianism as we're becoming increasingly aware of the benefits of eating from the earth.

Healthy diets from the earth can include meat, but some people prefer no meat in their own diet or their children's diet. Giving your baby a vegetarian diet in his first year of life isn't difficult, especially if you follow your doctor's nutritional guidelines.

If you are a vegetarian and plan to raise your child as one, check with your doctor to see what supplementation is best for your baby.

Vegan Diet

What is a vegan diet? A vegan diet eliminates all animal products, including eggs and dairy as well as meat and fish.

If you follow a vegan diet, ensure that your doctor tracks your baby's growth and nutritional status closely and advises you on supplementing her diet with appropriate vitamins. As your child grows, allow her to choose if she wants to follow a vegan diet. Babies and children on a vegan diet without adequate supervision may have more nutritional deficiencies than those who aren't vegan. Use care if you follow such a regimen.[14]

HERBAL SUPPLEMENTS

Many herbal remedies are unsafe for babies to use and often dosed without research guidelines. Ask your pediatrician to look at and approve of any herbal remedies you're considering for your baby. Herbs in our marketplace can be helpful, but, unfortunately, these supplements are not well tested in children for their dosages, and improper quantities can cause toxicity. Manufacturers are supposed to be responsible for stating the safe use of any vitamins or herbal supplements for both adults and babies. However, the Food and Drug Administration (FDA) does not routinely test or manage dietary supplements unless there's a concern expressed. The FDA sets standards for safety and has the authority to act against any dietary supplement considered medically harmful.[15]

Many parents believe they're helping by purchasing natural supplements for their children. However, it's best to consult a pediatrician before using them because they can be harmful for babies.

Until we have more information, herbal supplements should not be given to babies and children. It is true that many medicinal herbs and supplements have been used all over the world for centuries, and multiple studies have provided evidence for effective herbal treatment of many disorders in adults. However, more studies are needed to properly know the value of herbal supplements, especially in babies and children.

Chapter 23

PESTICIDES AND YOUR BABY

More toxins are present in our environment than ever before. Over the last century, a surge of processed chemicals have become available to us as pesticides, which are poisonous substances in various forms. What's more, toxins can be present in foods or simple products such as household cleaners or insect repellent.

Pesticides in foods come from potentially harmful chemicals used to kill insects while fruits and vegetables are growing. Other prevalent types of pesticides are those used for general insect control in parks, public places, and residential homes. According to a 2017 report by the EPA, Americans used more than a billion pounds of pesticides in 2012 for pest control.[1] Pesticides in and on foods have no nutritional value and can cause problems for your baby, so avoid them.

DANGERS OF PESTICIDES

It's difficult to detect the quantity of pesticide any one person is exposed to or ingests. Unfortunately, due to lack of information, we don't even know how much of a particular toxin is harmful—to either adults or babies. Pesticides are found *on* food and *in* food, but they're tasteless. For this reason, it's hard to say exactly how much toxin a child consumes. There's no known "safe" level of pesticide exposure for children.

Pregnant women are especially vulnerable because toxic chemicals can be passed to the baby in the womb. And later, babies can ingest pesticides through their mother's breast milk.[2, 3, 4] For this reason, I recommend pesticide elimination while pregnant and breastfeeding your baby.

Remember, even after babies are born, they are still growing and developing. Babies are growing more rapidly and eat more food in proportion to their body size than adults. Their digestive system may be impaired by the use of pesticides, blocking the absorption of essential nutrients necessary for their growth. In addition, a baby's kidneys aren't fully developed and capable of processing pesticides. This limits the body's ability to fully rid itself of the pesticides.[5, 6]

What this means is that pesticide poisoning can potentially cause permanent organ damage. A baby's developing body is at risk for long-term damage such as permanent brain injury, cancer, and asthma if she takes in too much of these chemicals. The list for potential damage includes all organ systems in the body.[7]

The Food Quality Protection Act passed in the United States in 1996 addresses the issue of pesticides and enforces safety standards for pesticides in foods. Many pesticides over the past decade have been voluntarily phased out or canceled. For example, children's exposure to carbamates from pesticides has been reduced in the past two decades by 70 percent.[8] Although the Food Quality Protection Act and the Environmental Protection Agency have taken steps to reduce pesticides, they are still found in milk, meat, fruits, and vegetables.

WHAT CAN YOU DO TO LIMIT EXPOSURE TO TOXINS?

Reduce your baby's exposure to toxic chemicals in foods. Toxins are present in our lives, and it can feel overwhelming to figure out how to totally avoid them, so the key word is *reduce.* You cannot live happily spending all of your time trying to figure out how to *eliminate* all toxins, so work on reducing their presence. You can dramatically limit your family's exposure to potentially harmful chemicals in foods.

Eat natural foods. Locally grown fruits and vegetables are best. If you shop at a farmer's market, ask the growers if they use pesticides on their produce. Should you buy organic foods? Organic meat, poultry, eggs, and dairy products come from animals that are given no antibiotics or growth hormones. Organic fruits and vegetables are grown without toxic pesticides.

Because organic foods can get quite expensive, look for items grown locally. Find people who grow their own food and garden with them. Or, if you lack the time (like me), look around for someone who has a garden and will sell you organic, homegrown fruits and vegetables for a reasonable price.

Buy hormone- and antibiotic-free milk when possible, even for cooking. Babies one year and younger are not drinking cow's milk yet, but they can eat products made with milk. If you can get organic, hormone-free milk and/or antibiotic-free milk, the risk of excess chemicals in your baby's body is reduced. Knowing you can introduce dairy products before age one to babies who aren't allergic to them, you can cook with milk freely. Hormone- and antibiotic-free milk is a better-safe-than-sorry approach to milk consumption for all children.

Never give any food with raw or unprocessed milk to your baby. This can contain bacteria that can harm the body and make your baby sick.

Cook meat that's nitrate-free and hormone-free, and trim off the fat. Nitrates are strongly associated with cancer, so avoid them. This is relatively easy to do. If you buy meat, look for meat that's labeled "natural" or "preservative-free." If you cook meat that's fresh, look at the package ingredients to ensure the meat contains no additives.

If your baby is eating meat in the first year of life, puree your own additive-free meat before he's nine months old and give him small, soft chunks after that age. Not only is trimming the fat a healthy habit because of the lack of nutritional value, but it gets rid of toxins that can be stored in the fat.

Clean your fruits and vegetables by rinsing them with running water before eating them. Don't assume foods you buy have been washed well. According to the National Pesticide Information Center (NPIC), using fresh water is the best way to rid your fruits and vegetables of pesticides and dirt. Don't soak your produce, because the pesticides will just sit in the water with your foods. Running water works best.[9]

Brush or rub produce to avoid bruising it during the rinsing process. Wash waxy or soft-skinned fruits well and then peel them before eating. (Pesticide residues can soak into the soft skins and be trapped under the wax.)

Dry your produce with a paper towel if the items will not be cooked. Gently drying your food after rinsing may help reduce bacteria.

Cleaning agents sometimes used on fruits and vegetables such as bleach or soap could add toxins to your produce, so don't use them. These chemicals can be trapped in the pores of your fruit or vegetables and later ingested. Cleaning foods with vinegar or baking soda may affect the flavor of food, and produce cleaning sprays are generally designed for post-harvest use before shipping. In summary, the best defense against pesticides and bacteria is rinsing, a gentle rub or brush, and drying items that won't be cooked with a paper towel.

Middle East: Family Group Cooking Practices

In the Middle East, two to four people might cook for a family of twenty or more. In many areas of the countryside, this tends to be more common than in the cities. Processed foods are in limited supply, which is a good thing. The people cook natural foods instead, often for the entire extended family. Not only does this save time and money, but the family also gets to share the meal. Family cooking teaches the younger generation kitchen skills and helps sustain traditional culinary practices.

Consider cooking cooperatively with family and friends, sharing homegrown, pesticide-free fruits and vegetables. An added bonus is the joy of group cooking and dining.

France: Fresh Foods

In France, many people go to the market one to three times a week to buy their fresh foods. This practice reduces pesticide residue, promotes healthy eating, and ensures the fruit and vegetables remain fresh and aren't wasted.

Yes, time is often an issue. But if you're able to get to the grocery store or market regularly, you can also shop more quickly than if you go only occasionally. If you buy small quantities of fresh foods frequently like the French do, you'll reduce food spoilage and not spend as much in the long run.

PESTICIDES IN AND AROUND THE HOME

As long as pests are in our environment, pesticides will be available to rid ourselves of them. This problem extends to the following list of potentially hazardous products:

- Insect repellents
- Insect-control products

- Rodent-control products
- Cleaning agents
- Lawn products
- Garden products
- Soil fumigants
- Pet products

The following tips can help your baby avoid contact with environmental toxins such as those listed:

Use toxin-free products. Various natural toxin-free products are available on the market—e.g., orange tree oil insect spray kills and repels insects. Remember, however, that even if a product is considered natural, it can be harmful to humans in excess. A good web source to check the potential for toxicity in natural products is the Environmental Protection Agency's Pesticide Product and Label System (https://iaspub.epa.gov/apex/pesticides/f?p=PPLS:1).

Block insects from entering your home. Use screens, caulk, and whatever else you need to keep them out. Trim back or remove excess shrubs around your house. One good way to send insects in a different direction is to use cedar mulch in your garden and yard. Cedar naturally repels insects and has a nice scent. If you use cedar in your garden, use a one-inch layer of shavings. If you put cedar mulch in your yard, sprinkle a layer in the grass. Avoid using cedar chips, though. The larger chips are a fire hazard and more expensive than smaller sizes.

I also spray orange oil along the baseboards in areas of our home where bugs seem to get in. If you spray a day before you plan to mop, it has twenty-four hours to do its job before you clean the residue. Effectiveness research reviews are mixed—orange oil is not as strong as toxic pesticides! However, I (and many other people) have found with weekly orange oil spraying, controlling insects entering our home is easy. You can make your own recipe by adding two ounces of orange oil to one gallon of water. You can also buy an already-mixed solution, such as Orange Guard Home Pest Control.

Lock all products containing pesticides away from children. Products should be sealed, closed, and out of reach. In particular, rodent-control products can cause rapid fatal poisoning when ingested. This is one example of many potentially toxic, fatal issues with the products kept in the home. Seal and close the containers, and then lock them away.

Keep the pesticides in their original containers. Moving pesticides to a different container can lead a person to mistake them for a safe product. Also, a new container might arouse curiosity in a baby who likes to explore.

Avoid using household cleaners or pesticide products when your baby is nearby. Don't clean the floor while your baby is crawling around or in the same room. Even if you have her contained, you have a recipe for exposure or accidental ingestion.

If pesticides are used, clean the floors to reduce the residue. Don't use pesticides in rooms where your baby plays, such as the kitchen, bedrooms, or living area. If you spray pesticides in the home, clean the floors after applying them to reduce as much residue as possible.

Cover your baby to avoid contact with insects. Babies who are exposed to areas with a large number of insects should be covered. Even in the summer, your baby will be cool enough wearing pants and lightweight cotton shirts with long sleeves.

Consider DEET-free insect repellents that have the ingredient IR3535. This substance has been safely used in Europe to repel insects for over two decades. There have been no reports of toxicity other than topical irritation. To avoid possible ingestion, insect repellants should not be applied to your baby's hands, feet, or face. (You can find an updated list of brand-name insect repellents that have the ingredient IR3535 at www.lisalewismd.com/safe-repellents.)

Consider Avon Skin So Soft lotion. You can apply a light coat of Avon Skin So Soft lotion to babies' skin six months and older. Avon products are typically bought from a distributor or certified Avon seller on the web. The insect repellent and sunscreen made by Avon is not recommended—only the lotion. Skin So Soft has a light fragrance that repels insects and has not been found to be toxic like agents such as N,N-Diethyl-meta-toluamide (DEET), found in insecticides.

Be aware of where your baby travels. Is she crawling on a surface that was just sprayed with an insect repellent or cleaned with a toxic agent? Is she moving toward an unidentified object on the floor? Keep your eyes open and watch where your baby goes. Go into your baby's world—literally. Get on your hands and knees and look around to everywhere your baby might go. Ensure she can reach no potentially harmful products or objects.

Babies put things in their mouth and play in areas close to the ground where pesticides are applied. They might even place their mouths on the floor. Those who crawl and put things in their mouths are at greater risk of exposure to applied pesticides than older children because they enjoy the taste and texture of inanimate objects.

Check places your baby visits outside the home. Ask about pesticide control and environmental toxins in the day care your child attends or home of a babysitter. How are they used? Where are they used? Will your baby play where the environmental toxins are applied? If an exterminator comes and treats the location, is the floor cleaned afterward? If disinfectants are applied to toys, are they rinsed after the application? Don't be embarrassed to check items outside your home; in fact, you can increase awareness for others and help them avoid harm.

Resources for Poison Control and Prevention

If your baby ingests any poisonous or toxic product, call the Poison Control Center immediately at 1-800-222-1222. For more information on pesticide prevention in your foods and home, check with the following two organizations:

Environmental Protection Agency (EPA) Office of Pesticide Programs

https://www.epa.gov/pesticide-contacts/forms/contact-us-about-pesticide-contacts-and-organizational-information

US Environmental Protection Agency
Office of Pesticide Programs, Mail Code 7506C
1200 Pennsylvania Ave. NW
Washington, DC 20460

US Food and Drug Administration (FDA), **Center for Food Safety and Applied Nutrition**

https://www.fda.gov/aboutfda/centersoffices/officeoffoods/cfsan/contactcfsan/default.htm
1-888-SAFEFOOD (1-888-723-3366)

US Food and Drug Administration
Center for Food Safety and Applied Nutrition Outreach and Information Center
5001 Campus Drive, HFS-009
College Park, MD 20740-3835

PART 4

Building Immunity
and Body Care

Some people care too much. I think it's called love.

—Winnie the Pooh

Chapter 24

BUILDING YOUR BABY'S IMMUNE SYSTEM

When your baby is born, many loved ones will want to shower her with affection and protection. Your baby will first bond with her parents, and as the months march on, she will learn to love the important people in your lives. It is important to socialize your baby with others and strengthen his immune system, but not too early.

BABY'S MONTHS ONE AND TWO

During the first two months of life, don't allow your baby to be around many people. It's important not to subject him to any adults or children who might be sick. He's working on building his immune system, and in the first two months of life, illness could progress rapidly and be difficult to detect. After the two-month checkup, if everything looks good and your baby has had his vaccines, your doctor will typically give the green light for your baby to be around other people. If your baby was born premature, ask when you can increase your baby's contact with others.

Still, you want to proceed with caution. Avoid crowded places, stores, airplanes, day cares, and any other place your baby may come into contact with illness. If you will be around people in his first two months of life and believe contact is inevitable, use a baby sling to carry him on your chest. This will minimize unwanted hands on your baby and reduce close contact with others. Avoid passing him around to others during this period. If you do, don't hesitate to give them hand sanitizer to use first or ask them to wash their hands in warm soapy water before holding your newborn baby. For more information on preventing and treatment of colds for your little one, check out "Aaaaachooooo! Treat and Prevent Baby Colds" from *Bloggy Moms.*[1]

During this time period, your baby will receive his vaccines. Vaccines protect your baby and will help strengthen his immune system to fight against life-threatening diseases. Our worldwide goal is to vaccinate as many babies, children, adolescents, and adults as possible. This practice helps establish "herd immunity." That's right—herd, as in cattle. Large groups of people who are all vaccinated and living in the same place can protect each other—and those living around them, such as cancer patients, who cannot be vaccinated. Think of it as a community advantage. Talk to your doctor about the appropriate vaccines for your baby. Most health care providers follow a research-backed schedule from the American Academy of Pediatrics. You can find the link to the immunization schedule in the Endnotes.[2]

BABY'S MONTH THREE

In his third month of life, gradually (when possible) introduce your baby to other people. Some babies go to day care during this time, and this is understandable. Day care centers are required to conform to standards for prevention of illness. Check to make sure your facility is up to date with measures to reduce the risk of disease in children.

Day Care Policies to Reduce Risk of Illness

These eleven requirements should be in place in day care centers.

1. Physical examination to enter day care plus routine ongoing health checks with doctor
2. Exclusion criteria for sick children (For example, children with fever, diarrhea, vomiting, or any obvious contagious illness are required to go home)
3. Immunizations required and up to date
4. Health Department notification of outbreaks
5. Parent notification of outbreaks
6. Food preparation area separate from children and bathrooms
7. Clean rooms and bathrooms; properly sanitized toys
8. Breast milk and formula labeled and properly stored
9. Hand washing mandated for children and adults before eating, after toileting, and after any change of activities
10. Hand washing mandated for day care employees and attending parents
11. Hand dryers or individual paper towels for personal use

For more day care information, see Chapter 12, "Child Care for Working Parents."

BABY'S MONTHS THREE TO TWELVE

After approximately three months, breathe a sigh of relief and know that building your baby's immune system can best happen through contact with the outside world. Some say our society is too "sterile," and I agree. Children who are placed in day care might have fewer instances of asthma than those who are isolated. The proposed reason for this is called the *hygiene hypothesis*. Industrialized nations such as the United States and European countries tend to have good access to hygiene prevention such as frequent hand washing, cleaner homes and facilities, and less crowding of children in one space. However, the current thinking is that a baby's immune system is better developed when tested by having contact with other individuals.

For example, a 2008 study in the *European Respiratory Journal* showed that children of mothers who lived on a farm during pregnancy had 50 percent less hay fever and eczema (allergic skin) than children born to urban mothers. This study suggests that mothers are able to pass immune benefits to their children during pregnancy that have lasting power well beyond birth.[3]

However, a study from the Netherlands in the 2009 *Journal of Respiratory and Critical Care Medicine* disputed the hygiene hypothesis. "We found no evidence for a protective or harmful effect of day care on the development of asthma symptoms, allergic sensitization, or airway hyper-responsiveness at the age of eight years," wrote Johan C. de Jongste, MD, PhD, of Erasmus University in the Netherlands.[4] To simplify, Dr. Jongste's research found no immune system benefits, good or bad, in children attending day care.

I think the answer lies somewhere in between. It would be irresponsible to have a neighborhood party and invite all the children who are ill. Yet our children need exposure to others to build a healthy immune system. More studies need to be conducted to clarify the role of immune system building in children by exposure to the environment.

Parents in many countries, including Vietnam as discussed in Chapter 5, have families and friends who help deliver prolonged care at home to reduce their baby's outside contact and the new mother's stress. Other countries, such as Belgium, may take their babies out into society in the first month of a baby's life.

Contact in the first year is a double-edged sword. It's good to have your older baby around other people. Placing the baby in isolation doesn't help build the immune system or stimulate the social skills needed for your baby to develop. However, the more people your baby is around, the more likely he is to pick up an illness—a normal part of childhood. Babies in day care will pick up, on average, seven to nine viral infections in a year. A healthy, diverse diet and breastfeeding will help build the immune system. In your baby's environment, frequent hand washing in adults and children remains the number one best defense to prevent contagious illness.

Chapter 25

YOUR BABY'S HEAD, EYES, AND EARS

T he small size of your baby may seem intimidating at first, but as time marches on, you will feel more and more comfortable caring for her body. The most accessible and delicate parts of the body—your baby's head, eyes, and ears—actually require very little maintenance.

KEEPING YOUR BABY HEALTHY

Head and Fontanel (Soft Spot)

A fontanel, also known as the soft spot, is located on your baby's head. Fontanels are membranous coverings between the cranial bones that allow the head and brain to grow to a normal shape and size. Your baby has two fontanels. The one on top of the head is the anterior fontanel; the other, on the back of the head, is the posterior fontanel. Yes, it's okay to touch them! Most fontanels make a small indention in the scalp, and this is normal. When a baby lies flat, the fontanel may appear full. When she's sitting up, the fontanel may appear more sunken or caved in due to the effects of gravity.

Should I worry about fontanel changes? A fontanel that appears sunken in the head (caved in) may be associated with dehydration. Babies who are dehydrated will have other signs as well, such as irritability, decreased urination, vomiting, and diarrhea. Typically, the first important marker of dehydration is decreased urination, so please take note if your child is ill and not urinating normally. A sunken fontanel associated with dehydration indicates severe illness and should urgently be evaluated.

Be aware that a bulging fontanel with fever could indicate meningitis while a bulging fontanel with no other symptoms could signify extra pressure around the brain. If you notice any kind of fontanel change, with or without a fever, take your baby to see a doctor or health care provider immediately.

By one year of age, you will notice your baby's fontanel is significantly smaller. Most fontanels close by the age of two years. A fontanel that closes too early can cause pressure buildup around the brain because the skull can't accommodate the extra growth. This condition, called craniosynostosis, is rare and requires surgical intervention. Prompt treatment with surgery typically alleviates the problem.

Should I worry about the size of my baby's fontanel? The size of the fontanel varies from baby to baby. Comparisons between babies mean little. A doctor will evaluate your baby's fontanel at checkups and sick visits to be sure the size and pressure feel normal. Pay attention to changes in the size and shape of the fontanel so that you can point them out to your doctor, but since problematic conditions are so uncommon, you don't need to worry.

What is the cause of cradle cap? The common condition of cradle cap is often called baby dandruff. It's when a baby's scalp has a dry, flaky, yellow appearance, and sometimes the flakes are crusted. Minimal redness is also associated with cradle cap. The true cause is unknown. Some babies with sensitive skin get cradle cap, which typically occurs in the first three months of life and is more common in the winter. One theory surmises that withdrawal from the hormones of pregnancy causes the sebaceous glands to react. Even yeast infection in babies has been associated with cradle cap. But cradle cap isn't harmful unless it's extensive and the baby's scalp becomes irritated.

Cradle cap treatment. One of the best remedies is a mild dandruff shampoo. In our clinic, we recommend Head & Shoulders. Your doctor can suggest a good brand for you. Scrub the scalp gently with a soft brush, leave the shampoo on for five minutes, and rinse. Use this every other day until the cradle cap improves and then drop back to one or two times a week. Confine the shampoo to the head so that it doesn't irritate the skin on your baby's body or his eyes. Have a dropper or spoon nearby in case you accidentally get shampoo in his eyes or skin area. If this occurs, lay your baby flat and rinse gently with warm water. Use the spoon to scoop water or use the dropper to gently cleanse the eye. If hats are needed—particularly in cold weather—use those that are made of cotton instead of polyester or wool.

Cradle cap may come and go until the first birthday. If your baby has a rash on his body or cradle cap that extends beyond his first year of life, have your doctor examine him. A rash could indicate infantile eczema, a condition often confused with or seen in association with cradle cap. This skin condition may need extensive treatment and preventive measures against further recurrences.

India: Treatment for Cradle Cap

Parents from India often treat cradle cap with pure coconut oil to hydrate the scalp and remove scales. Virgin coconut oil is best for this purpose. Before using coconut oil on any part of your baby's body, though, apply a patch about the size of a small coin on the head first, a day before treatment. This tests for any allergic reaction. If you see no rash after twenty-four hours, you can proceed.

On the day of treatment, wash your baby's hair with a gentle shampoo and remove scales with a soft brush. Apply a quarter-size amount of coconut oil to the area on the scalp and rub it in. Let the baby sleep overnight with the coconut oil on her head. This will hydrate the scalp and help remove the scaling caused by cradle cap.

Babies smell nice and sweet after a coconut oil treatment. Yum!

Symptoms Indicating a Problem Beyond Cradle Cap

Have your doctor check your baby's cradle cap if:

- The baby's scalp is bleeding.
- The cradle cap resists treatment.
- Your baby has a rash on her body.
- Your baby's tongue has a white film that looks like cottage cheese (possible thrush).
- The rash on the scalp appears warm, weepy, or painful.

Eyes

Crossed eyes. When your baby is first born, you may want her to gaze lovingly into your eyes—but she's looking everywhere else! She's learning to use her eye muscles. Every object and person in her environment attracts her attention, so she looks around all the time.

By age one month, she fixes her eyes for at least fifteen seconds while looking at you. Sometimes, it may look like her eyes cross, which is common up to age four months. One way to help her learn to use her eye muscles is to place different items and patterns in front of her face. Putting visual stimuli in front of her helps her learn to fix, track, and follow.

When your baby is examined by your doctor, point out crossed eyes. If your baby's crossed eyes recur, seek advice in case a medical condition needs to be addressed. Babies with visual problems can benefit greatly from treatment if these problems are detected early.

Eye color. A baby is usually born with eyes that are gray to gray-blue. Is this the exact color she'll have for the rest of her life? Hardly ever! If your baby's eyes look brown in the first few months, they're likely to stay brown. In many cases, it's difficult to tell eye color until approximately six months of age. Babies with gray or blue eyes remain a mystery. Even after six months, their eyes may change color. The most common eye color shift is to hazel or brown. Sometimes, they look lighter at six months, and then they take a more gold or green tone.

Eye color depends on a pigment called melanin. If melanin is in small supply, you'll see baby blues or gorgeous green eyes. If there's a midrange amount, eyes are typically a happy hazel. Having a large amount of melanin produces beautiful brown eyes.

Eye color is inherited from parents, but this doesn't mean every baby's eyes match the parents' eyes. The inheritance factor can go back several generations. Two blue-eyed parents are most likely to have a blue-eyed baby because they both carry what are called recessive traits. But if the baby has two brown-eyed parents or one brown-eyed and one blued-eyed parent, she could have any eye color.

The term "hazel" comes from the fruit nut of a hazel tree, originally from Europe. Hazelnuts, in fact, match the eye color. Hazel eyes have a different meaning in America than in other parts of the world. Most Europeans define hazel as the true color of a hazelnut—a mixture of brown, red, and gold. Americans view hazel eyes as being any combination of colors or changing colors—typically light brown, green, and some blue or gold.

Conjunctivitis. Commonly called "pink eye," conjunctivitis is not always contagious. The whites of the eyes look red. You may or may not see matting (discharge from the eye). Usually, conjunctivitis is present in both eyes, but one eye may look more affected than the other. Conjunctivitis may be caused by viral or bacterial eye infections, irritations, or allergens that affect the eye. This condition is not painful, but if the eyes are irritated, they may become itchy.

Pink eyes in a baby should be referred to your doctor for care. If your baby has an eye infection, the risk of contagiousness is high. Be sure to wash your hands with warm soapy water each time you touch the eye. Treatment revolves around finding the underlying cause.

Runny eyes. Tearing eyes are not always a sign of conjunctivitis. If a baby has a cold or is exposed to something new in the environment, her eyes may run. Runny eyes can also be a precursor to allergies later in life.

Sometimes, the eyes may be wet enough to cause a small layer of mucus to form, especially after napping. Mucus is white discharge that looks like a thin film of slimy material. If your baby is fussy with an eye that tears or is sensitive to light, the doctor should check the eye to be sure no trauma has occurred. Treatment for runny eyes with mucus is to keep the eyes clean with a warm, soft, wet washcloth.

Red eye that is painful. Any eye pain in a baby should be referred promptly to your doctor. This could indicate infection or trauma to the eye.

Blocked tear duct (dacryostenosis). In the newborn period and often beyond, blocked tear ducts are common. The cause is an underdeveloped tear duct, or nasolacrimal duct. Babies are commonly born with this condition.

Tears are necessary to hydrate and protect the eyes. Tears drain into a duct on the inner corner of the eye by the nose. If the duct is blocked, tears are unable to drain properly, and tearing may be mild or excessive. Often, one eye will appear watery or have excess mucus or discharge. The symptoms tend to increase after sleep or exposure to cold air. If a baby has a cold, the eye on the blocked side will tend to discharge or tear more. Typically, there is no accompanying redness on or around the eye unless the area is wiped excessively.

A doctor should check the eye to confirm the diagnosis and rule out any signs of infection. The biggest risk of a blocked tear duct is infection, which is not very common but does happen. If you see pus, which is thick green or yellow discharge with crusting increasing in frequency, you must have the eye rechecked.

Blocked tear duct treatment involves gentle massage along the lacrimal duct (the upper nasal bridge of the nose), warm compresses, and keeping the eyes clean to avoid infection.

Typically, the condition will resolve by age nine months to one year. Your baby will grow, and the tear duct will open naturally. If the condition does not resolve by nine months, your doctor will likely refer your baby to an ophthalmologist (eye doctor). Some babies need a procedure to open the lacrimal duct with a special probe. This procedure works in most cases. In the unusual instance that the procedure doesn't work, other surgical methods can be used to open the tear duct and allow the tears to drain properly.

There are some eye conditions that require urgent care:

- Eye is painful or swollen shut
- Eye condition with associated fever

Seek care within twenty-four hours if you notice these symptoms:

- Red swollen eye, but baby has no fever and is not fussy
- Eyes or eye with mucus
- One eye is tearing persistently for more than twenty-four hours
- Eye or eyes seem sensitive to light with tearing

Ears

Baby earwax, called cerumen, is very soft and tends to drain out of the ear on its own. Most parents train their children to keep the ears "clean." However, you need only remove excess wax that's visible from the outer ear.

Special glands in the outer ear canal produce wax that moisturizes the inside of the ear. It helps prevent infection and removes debris. Rarely does a baby have excessive wax that would impair hearing.

Cleaning your baby's ears. Use a soft tissue or wet washcloth to remove only the wax you can see. Safety cotton swabs are okay, too. Be careful not to poke and prod the ear, and never insert a swab in a baby's ear. It can cause damage or pack the wax in more tightly.

Signs to look for in ear infections. Babies are more prone to ear infections than at any other age due to the small size of the ear canals and the angle of the eardrums. Because these characteristics are inherited, it's common for ear infection tendencies to run in families. Babies are also more likely to get ear infections than older children because their immune systems are still developing.

A baby who's getting an ear infection may be excessively fussy, not sleep well, eat less food than normal, not hear well, or run a fever. Sometimes, ear infections are obvious, such as when green or yellow mucus runs out of the ear. Commonly, ear infections appear around the time the baby has a cold or viral illness. Of course, babies could show these behaviors for other reasons, including teething, but it never hurts to check. If you suspect an ear infection, have your doctor take a peek. Although no baby is guaranteed to *never* get an ear infection, the following methods can help reduce your baby's risk.

Vaccinations. A fully vaccinated child has less ear infections. Three vaccines are most helpful to prevent ear infections—pneumococcal polysaccharide, *Haemophilus influenzae*, and influenza (seasonal flu). Young babies who are high risk also receive the meningococcal vaccine. These vaccines not only help prevent ear infections but also reduce the risk of other bacterial infections such as pneumonia and meningitis.

Breastfeeding. Breastfeeding helps strengthen the immune system and thus prevent ear infections. Prolonged breastfeeding has been shown to continue to reduce ear infections and other types of infections.

Good nutrition. In addition to breastfeeding, eating natural foods from the earth strengthens the immune system and combats illness. In particular, fruits and vegetables have phytochemicals, special substances that can strengthen the immune system.

Not smoking. Smoking in a baby's environment increases the risk of ear infections by at least 50 percent. Secondhand smoke impairs a baby's immune system and causes excessive mucus production in the ear tube. This fluid can back up and lead to ear infections.

Hand washing. All adults caring for a baby should wash their hands regularly, especially when caring for more than one child. Hand washing is the best defense in preventing ear infections.

Not sharing sippy cups or bottles between children. Just one sip passed from the cup or bottle of a sick child can easily cause another child to pick up the same illness or infection. If you have twins, this is a hard task to accomplish! I say just do the best you can to keep cups and bottles separate.

Is My Baby Hearing Well?

How can you tell if your baby is hearing well? Does he startle at sudden noises? Does an older baby stir and move around when you walk into the room? Does he smile when music is played?

If you're not sure, stand behind your baby where he can't see you and clap your hands. Does he respond? If your baby doesn't hear well or you sense his hearing has changed, have your doctor check his hearing.

Newborn babies in America typically have a hearing screen in the hospital after birth. If your baby has not had a screen, ask your doctor about obtaining one. Once your baby has passed his hearing screen, you can take comfort in knowing he's unlikely to have a problem with hearing.

Chapter 26

YOUR BABY'S HAIR AND NAIL CARE

S ome infants are born with a large amount of hair, while others don't have much at all. You may notice that in the first six months, your infant's hair seems to get thinner. Don't despair. It's common for babies to lose hair in the first year of life. The hair will grow back—sometimes in a different color or texture!

HAIR CARE

The cause of hair loss in babies is most commonly a withdrawal from the hormones of pregnancy. Conditions such as cradle cap and other less common disorders may also thin your infant's hair. Be sure to mention any hair loss to your doctor or health care provider during your well-baby visits, though generally there's no problem.

Caring for Your Baby's Hair

Here are tips on caring for your baby's hair and preventing further hair loss.

- Don't wash your baby's hair every day. For most babies, two to three times a week is enough.
- Use a gentle shampoo and gently scrub it into the scalp.
- While your baby is awake and lying down, rotate her head position to avoid continual pressure on one spot of the head.
- Be gentle when brushing your baby's hair.
- Don't put items in your baby's hair such as rubber bands or headbands that can pull the hair tight.

Haircuts will not cause hair to grow back more quickly. Most babies don't need a haircut in the first year of life. Some parents, however, cut their baby's hair in the summer to cool her head. In the winter, if the hair is cut or the baby has little hair, she'll be more comfortable wearing a hat.

China: Ceremonial Haircuts

In many countries, babies and children are given haircuts with a ceremony at various stages of life. Traditional Chinese parents often provide haircuts to their baby at thirty days after birth. This period is considered to be the baby's first birthday, also known as their "full moon."[1] Each family has its own tradition—some cutting a small amount, others shaving the whole head except the crown. They might save the hair in an envelope or tied with a red ribbon.

Less traditional Chinese parents often wait and give the first haircut on the second day of the second month of the lunar calendar (usually in January or February in the Western calendar). The Chinese call this "Dragon Head-Raising Day." They believe if children get a haircut on this day, they will grow up to be healthy, prosperous adults.[2] This practice coincides with the Chinese New Year celebration.

Consider cutting a baby's or a toddler's hair a rite of passage to be enjoyed, documented, and celebrated. Many children's salons provide a certificate and wrap up the first lock of hair for the parents. You might want to start your own family haircutting ceremony. Snip a lock of your baby's hair yourself and have a celebration just like others enjoy around the world.

NAIL CARE

A newborn's nails are quite soft and often long because they were exposed to amniotic fluid, which kept them soft, in the womb. A little later, babies can easily scratch themselves because of their happy, waving arms. During the first month or so, you can put socks or special mittens on babies' hands to prevent them from scratching themselves. This will buy you time to get the hang of clipping their nails.

The best time to clip nails is while your baby is asleep. When babies are awake, they're sure to move their hands in response to clipping. If you choose to clip your baby's nails while he's awake, ask another person to hold his hand still.

Have your supplies ready. Place your nail clippers (or nail scissors), baby emery board, and gauze (just in case!) in easy reach. It's best to use special clippers made for babies. You can use baby nail scissors, but they require your baby's hand to be especially steady. They have a rounded edge to help prevent injury, but they can still jab him.

Go ahead and clip! Get yourself and your baby in a good position. The fingers should be accessible and at an angle you can reach. With your non-dominant hand, gently hold the baby's palm to ensure he doesn't pull back his hand and cause an injury. Even sleeping babies tend to move their fingers when you touch their hand.

Clip the excess portion of the nail to the tip of the finger, being careful not to nick the skin or flesh. You can then file any jagged edges with a baby emery board or nail file. Don't chew or tear the nails; this can cause injury or infection around the nail beds.

Most baby nails need to be clipped once a week. Some grow more quickly and require clipping twice a week. When you notice an edge on the nail between clipping sessions, you can gently file the nail instead of clipping.

If you nip the finger: Baby movement or an accidental clip can cause a bleeding finger. First, apply pressure with clean gauze. Clean the area with warm water, and then dab on hydrogen peroxide and hold the gauze over the area. A small nip will heal well. If you note excessive bleeding or a deep wound, though, consult your doctor.

Baby toenails are oddly shaped. After birth, the toes may appear curved in due to the position of the feet in your womb. They will stretch out in time. Baby toenails tend to grow in the shape of the toe. Little pudgy toes are normal, and their nails will bend, cave in or out, and often appear ingrown. An ingrown toenail in a baby is extremely uncommon, while an infected toenail, usually from injury, is more common.

If the toenails aren't causing your baby pain, then they're probably normal even if they're oddly shaped. However, if you notice pus or see red skin around the nail, have your doctor check the toe to determine if it needs treatment for infection.

Superstitions sometimes have a bit of truth to them. Soula Aman, a mother who was born in Greece and now lives in Belgium, has advice for fingernail disposal. "In Greece, it's believed you should not throw your baby's fingernails outside because the birds may use them for their nests. The babies could have pain in their head if this happens."[3]

I don't agree about the pain in the head, but it's lovely to think birds could scavenge your baby's fingernails to construct their nests. I see no reason not to dispose of clippings outside if you don't want to throw them in the trash.

Chapter 27

YOUR BABY'S ORAL HEALTH

In the first year of life, tooth care is relatively easy. Once the baby's bottom teeth have fully pushed through, you can use a soft finger brush on the teeth once a day. A small brush that fits on your finger, using a finger brush helps your baby get used to the brushing sensation and oral stimulation. If you don't have a finger brush, a small, soft toothbrush would work as well. Simply use water on the brush; no toothpaste is necessary. If you prefer, you can use a soft cloth to wipe the teeth.

Your baby's toothbrush should be rinsed in hot water after use and thrown away if your baby has had a recent illness.

If you're holding a baby toothbrush in your hand, it's okay for him to chew on it. This is actually comfortable for a teething baby. Just be sure you're in control of the brush since it could poke the back of his mouth and cause injury if the baby moves or falls.

Armenia: First-Tooth Ceremonies

In Armenia, it's common to have a first-tooth party, traditionally called *agra hadig*. *Agra* means tooth, and *hadig* is a dessert—a traditionally cooked wheat dish—made especially for the occasion.

Once a baby has cut a tooth, the family schedules a party to celebrate the baby's accomplishment. There's much celebrating, but the event signifies authentic concern for the baby's future. The baby is seated in a circle surrounded by various objects. A scarf is placed over the baby's eyes and *hadig* is sprinkled over the head, symbolizing preparation for a fruitful life.

After the objects are placed in front of him, everybody waits. The baby reaches for or crawls toward the object that symbolizes what his career will be. For example, if the baby selects a knife, his career will be in the medical field, such as a doctor or surgeon. Some objects might be little packages with a piece of paper revealing his profession.

Parents decide if they want to make this an afternoon or an evening event. An afternoon first-tooth party typically involves ladies only and sweets offered, while an evening event includes males and a full Armenian buffet.[1]

You can find inspiration from Armenian traditions to consider how to celebrate your baby's milestones. Pick your own objects to place in front of him, those that *you* consider fantastic careers for your baby!

CARING FOR TEETH AND GUMS

Your baby has the sweetest little gummy smile. It's easy to take care of that smile in the first year of life with these few simple tips.

After nine months of age, if your baby's upper teeth are fully erupted, brush them lightly twice a day. Many babies don't have teeth at this age, and the upper teeth are just erupting. If this is true, you don't have to start brushing until the upper teeth fully appear. If you notice swelling around the gums, this means she's still teething, so avoid this area with your finger brush. If you brush a swollen area, it can be painful or even bleed.

Clean gums and teeth with water. You can wipe your baby's gums with a warm cloth. Though it's not necessary, if you wipe away any extra residue, it's helpful for your baby's comfort. Babies over age nine months can drink one or two ounces of water after meals—a good habit to get into, as water naturally helps clean the teeth.

Juice is not good for teeth. Because juice can cause cavities and decay, it is not routinely recommended unless used to help with constipation. Give your baby only breast milk, formula, or water. Her teeth will be healthier if she eats fruits and vegetables instead of drinking juice. This habit can start preventing cavities early. Sugary drinks and juice taste great, but they aren't doing your baby's teeth any good. So, if you decide to have your own Armenian-style teething ceremony, let your baby have a little *hadig*, but skip the juice.

Put your baby to sleep without a bottle. If she falls asleep with the bottle, it will become difficult to keep her upper teeth clean as she gets older. You will literally have to get in behind her to clean those teeth after she falls asleep. At an early age, help her learn to settle herself to sleep without a bottle. You can use a pacifier to soothe her to sleep, but don't coat it with sweet syrup or sugar, as this can also cause cavities.

Start a sippy cup early. Once her teeth are in, drinking from a bottle increases the risk of cavities. Learning to use a sippy cup helps decrease bottle use and makes weaning off the bottle easier on your baby. Between six and nine months, work with your baby during the day to help her use a sippy cup filled with water, formula, or breast milk. Most babies don't get the hang of the cup until nine to twelve months, but the earlier you start, the better. Buy a sippy cup with a removable valve so you can take out the valve and gently tip the cup. That will help her learn to drink from the cup.

Do you have enough fluoride in your water? Babies under six months don't need fluoride, while those over six months do. The purpose of fluoride is to maintain healthy teeth. Your options are to supplement with prescription fluoride drops or give her the right amount of water daily. Each geographic area is different, so requirements vary from one county to the next. Some counties have too much fluoride in the water, while others have none or not enough. Your doctor or pediatric dentist can provide you with directions for adding fluoride to your baby's diet as necessary.

When should I take my baby to the dentist? The American Dental Association (ADA) recommends a first visit to the dentist by one year (or earlier if any problems need to be addressed). Your doctor will check your baby's teeth and let you know if an earlier visit is warranted.

When will my baby cut teeth? Most babies cut their first lower teeth at approximately six months, though some do it earlier and others around one year. There's nothing wrong with your baby if she cuts her teeth early or late. Tooth eruption tendencies are genetic. If a baby is born with a tooth, it can easily loosen and become a choking hazard, so be sure this natal tooth is removed.

Symptoms associated with teething. In the clinic, I hear many complaints about teething symptoms, including drooling, chewing, swollen gums, fussiness, and mildly elevated temperature (usually not over 100 degrees Fahrenheit). Some think loose stools are associated with teething, although this hasn't been proven in research. There is no specific treatment except to console your baby using the following strategies.

Teething Treatment

Teething rings or toys. These are made specifically for babies to chew on. Buy new teething rings or toys labeled free of toxins rather than inherited ones because, in the past, some have been found to contain lead.

Gum massage or light rubbing. A gentle insertion of your clean finger into your baby's mouth might console her. If you touch her gum, be sure it's not in a swollen area. Massage the pre-teething area, not a freshly swollen area. Let her chew on your finger if she'd like (and if it's not uncomfortable for you!).

Pain-relieving agents. It's okay to use Tylenol in appropriate doses and limited quantities. At the time of this writing, ongoing studies question if fever and pain reducers weaken the immune system. Only with your doctor's approval should you use Tylenol, and even then, use it sparingly, reserving it for significant pain.

Topical pain reducers. Topical agents are designed to give quick relief, but they can be toxic in excess quantity. I don't recommend using them due to the increased risk of toxic side effects.

The Caribbean: A Cold Compress Teething Remedy

Brigitte Assing, a mother of one in Grenada, an island country in the Caribbean, recommends a cold compress for babies who are teething. Brigitte says, "Place a clean cotton cloth in the freezer, having wet it with boiled water (fold it into a 1" x 2" size). Once the cotton is frozen, then the child can bite on it. Kind of like a teething ring—but softer."[2] It sounds simple, and the cold will help numb the pain. I would suggest using the cold compress only if your baby is soothed. Some babies don't like cold; others will be delighted by quick relief!

Chapter 28

YOUR BABY'S UMBILICAL CORD

The umbilical cord is literally the life connection between mother and baby in the womb. While the baby is developing, nutrients and oxygen from the mother are provided through the umbilical cord. It's attached to the placenta, an organ connected to the womb that provides ongoing nourishment to the unborn baby. Once your baby comes out of the birth canal, the connection is cut at the umbilicus, producing the umbilical cord "stump."

CUTTING THE CORD

In many cultures, cutting the cord is a symbolic gesture that's typically performed by the doctor or midwife assisting with the baby's birth. In some cases, a father can have the honor of cutting the cord. At this time, if you have arranged in advance to store your baby's cord blood in a cord blood bank, the blood will be collected. Cord blood is rich in stem cells, which can be used later if there's a health problem with the baby or another person in need of stem cells. For accurate information about storing cord blood, reference the FDA's page on cord blood banking (https://www.fda.gov/biologicsbloodvaccines/resourcesforyou/consumers/ucm236044.htm).

Avoiding infection. Infections can be prevented with a substance called triple dye, which may be applied to the cord while it's still attached. However, the cord is unlikely to get infected if the area is kept clean and covered, even if triple dye is not applied.

Cord appearance. The cord is cut just below the baby's umbilical opening. This will leave a small amount of the placenta tissue (remnants of the cord) protruding through the belly button opening.

After your baby comes home, what's left of the cord will dry up and begin to look crusty. Between seven and fourteen days after birth, the rest of the umbilical cord will fall off. Yellow drainage or mild bleeding could occur, and the area where the cord fell off might look raw.

Easy care. Keeping the cord clean and dry will help it fall off. To clean it, apply peroxide once daily with a clean cotton swab or gauze unless instructed otherwise by your doctor. (Stay away from alcohol because it can sting the area as the cord starts to separate. Peroxide doesn't cause this side effect.)

Don't submerge your baby in a full bath (getting the cord wet) until one week after the cord has fallen off. Before this, sponge baths are sufficient and keep the cord dry. Keep in mind: babies don't need baths every day. In fact, the chemicals in most water supplies can overdry their skin.

Samoa: Traditions Surrounding the Placenta

In different parts of the world, what happens to the umbilical cord and placenta is an important responsibility. In the West, we often throw out the umbilical cord—after all, it's no longer needed outside of the womb. In Samoa, discarding the umbilical cord and placenta could be considered very risky. The newborn is considered at risk if the placenta is not treated with care. After a baby in Samoa is born, the placenta is offered to the parents. The parents may then wrap the placenta in a cloth and bury it or even throw it into the sea.[1]

REASONS TO CALL THE DOCTOR

If you notice any of these seven signs, make sure that you take your little one in to see the doctor. Even though serious problems with the umbilical cord are uncommon, it's important to keep an eye on the umbilical cord healing process.

- Large amount of drainage
- Tenderness around the umbilicus; excessive crying when area is touched
- Large amount of bleeding; continuous bleeding and oozing
- Foul-smelling discharge
- Pus oozing from the area
- Fever over 100.4 degrees Fahrenheit

One week after the cord falling off, if you see a red, raw-looking area, contact your doctor to assess it. This could be a granuloma, which needs to be treated. (A granuloma is a bit of healing tissue that can stay behind during the healing process.)

The attached umbilical cord is not an object to be feared; it should be embraced as part of your baby's nourishment in the womb. I've seen some families keep the umbilical cord, while others merely toss it in the trash. Is your baby's umbilical cord worth placing in a box for safekeeping or burying in your backyard? That's the beauty of parenting. You get to decide.

APPENDIX

HELPFUL LIST: SHOPPING FOR YOUR BABY

Feeding

Baby bowls
Baby spoons
Bottle nipples
Bottles
Formula
High chair
Sippy cups

Changing and Sleeping

Changing pad
Changing table
Sleep area: co-sleeper, crib, bassinet

Safety

Cabinet and door latches
Outlet covers
Rear-facing car seat

Safety gates
Sun shields for car

Entertainment

Baby board books
Rattles
Teething toys

Clothing

Diapers: three dozen initially; stock up on sale in various sizes
Gowns or one-piece sleepers: four to six
Jacket: if seasonally required
Laundry detergent: dye-free, perfume-free
Onesies: four to six
Pants: three or four pairs
Receiving blankets: three or four
Shirts: four to six
Shoes (optional)
Small cotton hat: one
Socks: four to six pairs

Extras

Baby bathtub
Baby book/scrapbook
Baby monitor
Diaper bag
Diaper pail
Infant sling or body carrier
Stroller

Nestling Kit

Adhesive bandages
Antibiotic ointment

Baby lotion (unscented only)
Baby nail scissors
Baby shampoo
Baby sunscreen (oxybenzone- and retinyl palmitate–free)
Baby wipes
Box of 4 x 4 gauze
Bulb syringe
Diaper covers (if using cloth diapers)
Diapers
Emery board and nail file
Ice pack
Medical tape
Pacifiers
Small scissors
Tweezers
Thermometer

Medicine

Use only with doctor's advice.

Acetaminophen (Tylenol)
Diaper rash cream
Diphenhydramine (Benadryl)
Ibuprofen (Advil, Motrin)
Pedialyte
Saline nose drops
Simethicone drops (Mylicon for excessive gas)

For Mom

Clothing that's comfortable and provides easy nursing access
Lanolin cream for sore nipples
Nursing bras
Nursing pads, breast pads

HELPFUL LIST: FINGER FOODS AND HEALTHY INGREDIENTS FOR PUREES

Fruits

Apple
Blueberries
Cherries
Grapes
Kiwi
Mango
Papaya
Peaches
Pears
Prunes
Soft banana

Vegetables

Avocado
Beets
Broccoli
Carrots
Cauliflower
Green beans
Olives, sliced
Onions, minced
Peas
Pumpkin
Squash
Sweet potato

Meats/Protein

Chicken (slow cooked, finely chopped, or pureed)
Eggs (scrambled)
Fish (exclude tuna, swordfish, shark, and other large fish, which could be high in mercury)
Nut pastes
Red meat (slow cooked, finely chopped, or pureed)
Turkey

Legumes

Black beans
Garbanzo beans (chickpeas)
Lentils
Pinto beans
Split peas

Starch/Grains

Bread
Brown rice
Cereal (barley, wheat, oats—low sugar)
Pasta
Tofu
White rice

Dairy

Cheese (soft chunks or grated)
Cottage cheese
Yogurt

Add these herbs and oils to taste when preparing pureed or finger food:

Oils

Coconut oil
Grapeseed oil
Olive oil

Herbs and Spices

Basil
Cilantro
Cinnamon
Cumin
Garlic
Ginger
Mint
Parsley
Rosemary
Saffron
Thyme
Turmeric

BABY FOOD RECIPES FROM AROUND THE WORLD

The following recipes are wonderful foods to introduce to your baby between six and nine months, but they are also great recipes to be enjoyed by the whole family! Unless you like really mushy foods, your portion doesn't have to be pureed. And if a baby doesn't like a flavor, try again once a week or even once daily. The taste buds are likely to adjust over time.

FOR BABIES SIX MONTHS AND OLDER

America: Vegetable Soup

6 cups organic chicken broth
1/4 cup diced onions
1/2 cup diced carrots
2 garlic cloves, diced or minced
1/2 cup diced celery
Pinch of salt

1. Bring chicken broth to boil. Add the rest of the ingredients. Cook for 45 minutes to ensure the vegetables are soft.
2. Allow to cool. Pour soup into your baby's bowl using a strainer. Enjoy. The soft vegetables may be eaten by older babies and toddlers.

China: Rice *Congee*

1 cup long-grain, round rice
12 cups water
Pinch of salt

1. Using a large pot, cook rice in water on high until mixture is boiling. Stir continually for 5 minutes. Add a pinch of salt. Then turn the heat down to low and place a lid on the pot. Some steam should be allowed to escape. (If your lid does not allow steam to escape, tilt the lid.) Cook for 2 hours.

2. Allow the *congee* to cool before feeding to your baby. Different grains of rice produce a different consistency of soup. If your *congee* appears thicker than applesauce consistency, you can reheat with more water. Add any pureed vegetables or meats to the soup.

3. Allow to cool. Pour soup into your baby's bowl using a strainer. As your baby moves toward chunky foods, add more soft vegetables and meat.

India: Easy Garam Masala Chicken and Vegetables

1/8 teaspoon garam masala
1 tablespoon olive oil
1 cup diced chicken
2 cups vegetables (mixture of squash, carrots, and cauliflower)

Garam Masala Ingredients[1]

1 tablespoon cumin
1 1/2 teaspoons ground coriander
1 1/2 teaspoons ground cardamom
1 1/2 teaspoons ground black pepper
1 teaspoon ground cinnamon
1/2 teaspoon ground cloves
1/2 teaspoon ground nutmeg

1. Mix all garam masala spices in a bowl. Place in an airtight container and store in a cool, dry place.

2. Place olive oil in a pan. Heat on low. Add chicken and garam masala and cook for 5 minutes. Add vegetables and

cook until limp. As your baby gets older, you can add more garam masala to taste. Puree to feed babies six months and up; may serve in small chunks to ages nine months and up.

Lebanon: Hummus

By Laura Jaafar, San Antonio, Texas

This recipe is not as "strong" as a traditionally prepared recipe so that the baby can get used to the flavor. Hummus can also be mixed with plain yogurt for a recipe variation. For toddlers who are not used to the taste of hummus, you can try dipping a small piece of whole-grain bread into the hummus to introduce them to the flavor.

2 (15.5 ounce) cans unsalted garbanzo beans (chickpeas), rinsed and drained
1 garlic clove, crushed
1/2 cup water
1/8 cup tahini (sesame seed paste)
2 tablespoons fresh lemon juice
2 tablespoons extra-virgin olive oil
1/2 teaspoon salt
1/8 teaspoon black pepper

1. Place beans and garlic in a food processor or blender. Process or blend until chopped.
2. Add 1/2 cup water and remaining ingredients. Blend until smooth; scrape down sides as needed.

Uganda: Pumpkin Puree

1 whole pumpkin

1. Preheat oven to 350 degrees Fahrenheit (177 degrees Celsius). Wash pumpkin and cut into four parts (excluding stem). Remove visible seeds and pulp.

2. Wrap each piece of pumpkin in aluminum foil. Place one cup of water in the bottom of a long baking dish. Place the pumpkin in the dish. Cook for approximately one hour or until soft.

3. Remove the pumpkin flesh from the outer shell. Use blender to puree. Strain any excess pulp or seeds before feeding.

4. Alternate recipe for babies eating chunky foods: After baking, allow the pumpkin to cool. Remove pumpkin flesh from shell, cut in cubes, and serve.

FOR BABIES NINE MONTHS AND UP WHO HAVE STARTED SOFT, CHUNKY FOODS

Costa Rica: *Picadillo de Chayote*

By Christa Jimenez, Blogger, Pura Vida Moms (http://www.puravidamoms.com)

2 tablespoons butter (salted or unsalted doesn't seem to matter)
1/2 white onion
3 garlic cloves
2 chayotes*
1–1 1/2 teaspoons salt
1/2 can whole kernel corn
Heavy cream, to preference
1/2 bunch cilantro

*I find chayotes locally at Sprouts, King Soopers, and most Mexican supermarkets. Be prepared for your cashier to have no idea what they are or how to ring them up. They're also known as pear squash, mirlitons, cho-cho, chouchoute, or choko.

1. As with most recipes, this one starts with a *sofrito* (a seasoned tomato-based sauce used as a foundation in Caribbean, Latin American, and Spanish cooking). In a heavy saucepan, heat the butter on medium-low. (Costa Ricans would actually use Numar margarine, but I prefer using butter instead of margarine.) While it's warming, chop the onion into fine pieces and mince the garlic. (I put it in a garlic press.) Raise the heat to a good medium, add the onion and garlic, and cook until the onion is transparent. You've just made a *sofrito*!

2. While that is heating, wash and chop your chayotes. There are probably a zillion ways to do this, but I like to make each piece even to make the dish look pleasing visually.

3. After you've diced the chayotes, add them to the pot, cover it, and turn up the heat to a good medium high. Chayotes are mostly water, so you want to cook the water out. I cover the pot to let them boil a bit until almost completely tender and dry. The chayote will often cook all the water out and begin to brown on the bottom of the pan. Brown is not good, so to combat the dryness, I open the can of corn and add about a half cup of the liquid to the pan, then let it keep cooking. (You could add water here, but I prefer to use the liquid from the corn because it adds a nice flavor.)

4. Once tender, add salt and half of the canned corn. (You can definitely use fresh sweet corn here, but I don't have the patience for it.)

5. Cover with heavy cream (or put in as much as you want) and heat thoroughly. Chop up some cilantro and stir it in about 10 minutes before serving.

Option: serve with mashed beans and soft pieces of tortilla.
Buen provecho!

India: Baby-Friendly Zucchini Sticks

By Puneeta Chhitwal-Varma, Writer, Founder of
Maple and Marigold (www.mapleandmarigold.com)

My mother is a big believer in eating and living healthy, and she started both my brother and me on this track early in our lives. Years ago, as I became a mother and started to navigate this new world of parenting, old habits that my mom had inculcated in me early on came to my rescue.

Like all parents, I want to give my kids the best start possible. A big part of that best start is introducing healthy foods at an early age. The other thing I wanted was to help them actually like vegetables. There is a tendency for parents to hide vegetables in food because we assume kids will hate the taste. The thing is, though, vegetables are delicious and deserve to shine on the plate. Kids will love different flavors and textures if we give them a chance and offer veggies that are cooked the way they were meant to be. Zucchini is a great example. Often maligned for being soggy and flavorless, you will be surprised to learn that zucchini was one of the first few vegetables that my kids liked. And even today at ages eleven and six, they will eat it with no complaints.

A delicious and underrated vegetable, zucchini comes chock full of vitamins and minerals and makes a great start for a child's dietary journey.

Cut the zucchini in sticks so that our wee ones are able to hold them and feed themselves. It will be messy at the beginning, but slowly they will develop a taste for it. This dish is appropriate for kids who are comfortable eating solids.

Half a zucchini, cut in long fingerlike pieces 1 centimeter or 1/2 inch thick
1 teaspoon oil or butter for the pan (use the latter if your baby has already started milk)

1. Heat the pan to medium and toss the zucchini sticks in. Sauté gently for 5–8 minutes, cooking till the sticks are still just a little crunchy. Don't let the zucchini turn soggy; it will lose its flavor.
2. Cool and leave in front of your child. I promise they will reach for it.

Middle East: Lentils with Onion, Garlic, and Turmeric

1 cup brown lentils, dry
1 tablespoon virgin olive oil
1/4 cup minced onion
1 tablespoon minced garlic
1/8 teaspoon turmeric
3 cups chicken broth

1. Rinse lentils. Heat olive oil in a saucepan. Add and sauté onion and garlic on low heat for 2 minutes.
2. Add lentils and turmeric, sautéing mixture for 2 additional minutes.
3. Add water and cook for 20 minutes or until tender. May serve to ages nine months and up; or, to feed babies six months and up, puree until lentils and onions are no longer chunky. As your baby gets older and continues to enjoy lentils, you can increase the proportions of garlic, onion, and turmeric to taste.

ENDNOTES

Chapter 1

1. Gottlieb, Alma, and Judy S. Delaoche. *A World of Babies*, 1st edition. Cambridge University Press, 2008, p. 105.

2. Feldman, Ruth, Arthur I. Eidelman, Lea Sirota, and Aron Weller. "Comparison of Skin-to-Skin (Kangaroo) and Traditional Care: Parenting Outcomes and Preterm Infant Development." *Pediatrics* 110, no. 1 (2002): 16–26. http://pediatrics.aappublications.org/content/110/1/16.

Chapter 2

1. Ronit Lubetzky, Francis B. Mimouni, Shaul Dollberg, Ram Reifen, Gina Ashbel, and Dror Mandel. "Effect of Music by Mozart on Energy Expenditure in Growing Preterm Infants." *Pediatrics* 125, no. 1 (January 2010): e24–8. http://pediatrics.aappublications.org/content/pediatrics/125/1/e24.full.pdf.

2. National Early Literacy Panel. "Developing Early Literacy: Report of the National Early Literacy Panel." National Institute for Literacy, 2008. https://www.nichd.nih.gov/publications/pubs/documents/NELPReport09.pdf.

3. McClure, Max. "Infants Process Faces Long Before They Recognize Other Objects, Stanford Vision Researchers Find." *Stanford Report*, December 11, 2012. http://news.stanford.edu/news/2012/december/infants-process-faces-121112.html.

4. The Global Fund for Children. *Global Babies*. Watertown, MA: Charlesbridge, 2007.

Chapter 3

1. Contributor Ijeoma Nnamani, Ivy Children's Clinic, Euless, Texas.

2. Contributor Charu Chhitwal, cofounder of www.ketchupmoms.com

Chapter 4

1. Levine, Robert A., New, Rebecca S., *Anthropology and Child Development, A Cross-Cultural Reader.* Blackwell Publishing, 2008, p. 67–68.

2. Contributor Lisa Yannucci, *Mama Lisa's World: International Music and Culture.* http://www.mamalisa.com.

3. Alexander, Heather. *A Child's Introduction to the World: Geography, Cultures, and People—From the Grand Canyon to the Great Wall of China.* New York: Black Dog & Leventhal Publishers, 2010, p. 34.

4. Contributor Sara Sierra, RN, pediatric nurse practitioner.

5. Contributor Patricia Grimaldos, dentist and artist.

Chapter 5

1. Miller, Craig D., ed., and the editors of Harvard Health Publications. "Understanding Depression: A Harvard Medical School Special Health Report." *Harvard Health Publications*, 2005.

2. Contributor Maybelline Valenti.

3. Mira, Karen. "How to Avoid Sibling Rivalry So Your Children Are Best Friends as Adults." *The Asian Parent.* http://sg.theasianparent.com/avoiding-sibling-rivalry/.

Chapter 6

1. Contributor Maria Babin, born in the United States, expat in France. www.trilingualmama.com.

2. Ybarra, Gabriel J., Richard H. Passman, and Carl S. Eisenberg. "The Presence of Security Blankets or Mothers (or Both) Affects Distress During Pediatric Examinations." *Journal of Consulting and Clinical Psychology* 68, no. 2 (April 2000): 322–30.

3. "Over a Third of British Adults Still Sleep with a Teddy Bear." Travelodge, August 16, 2010. https://www.travelodge.co.uk/press-centre/press-releases/over-third-british-adults-still-sleep-teddy-bear.

4. Contributor Siobhan Louise Twissel, nanny, England.

Chapter 7

1. Levine, Robert A., and Rebecca S. New. *Anthropology and Child Development: A Cross-Cultural Reader*. Malden, MA: Blackwell Publishing, 2008, p. 216–217.

2. Contributor Galina Nikitina.

3. Maiden Brown, Anne, Edie Barwell, and Dickey Nyerongsha. *The Tibetan Art of Parenting: From Before Conception Through Early Childhood*. Somerville, MA: Wisdom Publications, 2008, p. 122–123

Chapter 8

1. Small, Meredith, F. *Our Babies, Ourselves: How Biology and Culture Shape the Way We Parent*. 1st ed. New York: Anchor Books, 1998, p. 118–120.

2. Harkness, S., C. M. Super, C. H. Keefer, N. van Tijin, and E. van der Vlugt. "Cultural Influences on Sleep Patterns in Infancy and Early Childhood." Paper presented at the meeting of the American Association for the Advancement of Science Symposium on Ethnopediatrics: Cultural Factors in Child Survival and Growth, Atlanta, GA, February 1995.

3. Gottlieb, Alma, and Judy Deloache. *A World of Babies*, 2nd edition, Cambridge University Press, 2017, p. 280.

4. Levine, Robert A., and Sara Levine. *Do Parents Matter?* Public Affairs, New York, 2016, p. 62–64.

5. "Sudden Unexpected Infant Death and Sudden Infant Death Syndrome: Data and Statistics." Centers for Disease Control and Prevention, last updated April 17, 2017. https://www.cdc.gov/sids/data.htm.

6. Coleman-Phox, Kimberly, Roxana Odouli, and De-Kun Li. "Use of a Fan During Sleep and the Risk of Sudden Infant Death Syndrome," *Archives of Pediatric and Adolescent Medicine* 162, no. 10 (October 6, 2008): 963–8. http://jamanetwork.com/journals/jamapediatrics/fullarticle/380273.

7. Eidelman, Arthur I., Richard J. Schanler, and the American Academy of Pediatrics. "Policy Statement: Breastfeeding and the Use of Human Milk." *Pediatrics* 129, no. 3 (March 2012): e827–41. http://pediatrics.aappublications.org/content/pediatrics/129/3/e827.full.pdf.

8. Hauck, Fern R., Olanrewaju O. Omojokun, and Mir S. Siadaty. "Do Pacifiers Reduce the Risk of Sudden Infant Death Syndrome? A Meta-analysis."

Pediatrics 116, no. 5 (2005): e716–23. http://pediatrics.aappublications.org/
content/pediatrics/116/5/e716.full.pdf.

9. American Academy of Pediatrics Task Force on Sudden Infant Death
Syndrome. "The Changing Concept of Sudden Infant Death Syndrome:
Diagnostic Coding Shifts, Controversies Regarding the Sleeping Environment,
and New Variables to Consider in Reducing Risk." *Pediatrics* 116, no. 5
(November 2005): 1245–55. http://pediatrics.aappublications.org/content/
pediatrics/116/5/1245.full.pdf.

10. Contributor Lisa Ferland, Sweden, author of *Knocked Up Abroad: Stories of
Pregnancy, Birth, and Raising a Family in a Foreign Country* (self-published,
2016).

11. "Vaccine Safety: Sudden Infant Death Syndrome." Centers for Disease Control
and Prevention, last updated August 28, 2015. http://www.cdc.gov/vaccine-
safety/concerns/sids.html.

12. Machaalani, Rita, and Karen A. Waters. "Neuronal Cell Death in the Sudden
Infant Death Syndrome Brainstem and Associations with Risk Factors."
Brain 131, no. 1 (January 1, 2008): 218–28. https://academic.oup.com/brain/
article-lookup/doi/10.1093/brain/awm290.

13. Blair, Peter S., Peter Sidebotham, Carol Evason-Coombe, Margaret Edmonds,
Ellen M. A. Heckstall-Smith, and Peter Fleming. "Hazardous Cosleeping
Environments and Risk Factors Amenable to Change: Case-Control Study of
SIDS in South West England." *British Medical Journal* 339 (2009): b3666.

14. MacDorman, Marian F., T. J. Mathews, Ashna D. Mohangoo, and Jennifer
Zeitlin. "International Comparisons of Infant Mortality and Related Factors:
United States and Europe, 2010." *National Vital Statistics Reports* 63, no.
5 (September 24, 2014): 1–6. https://www.cdc.gov/nchs/data/nvsr/nvsr63/
nvsr63_05.pdf.

Chapter 9

1. Cox, Jeanine. "Baby Naming Traditions around the World." *Babble*,
courtesy of Disney, 2011. http://www.babble.com/baby-name-articles/
baby-naming-traditions/.

2. Companez, Rabbi Karen. "What to Expect at a Baby Naming." *ReformJudaism.
org*. http://www.reformjudaism.org/what-expect-baby-naming.

Chapter 10

1. Goddard, Joanna. "17 Surprising Things about Parenting in Spain." Interview with Adrienne. *A Cup of Jo*, August 13, 2015. https://cupofjo.com/2015/08/parenting-in-spain/.

2. "Pacifiers & Thumb Sucking." *Canadian Dental Association*. http://www.cda-adc.ca/en/oral_health/cfyt/dental_care_children/pacifiers.asp.

3. Task Force on Sudden Infant Death Syndrome, "The Changing Concept of Sudden Infant Death Syndrome."

Chapter 11

1. American Academy of Pediatrics Task Force on Circumcision. "Circumcision Policy Statement."*Pediatrics* 130, no. 3 (September 2012): 585–6. http://pediatrics.aappublications.org/content/pediatrics/130/3/585.full.pdf.

2. Sorokan, S. Todd, Jane C. Finlay, Ann L. Jefferies, and the Canadian Paediatric Society, Fetus and Newborn Committee, Infectious Diseases and Immunization Committee. "CPS Position Statement: Newborn Male Circumcision." *Paediatrics & Child Health* 20, no. 6 (August/September 2015): 311–5. https://www.ncbi.nlm.nih.gov/pmc/articles/PMC4578472/pdf/pch-20-311.pdf.

3. Contributor Ovais Mohiuddin, MD, Honey Pediatrics, Dallas, TX.

Chapter 12

1. Daniel Detzner, Blong Xiong, and Patricia A. Eliason. "Background on Southeast Asian Parenting." *Conversations on Vietnam Development*, posted July 17, 2017 by Đào Thu Hằng. Reviewed April 2010 by the author. Originally published as part of the series *Helping Youth Succeed: Bicultural Parenting for Southeast Asian Families Facilitator Manual*, University of Minnesota Extension (1999): 1–7. https://cvdvn.net/2016/07/17/background-on-southeast-asian-parenting-helping-youth-succeed-bicultural-parenting-for-southeast-asian-families/.

2. Gurka, Matthew J., Blackman, James A., Heymann, Peter W. "Risk of Childhood Asthma in Relation to the Timing of Early Child Care Exposures." *Journal of Pediatrics*, 155(6): 781–787. https://www.ncbi.nlm.nih.gov/pmc/articles/PMC2783908/.

3. Montessori, Maria. *The Absorbent Mind*. New York: Holt Paperbacks, reprint edition, 1995.

Chapter 13

1. Grimshaw, Kate E. C., Joe Maskell, Erin M. Oliver, Ruth C. G. Morris, Keith D. Foote, E. N. Clare Mills, Graham Roberts, and Barrie M. Margetts. "Introduction of Complementary Foods and the Relationship to Food Allergy." *Pediatrics* 132, no. 6 (December 2013): e1529–38. http://pediatrics. aappublications.org/content/pediatrics/early/2013/11/12/peds.2012-3692.full. pdf.

2. Silverberg, Jonathan I., Eric L. Simpson, Helen G. Durkin, and Rauno Joks. "Prevalence of Allergic Disease in Foreign-Born American Children." *JAMA Pediatrics* 167, no. 6 (2013): 554–60.

3. Ehrlich, Steven D. "Turmeric: Overview." University of Maryland Medical Center Medical Reference Guide, last reviewed June 26, 2014. http://www. umm.edu/health/medical/altmed/herb/turmeric.

Chapter 16

1. Eidelman, Arthur and Richard Schanler, "Breastfeeding and the Use of Human Milk." *Pediatrics* 129, no. 3 (2012): 827-841. http://pediatrics.aappublications. org/content/pediatrics/129/3/e827.full.pdf.

2. Belfort, Mandy B., Sheryl L. Rifas-Shiman, Ken P. Kleinman, Lauren B. Guthrie, David C. Bellinger, Elsie M. Taveras, Matthew W. Gillman, and Emily Oken. "Infant Feeding and Childhood Cognition at Ages 3 and 7 Years: Effects of Breastfeeding Duration and Exclusivity." *JAMA Pediatrics* 167, no. 9 (September 2013): 836–44. https://www.ncbi.nlm.nih.gov/pmc/articles/ PMC3998659/pdf/nihms571352.pdf.

3. Eidelman, et al. "Breastfeeding and the Use of Human Milk."

4. Dieterich, Christine M., Julia P. Felice, Elizabeth O'Sullivan, and Kathleen M. Rasmussen. "Breastfeeding and Health Outcomes for the Mother-Infant Dyad." *Pediatric Clinics of North America* 60, no. 1 (February 2013): 31–48.

5. The National Executive Committee of the Department of Health. "Administrative Order 2006-102: Revised Implementing Rules and Regulations of Executive Order No. 51, Otherwise Known as The 'Milk

Code', Relevant International Agreements, Penalizing Violations Thereof, and for Other Purposes." Office of the Secretary, Republic of the Philippines Department of Health, May 15, 2006. http://pcij.org/blog/wp-docs/a02006-0012.pdf.

6. Contributor Kimmy Ramos, Philippines.

7. Contributor Kris Pua Posadas, Philippines.

Chapter 17

1. "Half-Day Information Session on Breastfeeding at the CHPG." *Gouverner Princier*. October 18, 2012. http://en.gouv.mc/Policy-Practice/Social-Affairs-and-Health/News/Half-Day-Information-Session-on-Breastfeeding-at-the-CHPG

2. Paritakul, P., K. Ruangrongmorakot, W. Laosooksathit, M. Suksamarnwong, and P. Puapornpong. "The Effect of Ginger on Breast Milk Volume in the Early Postpartum Period: A Randomized, Double-Blind Controlled Trial." *Breastfeeding Medicine* 11 (September 2016): 361–5.

Chapter 18

1. Bhatia, Jatinder, Frank Greer, and the American Academy of Pediatrics Committee on Nutrition. "Clinical Report: Use of Soy Protein-Based Formulas in Infant Feeding." *Pediatrics* 121, no. 5 (2008): 1062–8. http://pediatrics.aappublications.org/content/pediatrics/121/5/1062.full.pdf.

2. Vandenplas, Yvan, Martin Brueton, Christophe Dupont, David Hill, Erika Isolauri, Sibylle Koletzko, Arnold P. Oranje, and Annamaria Staiano. "Guidelines for the Diagnosis and Management of Cow's Milk Protein Allergy in Infants." *Archives of Disease in Childhood* 92, no. 10 (2007): 902–8. https://www.ncbi.nlm.nih.gov/pmc/articles/PMC2083222/pdf/902.pdf.

Chapter 19

1. Contributor Blanca Santos Ruiz, MD, Granada, Spain.

Chapter 20

1. Korioth, Trisha. "Simple Remedies Often Best for Common Colds in Young Children." *AAP News*, November 27, 2011. http://www.aappublications.org/content/32/12/32.5.

2. Kikafunda, J. K., A. F. Walker, and J. K. Tumwine. "Weaning Foods and Practices in Central Uganda: A Cross-Sectional Study." *African Journal of Food, Agriculture, Nutrition and Development* 3, no. 2 (2003).

3. Contributor Clare Monson, blogger at ParentTribe.net, Portugal.

Chapter 21

1. Radesky, Jenny, Dimitri Christakis, and the American Academy of Pediatrics Council on Communications and Media. "Policy Statement: Media and Young Minds." *Pediatrics* 138, no. 5 (November 2016): 1–6. http://pediatrics.aappublications.org/content/pediatrics/early/2016/10/19/peds.2016-2591.full.pdf.

2. World Health Organization. "Japan Has the Highest Life Expectancy: The World Health Organization 2017 Statistics Report." WHO Kobe Center, May 22, 2017. http://www.who.int/kobe_centre/mediacentre/whs/en/. The 2017 Report is accessible at http://apps.who.int/iris/bitstream/10665/255336/1/9789241565486-eng.pdf.

3. Anderson, Charlotte. *The Little Book of Japan*. North Clarendon, VT: Tuttle Publishing, 2013.

Chapter 22

1. Wagner, Carol L., Frank R. Greer, and the American Academy of Pediatrics Section on Breastfeeding and Committee on Nutrition. "Prevention of Rickets and Vitamin D Deficiency in Infants, Children, and Adolescents." *Pediatrics* 122, no. 5 (November 2008): 1142–52. http://pediatrics.aappublications.org/content/pediatrics/122/5/1142.full.pdf.

2. Ibid.

3. Lange, Nancy E., Augusto Litonjua, Catherine M. Hawrylowicz, and Scott Weiss. "Vitamin D, the Immune System and Asthma." *Expert Review of Clinical Immunology* 5, no. 6 (November 2009): 693–702. https://www.ncbi.nlm.nih.gov/pmc/articles/PMC2812815/pdf/nihms-169091.pdf.

4. Wagner et al., "Prevention of Rickets and Vitamin D Deficiency in Infants, Children, and Adolescents."

5. Centers for Disease Control and Prevention. "Recommendations to Prevent and Control Iron Deficiency in the United States." *Morbidity and Mortality Weekly Report* 47, no. RR-3 (April 3, 1998): 1–36. https://www.cdc.gov/mmwr/pdf/rr/rr4703.pdf.

6. Baack, Michelle L., Susan E. Puumala, Stephen E. Messier, Deborah K. Pritchett, and William S. Harris. "What Is the Relationship between Gestational Age and Docosahexaenoic Acid (DHA) and Arachidonic Acid (ARA) Levels?" *Prostaglandins, Leukotrienes and Essential Fatty Acids* 100 (2015): 5–11. https://ac.els-cdn.com/S0952327815001210/1-s2.0-S0952327815001210-main.pdf?_tid=e8059c2c-a29a-11e7-ae69-0000 0aabofo1&acdnat=1506417366_3f8d91632c00c268df2764c27ed36d71.

7. "Long Chain Polyunsaturated Fatty Acid Supplementation of Infant Formula." American Council on Science and Health, July 1, 2002. https://www.acsh.org/news/2002/07/01/long-chain-polyunsaturated-fatty-acid-supplementation-of-infant-formula.

8. The US Department of Agriculture and the US Department of Health and Human Services. *Dietary Guidelines for Americans*, 7th ed. Washington, DC: US Government Printing Office, December 2010. P. 39. https://health.gov/dietaryguidelines/dga2010/dietaryguidelines2010.pdf.

9. "Choose the Right Fish to Lower Mercury Risk Exposure." *Consumer Reports*, August 2014. https://www.consumerreports.org/cro/magazine/2014/10/can-eating-the-wrong-fish-put-you-at-higher-risk-for-mercury-exposure/index.htm.

10. "Which Fish Are Safe for Pregnant Women?" *Consumer Reports*, January 27, 2017. https://www.consumerreports.org/food-safety/safe-fish-for-pregnant-women/.

11. The US Food and Drug Administration and the US Environmental Protection Agency. "Eating Fish: What Pregnant Women and Parents Should Know." FDA.gov, January 2017. https://www.fda.gov/downloads/Food/FoodborneIllnessContaminants/Metals/UCM537120.pdf.

12. Menon, Shanti. "Tip: Mercury Guide." The Natural Resources Defense Council, March 10, 2016. https://www.nrdc.org/stories/mercury-guide.

13. Innis, S. M., D. H. Adamkin, R. T. Hall, S. C. Kalhan, C. Lair, M. Lim, D. C. Stevens, P. F. Twist, D. A. Diersen-Schade, C. L. Harris, K. L. Merkel, and J.

W. Hansen. "Docosahexaenoic Acid and Arachidonic Acid Enhance Growth with No Adverse Effects in Preterm Infants Fed Formula." *The Journal of Pediatrics* 140, no. 5 (May 2002): 547–54. http://www.jpeds.com/article/ S0022-3476(02)58526-7/abstract.

14. Di Genova, Tanya, and Harvey Guyda. "Infants and Children Consuming Atypical Diets: Vegetarianism and Macrobiotics." *Paediatrics & Child Health* 12, no. 3 (March 2007): 185–8. https://www.ncbi.nlm.nih.gov/pmc/articles/ PMC2528709/pdf/pch12185.pdf.

15. US Food and Drug Administration. "Questions and Answers on Dietary Supplements." FDA.gov, last updated January 13, 2016. https://www. fda.gov/food/dietarysupplements/usingdietarysupplements/ucm480069. htm#FDA_role.

Chapter 23

1. Atwood, Donald, Claire Paisley-Jones, and the Biological and Economic Analysis Division, Office of Pesticide Programs, and Office of Chemical Safety and Pollution Prevention of the US Environmental Protection Agency. "Pesticides Industry Sales and Usage: 2008–2012 Market Estimates." EPA, 2017. https://www.epa.gov/sites/production/files/2017-01/documents/pesti- cides-industry-sales-usage-2016_0.pdf.

2. Eskenazi, Brenda, Lisa G. Rosas, Amy R. Marks, Asa Bradman, Kim Harley, Nina Holland, Caroline Johnson, Laura Fenster, and Dana B. Barr. "Pesticide Toxicity and the Developing Brain." *Basic & Clinical Pharmacology & Toxicity* 102, no. 2 (February 2008): 228–36. http://onlinelibrary.wiley.com/ doi/10.1111/j.1742-7843.2007.00171.x/epdf.

3. The National Institute for Occupational Safety and Health Division of Surveillance, Hazard Evaluations and Field Study. "Reproductive Health in the Workplace: Pesticides." The Centers for Disease Control and Prevention, last updated April 20, 2017. https://www.cdc.gov/niosh/topics/repro/pesticides. html.

4. Roberts, James R., and J. Routt Reigart, eds. *Recognition and Management of Pesticide Poisonings.* 6th ed. US Environmental Protection Agency Office of Pesticide Programs, 2013. https://www.epa.gov/sites/production/files/2015-01/ documents/rmpp_6thed_final_lowresopt.pdf.

5. Committee on Pesticides in the Diets of Infants and Children, National Research Council. "Pesticides in the Diets of Infants and Children."

Washington, DC: National Academies Press, 1993. https://www.ncbi.nlm.nih.gov/books/NBK236275/pdf/Bookshelf_NBK236275.pdf.

6. "Reducing Pesticide Exposure in Children and Pregnant Women." *Northwest Bulletin: Family and Child Health* 21, no. 1 (Fall/Winter 2006): 1–15. http://depts.washington.edu/nwbfch/PDFs/NWBv21n1.pdf.

7. Landrigan, Philip J., Clyde B. Schechter, Jeffrey M. Lipton, Marianne C. Fahs, and Joel Schwartz. "Environmental Pollutants and Disease in American Children: Estimates of Morbidity, Mortality, and Costs for Lead Poisoning, Asthma, Cancer, and Developmental Disabilities." *Environmental Health Perspectives* 110, no. 7 (July 2002): 721–8. https://www.ncbi.nlm.nih.gov/pmc/articles/PMC1240919/pdf/ehp0110-000721.pdf.

8. US Environmental Protection Agency. "Food and Pesticides." EPA.gov, last updated March 14, 2017. https://www.epa.gov/safepestcontrol/food-and-pesticides.

9. "Minimizing Pesticide Residues in Food." National Pesticide Information Center, last updated November 6, 2015. http://npic.orst.edu/health/foodprac.html.

Chapter 24

1. Lewis, Lisa. "Aaaaachooooo! Treat and Prevent Baby Colds." *Bloggy Moms*, 2016. http://bloggymoms.com/aaaaachooooo-treat-prevent-baby-colds/.

2. "Recommended Immunization Schedule for Children and Adolescents Aged 18 Years or Younger, United States, 2017." The American Academy of Pediatrics, in effect as of January 1, 2017. https://www.aap.org/en-us/Documents/immunizationschedule2017.pdf.

3. Douwes, J., S. Cheng, N. Travier, C. Cohet, A. Niesink, J. McKenzie, C. Cunningham, G. Le Gros, E. von Mutius, and N. Pearce. "Farm Exposure In Utero May Protect against Asthma, Hay Fever and Eczema." *European Respiratory Journal* 32, no. 3 (2008): 603–11. http://erj.ersjournals.com/content/32/3/603.long.

4. Caudri, Daan, Alet Wijga, Salome Scholtens, Marjan Kerkhof, Jorrit Gerritsen, Jopje M. Ruskamp, Bert Brunekreef, Henriette A. Smit, and Johan C. de Jongste. "Early Daycare Is Associated with an Increase in Airway Symptoms in Early Childhood but Is No Protection against Asthma or Atopy at 8 Years." *American Journal of Respiratory and Critical Care Medicine* 80, no.

6 (September 2009): 491–8. http://www.atsjournals.org/doi/full/10.1164/rccm.200903-0327OC#readcube-epdf.

Chapter 26

1. Yeo, Teresa Rebecca. "Heritage and Culture: Chinese Birth Rituals." National Library Board of Singapore's *Singapore Infopedia*, May 14, 2013. http://eresources.nlb.gov.sg/infopedia/articles/SIP_2013-05-14_113920.html.

2. Xiao, Zhao. "Haircut Boom on Dragon Head-Raising Day." *China Daily*, updated March 1, 2017. http://www.chinadaily.com.cn/m/innermongolia/2017-03/01/content_28396698.htm.

3. Contributor Soula Aman, Belgium.

Chapter 27

1. Rogan, Jim. "Armenian First Tooth." The Library of Congress's *Local Legacies*, Spring 2000. http://memory.loc.gov/diglib/legacies/loc.afc.afc-legacies.200002748/.

2. Contributor Brigitte Assing, St. George's, Grenada.

Chapter 28

1. Queensland Heath. "Cultural Dimensions of Pregnancy, Birth, and Post-Natal Care: Samoan Profile." QLD.gov, October 27, 2009. https://www.health.qld.gov.au/__data/assets/pdf_file/0034/158569/samoan-preg-prof.pdf.

Appendix

1. "Garam Masala." Reprinted with permission from allrecipes.com. http://allrecipes.com/recipe/142967/easy-garam-masala/.

Acknowledgments

Parent education across cultures has been my heart for many years. I am grateful for the support of numerous people. Brooke Jorden responded to my manuscript submission quickly and with grand enthusiasm. Familius editor Lindsay Sandberg listened patiently to my questions and expertly fine-tuned my grammar. Thank you, Familius. Your commitment, *helping families be happy*, is an important value displayed in this book.

I am grateful to the American Academy of Pediatrics for continuing to educate health care providers in America and around the world. Each contributor provided insight and had an important role. They are individually named in the book and greatly appreciated. My dear friend Professor Malinda Seymore has been a sounding board and source of tremendous support from the book's inception. Dr. Melissa Asgaonkar, colleague and friend, meticulously read the manuscript and offered helpful suggestions. Heartfelt appreciation to those who encouraged this project for many years: Paula Craig, Jennifer Flippo, Dr. Omar and Bertha Gomez, Barbara and Jack Lewis, Marilyn Menchaca, Monica Rodriguez, and Fran Seymore. To my sister, Laura Jaafar, and brother, Greg Ehl, thank you for your devotion and guidance. I'll always be grateful for my father's enthusiasm and pride. My mother believed I could accomplish anything, and that support has sustained me for a lifetime. John, Sydney, and Jack: thank you for the unconditional love and joy you bring to my life.

ABOUT THE AUTHOR

DR. LISA LEWIS has been a practicing pediatrician for over twenty years. Dr. Lewis has traveled the world extensively and has a keen interest in the medical and parenting philosophies of other countries. She has been chosen as a Mom-Approved Pediatrician by *Dallas Fort Worth Child Magazine* in 2016 and 2017. From her experience, she writes about child health and parenting across cultures. Dr. Lewis frequently contributes to blogs and websites, including *New Parent Magazine, Bloggy Moms*, and *Multicultural Kid Blogs*.

Dr. Lewis attended medical school abroad at the American University of the Caribbean School of Medicine. During her third and fourth years of medical studies, she performed her clinical rotations at London Hospital Medical College in England, where she received clinical honors. She completed her pediatric residency at Texas A&M University Health Science Center, Scott and White Memorial Hospital in Temple, Texas, where she served as Chief Resident. For two years after her residency, she was Assistant Professor in the Department of Pediatrics at Texas A&M University Health Science Center. Dr. Lewis is currently in practice at Kid Care Pediatrics, Fort Worth, Texas. She is board certified in pediatrics by the American Board of Pediatrics and is a Fellow of the American Academy of Pediatrics.

Dr. Lewis is happily married and has two amazing children. She loves traveling with her family and gardening. To read more from Dr. Lewis, go to her website, www.lisalewismd.com.

ABOUT FAMILIUS

Visit Our Website: www.familius.com

Join Our Family

There are lots of ways to connect with us! Subscribe to our newsletters at www.familius.com to receive uplifting daily inspiration, essays from our Pater Familius, a free ebook every month, and the first word on special discounts and Familius news.

Get Bulk Discounts

If you feel a few friends and family might benefit from what you've read, let us know and we'll be happy to provide you with quantity discounts. Simply email us at orders@familius.com.

Connect

- Facebook: www.facebook.com/paterfamilius
- Twitter: @familiustalk, @paterfamilius1
- Pinterest: www.pinterest.com/familius
- Instagram: @familiustalk

FAMILIUS

---

*The most important work you ever do will
be within the walls of your own home.*

CPSIA information can be obtained
at www.ICGtesting.com
Printed in the USA
FFOW02n1434150318
45700738-46549FF